HISTORY OF LITERATURE SERIES

NINETEENTH-CENTURY ENGLISH LITERATURE

Margaret Stonyk

Schocken Books · New York

First American edition published by Schocken Books 1984
10 9 8 7 6 5 4 3 2 1   84 85 86 87
Copyright © Margaret Stonyk 1983
Published by agreement with The Macmillan Press Ltd., London

Library of Congress Cataloging in Publication Data

Stonyk, Margaret.
  Nineteenth-century English literature.

  (History of literature series)
  Bibliography: p.
  Includes index.
  1. English literature — 19th century — History and
criticism.   I. Title.   II. Series.
PR451.S85   1984   820'.9'007   83-20224

Printed in Hong Kong

ISBN 0-8052-3889-1

Contents

List of Plates

The author and publishers are grateful to the copyright holders listed above for their permission to reproduce these illustrations.

Editor's Preface

THE study of literature requires knowledge of contexts as well as of texts. What kind of person wrote the poem, the play, the novel, the essay? What forces acted upon them as they wrote? What was the historical, the political, the philosophical, the economic, the cultural background? Was the writer accepting or rejecting the literary conventions of the time, or developing them, or creating entirely new kinds of literary expression? Are there interactions between literature and the art, music or architecture of its period? Was the writer affected by contemporaries or isolated?

Such questions stress the need for students to go beyond the reading of set texts, to extend their knowledge by developing a sense of chronology, of action and reaction, and of the varying relationships between writers and society.

Histories of literature can encourage students to make comparisons, can aid in understanding the purposes of individual authors and in assessing the totality of their achievements. Their development can be better understood and appreciated with some knowledge of the background of their time. And histories of literature, apart from their valuable function as reference books, can demonstrate the great wealth of writing in English that there is to be enjoyed. They can guide the reader who wishes to explore it more fully and to gain in the process deeper insights into the rich diversity not only of literature but of human life itself.

A. NORMAN JEFFARES

. . . the function of the nineteenth century was to disentangle the disinterested intelligence, to release it from the entanglements of party and sect – one might almost add, of sex – and to set it operating over the whole range of human life and circumstance. In England we see this spirit issuing from, and often at war with, a society most stoutly tenacious of old ways and forms, and yet most deeply immersed in its new business of acquisition.

G. M. Young, *Victorian England: Portrait of an Age* (1936)

The movement that is going on is so continuous, the variety so great, that every historical comment seems fumbling and inaccurate, every generalisation inconclusive and incomplete.

G. Kitson Clark, *The Making of Victorian England* (1962)

We live notoriously, as I suppose every age lives, in an 'epoch of transition'. . . .

Henry James, Preface to *The Awkward Age* (1899)

There is nothing that requires more discretion than the paying of compliments to great men.

Bernard Shaw in *The Saturday Review* (1898)

I bless my stars for a taste so catholic, so unexcluding.

Charles Lamb, 'Detached Thoughts on Books and Reading' (1823)

Introduction

IN *Orlando* (1928), Virginia Woolf's lively fantasy of the English literary sensibility transforming itself over four centuries, her hero, suddenly a woman, finds herself in the middle of Victorian England and demands to see its books.

Accustomed to the little literatures of the sixteenth, seventeenth and eighteenth centuries, Orlando was appalled by the consequences of her order. For, of course, to the Victorians themselves literature meant not merely four great names separate and distinct but four great names sunk and embedded in a mass of Alexander Smiths, Dixons, Blacks, Milmans, Buckles, Taines, Paynes, Tuppers, Jamesons – all vocal, all clamorous, prominent, and requiring as much print as anyone else.

Virginia Woolf (1882–1941), the daughter of the formidable Victorian critic Sir Leslie Stephen (1832–1904) and herself the dashing evaluator of the period's literature in her *Common Reader* series, went on:

. . . it is clear that there are only two ways of coming to a conclusion upon Victorian literature – one is to write it out in sixty volumes octavo, the other is to squeeze it into six lines the length of this one.

When the problem of 'coming to a conclusion' is compounded by the nearly forty years that elapse between the publication of *Lyrical Ballads* in 1798 and the start of the Victorian era itself, the task of combining a selective brevity with justice becomes even more daunting. But a literary history can at least be a stellar chart to the century. The great luminaries can be seen in constellations of minor figures who have contributed something to their brilliance and perhaps been forgotten, as Dickens owed something of his lustre to Bulwer Lytton and to Ainsworth, and Tennyson to Keble. Figures of considerable magnitude, now in eclipse through changes of fashion, deserve rediscovery: the Romantic essayists. And occasionally a new star, already long in existence, may be reborn in the reader's mind outside the familiar heavens of the syllabus: a Beddoes, a Le Fanu, a Clare or a Blunt.

1

'The most glorious years: 1800–30

The Romantic Context

FROM the 1770s to the 1830s literary movements took place in Europe which involved a sympathy for political liberalism, an intellectual self-consciousness, a discriminating or flamboyant cultivation of emotion, a mingled sense of obligation and aversion towards society as a whole, and an idealistic passion for landscape.

English Romanticism was unusual in Europe for the rapidity with which it found a sympathetic audience. It had been preceded in the 1770s by the volatile and emotional German equivalent in the *Sturm und Drang* movement of the young Johann Wolfgang von Goethe (1749–1832), Friedrich von Schiller (1759–1805) and the unbalanced and morbidly sensitive Jakob Lenz (1751–92). This had been an impassioned rejection of the values of the European Enlightenment favoured by the closed circle of hereditary aristocrats that kept political power out of the hands of a fiercely intellectual German middle class, so that writers began to focus on their inner lives as a substitute for action. The *Frühromantiker* of the early nineteenth century took this inwardness still further, and Ludwig Tieck (1773–1853) and Novalis (the pseudonym of Friedrich von Hardenberg, 1772–1801) cultivated an idea of life as a dream or theatrical illusion that finds its only English expression in the bizarre yet compelling art of the germanophile Thomas Beddoes.

Romanticism in France was postponed by the revolution of 1789, so that in the 1820s the developing form was coloured by English writers brought back by the emigrés: Scott, Byron and Shakespeare. These anglophile influences joined with native trends in Jean-Jacques Rousseau (1712–78) as they developed through René de Chateaubriand (1768–1848) and Alphonse de Lamartine (1790–1869) into a vague but potent fusion of love, nature and religious ardour. The French Romantic poet was soon at odds with a newly industrialised society of bankers and the haute bourgeoisie that was unfriendly to liberal reform and to any art which did not serve the purposes of ostentation. After the political disappointments of 1830 and 1848, poetry turned more and more to expressing its separation from a hostile or indifferent milieu. Victor Hugo (1802–85) narrowed the revolutionary sentiments of his early drama to a mystical retreat to 'my house, my fields, and my loves'; Alfred de Vigny (1797–1863) adopted a stoical pose; Théophile Gautier (1811–72) developed the amoral doctrine that 'art for us is not the means, but the end'; Charles Baudelaire (1821–67) evolved whole rituals of self-protective artifice, a magical theory of language, and the presentation of the poet as an unacknowledged aristocrat whose gifts are spurned by the mob. English Romanticism developed along less embattled lines; its poets, so different from one another in their styles and theories, were united in their belief that (in Shelley's happy phrase) they were 'the unacknowledged legislators of mankind'. This conviction remained in place until the mid-century, and informs the poetry of Tennyson and Arnold as much as that of Wordsworth.

As far back as the 1760s in England a new sensibility with its emphasis on individual, even idiosyncratic experience, had begun to replace the formal Augustan presentation of human nature in terms of general truths and an essentially social existence that had been expressed in the poetry of John Dryden (1631–1700), Alexander Pope (1688–1744) and their defender Samuel Johnson (1709–84). This shift in attitude was prompted by the liberal values of the French Enlightenment, at a time when fresh developments in culture and political theory passed across borders without hindrance to all members of the educated classes. The most profound influence on this new sensibility was Rousseau himself, and Samuel Johnson, sensing his natural enemy, spoke his intense disapproval of the captivating novels, essays and speculative political constitutions that argued for personal and social relationships based on the truth of instinct. Johnson, as an Augustan, saw 'civilised society' as the greatest good, and insisted that 'our happiness is very much owing to the good opinion of others' which is based on the 'external advantages' that tell of rank.

Johnson's own finely melancholy display of Augustan values in his superb long poem *The Vanity of Human Wishes* (1749) was to be supplanted by a more supple and simplified verse, drawn from folk idioms such as the *ballad* (favoured by Thomas Gray), or from Elizabethan and Miltonic *blank verse* (used in James Thomson's influential *The Seasons* begun in 1730), and in the personal *sonnet* tentatively explored by Coleridge's predecessor W. L. Bowles (1762–1850). All these forms remained favourites with the English Romantic poets. Subject matter underwent a change in the later eighteenth century; there was an interest in the past, and in mythology, and a sympathy for the primitive, including the joys and sorrows of village life conveyed most gracefully in the deft and modish sentimentalism of Goldsmith's *The Deserted Village* (1770). There was a tendency to dwell on single, individualised characters rather than on social types, and to allow the poet to explore his own sensations. William Cowper (1731–1800), the most influential Romantic precursor, had begun to treat daily events as the starting-point for a meditation that disclosed the emotional waverings and the moral attitudes of the poet, and *The Task* (1785) has something of the pressure of thought that fills Wordsworth's *Lines Composed a Few Miles Above Tintern Abbey* (1798) and Coleridge's conversation-poems of the same decade.

The publication of *Lyrical Ballads* by Wordsworth and Coleridge in 1798 was not in itself the epoch-making event that literary history has made it out to be. It was its appearance at a time of severe political reaction to the dangerous example of France, and the preface by Wordsworth which laid claim to a general rather than an educated audience, that drew the fire of the critic Francis Jeffrey (1773–1850) in the weighty *Edinburgh Review*; Scottish intellectuals, thrust by the sudden in-accessibility of European ideas into a prominence they fully justified, were still committed to the rationalism of the Enlightenment and its conviction that literature was inseparable from social influence. Wordsworth appeared to be appealing to those levelling tendencies that had caused the plague in France, and from which England must be preserved. Jeffrey had no objection to the sober introspection of *Tintern Abbey*, but he found the subjects of poems such as 'The Idiot Boy' downright incendiary when read in the light of Wordsworth's assertion in the Preface that in 'humble and rustic life'

> the essential passions of the heart find a better soil in which they can attain their maturity, are under less restraint, and speak a plainer and more emphatic language.

The modern reader can understand that Wordsworth is writing of the need to find a form of expression for essentially private thought: 'the spontaneous overflow of powerful feelings'. But to the contemporary reader of the Preface, it seemed that Wordsworth was speaking only too pointedly of 'the great national events which are daily taking place', and ranging himself and his co-author on the side of Revolution.

The Revolution, so vehemently denounced in Edmund Burke's conservative *Reflections on the Late Revolution in France* (1790), put an end to the ties of English Romanticism to French liberalism. The flood of books from across the Channel thinned to a mere trickle, and the sentimentalism of late eighteenth-century fiction, plays and poetry was amplified into a cult of domestic virtue and social tranquillity that was the best preventive of large ideas of liberty and equality. The unfriendly reception of *Lyrical Ballads* caused Wordsworth to develop a Miltonic style that suggested a noble puritanical patriotism in his public verse, and he gradually developed a sense of human beings existing (like his Michael and the Leech-Gatherer) independently of their social context. There was nothing forced in this evolution, which is explained in detail in the last four books of *The Prelude* (finally published in 1850), earlier in *The Excursion* (1814), and first articulated in the 'Ode to Duty' (1807).

> I, loving freedom, and untried,
> No sport of every random gust,
> Yet being to myself a guide,
> Too blindly have reposed my trust;
> And oft, when in my heart was heard
> Thy timely mandate, I deferred
> The task, in smoother walks to stray;
> But thee I now would serve more strictly, if I may.

Coleridge's flight from the bloody and threatening events in

France was more precipitate: he felt a danger to his own sensitive perception of 'the Great' and 'the Whole' through his natural mysticism and 'the constant testimony of the senses', both of which were held cheap by the atheistical systematising of revolution.

The next generation of English Romantics, not personally betrayed by the Terror which had turned the Revolution from a 'pleasant exercise of hope and joy' to 'outrage and bloody power', experimented with ideas from which Wordsworth and Coleridge had turned in distaste, as distractions from their intuitive arts. Keats played with the intellectual freedom of a paganism that challenged a traditional Christian distrust of sensory delight, and Shelley zestfully publicised his atheism and hatred of tyranny, referring to Wordsworth's revulsion from his own youthful revolutionary ardour as the act of 'a slave'. Byron, like Shelley, avoided a period of reaction in England by exiling himself to the Continent during the particularly grim year of 1816, when a spate of civil disorders and agitation for reform brought down a vengeful and moralistic reaction. The corsairs and brigands of his Eastern tales had presented Bonaparte's ruthless déclassé egotism in a tactfully Levantine setting, and so exploited the fascinated fear of the dictator; Byron's more serious poetry was a blend of Romantic self-interest and that Augustan concern with social roles that he was apt to defend in a captious dislike of the new middle-class spirit in poetry. The Romantics, so often treated as a solid phalanx, were in fact men of two generations, often mutually unsympathetic and sometimes openly at war, forming unstable alliances as long as these were useful, and united not in the themes and styles of their poetry, but in their sense of the poet himself as the most important element of his art.

Romanticism in England included the rise of two new forms of literature that had a crucial role to play in making the new attitudes acceptable to a growing readership. The political journals that developed in the opening years of the century, with the cautiously liberal *Edinburgh Review* and the Tory *Quarterly Review*, adopted the weighty tones of public judgement learned from the *philosophes* of the French Enlightenment, and so created an audience for the temperate discussion of new theories of science, economics, the arts and politics. The Reviews enhanced the pleasure that educated citizens had learned to receive from the gregariousness of the late eighteenth century, when the 'Gothic haughtiness' of good society was banished and much time was spent in talk in the coffee-houses, the conversaziones and the learned societies of London and the provinces. The Victorian social philosophers Carlyle and Macaulay were to build on this appetite for responsible intellectual speculation in print.

In general, although the first two decades of the nineteenth century witnessed an irresistible move towards parliamentary reform that was preferable to revolution, there was a tacit understanding that political discussion ought to be restricted under the present emergency, and a growing feeling that the individual no longer had very much influence over public affairs. A style of personal Romantic prose developed that withdrew ostentatiously from politics and concentrated instead on the personality of the writer, inventing the idea of the man of letters as a being of surpassing interest to the reading public; a mediator, as critic, amateur and practitioner of poetry, between the austere genius of Wordsworth and Coleridge and the consumer of literature. Charles Lamb, William Hazlitt and Thomas De Quincey created the readership that Charles Dickens would inherit in the 1830s, eager for contact with a remarkable and confident mind that could see extraordinary significance in the shared events of daily life. The novel itself had not flourished during the aftermath of revolution, and the fictions of Sir Walter Scott and Jane Austen that appeared in the prudent years of the second decade are deeply conservative in spirit, arguing the need to reinvigorate the established social hierarchy and to protect society against an unscrupulous individualism.

The old system of oligarchic rule by landowners was ending peacefully in England, and the change was ratified in the Reform Act of 1832. Before then, the booming economy of England above the level of the middle class gave the initial impetus to the Industrial Revolution, as roads, canals and new towns were built and agricultural reforms put through with a fine disregard for the lower orders. This increasing prosperity within the more favoured classes led to a rapid growth of interest in acquiring the desirable products of trade and manufacturing; until the nineteenth century, those who were

rich could enjoy luxury but did not expect comfort or that
refinement in small pleasures which the late arrivals to
gentility in Jane Austen's novels praise with 'the greatest
alacrity and enjoyment'.

> 'What an excellent device', said he, 'the use of a sheepskin in carriages.
> How very comfortable they make it; impossible to feel cold with such
> precautions. The contrivances of modern days, indeed, have rendered a
> gentleman's carriage perfectly complete. . . .'

With private homes so comfortable, and a new and welcome
fashion for rooms set aside for individual inhabitation and
single functions rather than for the random use of a family and
its visitors, it is not surprising that the idea of home as a
sanctum filled with objects purchased for the sheer joy of
ownership eventually forced a reaction in favour of strict
simplicity in the aesthetic reforms of the 1860s and after.

While the middle class was enjoying this new comfort, the
lower classes endured a new wretchedness brought about by
the economic upheavals of the Napoleonic wars, a policy of
forced conscription, a high military death-rate, and the
callousness of demobilisation after the peace. Even Jane
Austen's socially unreflective Emma is aware of the misery on
the outskirts of her village, and these sufferers are the objects of
Wordsworth's ruminative studies of humanity reduced to its
basic attributes and Coleridge's active social conscience.
Despite this compassion and the very occasional rare voice
from outside the middle class (such as John Clare or William
Cobbett), the working class does not come into its own as a
subject for literary treatment until the 1840s.

Among the new possessions a gentleman and his family
could enjoy were books, now produced with greater ease owing
to improvements in manufacturing. This changed the
relationship between writer and reader from something stable
(in that purchasers were likely to rub shoulders in the crescents
of Bath and the drawing-rooms of London) to the uncertainties
of an amorphous 'public'. Society was becoming more
complex and less intimate, and publishing mirrored its
changes faithfully.

In one significant respect, the Romantic flowering in
England differed from those of the rest of Europe. Germans
were fond of referring to England as 'a land without music',

and while French Romanticism is inseparable from the achievement of Hector Berlioz (1803–69) and that of Germany is as rich in musical excellence as it is in its literature, English indifference to music placed a peculiar and eventually strangely beneficial stress on the verbal and visual expression of experience, and the constant and critical fitting of unadorned language to innate feeling.

'The vision splendid': the Romantic poets

William Wordsworth (1770–1850), like the great seventeenth-century poet John Milton (1608–74), whose style he adopted in the meditative autobiography *The Prelude* and whose muse he invokes in the Preface to *The Excursion* (1814), conscientiously set out to redeem his art from triviality and the 'judgements of the wealthy Few, who see / By artificial lights' and apply it instead to reconciling alienated and questioning man to the benign power within the universe.

> Of Truth, of Grandeur, Beauty, Love, and Hope,
> And melancholy Fear subdued by Faith;
> Of blessed consolations in distress;
> Of moral strength, and intellectual power;
> Of joy in widest commonalty spread;
> Of the individual mind that keeps her own
> Inviolate retirement, subject there
> To Conscience only, and the law supreme
> Of that Intelligence which governs all –
> I sing: – 'fit audience let me find, though few'.

'The egotism of such a man', wrote Coleridge of Milton, 'is a revelation of spirit', and it was 'the egotistical sublime', the assured and elevated tone in which a keen independent vision of the world was conveyed that gave Wordsworth and Coleridge, his collaborator on *Lyrical Ballads* (1798), their authority to shape the sensibility of the century to come.

Wordsworth's life was outwardly uninteresting, except for his much discussed but unimportant liaison with a Frenchwoman during his youthful burst of sympathy for the Revolution. His existence was instinctively shaped so as to nurture his poetic gifts and protect his sensibility; an extraordinary serendipity threw him in the way of an education in his native surroundings, a legacy that meant leisured retirement, a deeply affectionate sister, half-housekeeper, half-muse, and the indispensable friendship of Coleridge. Wordsworth's life, in the south of England and then in the Lake District of his boyhood, settled into a tranquillity free of 'outward accidents' which would have disturbed the placid reconstruction of his mental growth. But despite a long life and increasing honours (he was appointed poet laureate in 1843), his actual poetic career was a short one, ending effectively in 1807 with brief later flares in the sonnet 'Surprised by joy . . .' (1815) and the 'Extempore Effusion on the Death of James Hogg' (1835), which recapture the old, deeply personal note, where the death of an individual implicated in Wordsworth's creative life strikes into being one of those moments of remembered emotion and heightened awareness.

After 1807 the moments of recollected vision grow rarer, and the perilously achieved stance of calm authority becomes a pose; the dogmatic imperturbability of the *Ecclesiastical Sonnets* is a parody of the dynamic tranquillity of 'Nuns fret not . . .' and 'Earth has not anything to show more fair'. This notorious decline was a natural evolution that the poet had foreseen, notably in the valedictory *Ode on the Intimations of Immortality* (1807). Wordsworth's art, like that of his contemporary, the landscape painter John Constable (1776–1837) was not destined to evolve unceasingly, but was based on a vast bank of sensory impressions and a lesser supply of privileged visions which were used or faded, and which were not replenished after youth.

Wordsworth was the great investigator of change and growth in a century obsessed with its own rapid development. *The Prelude*, which he altered and adapted continuously so that it was not published until the year of his death, is 'the history of a Poet's mind', illustrating with passionate detail the progress from the unquestioned sensations of childhood to imaginative maturity nourished by experience, chastened by the misjudgements of a vain intellect, and supported by reading and human affection. Despite the awesomely authoritative tone – Wordsworth is the least ironic of poets – there is no offensive intellectual pride but rather a sense of wonder at the heroic potential of man, and a hunger to realise

the vision before the poet's insight fails with increasing
distance from the source.

> Oh! mystery of man, from what a depth
> Proceed thy honours. I am lost, but see
> In simple childhood something of the base
> On which thy greatness stands; but this I feel,
> That from thyself it comes, that thou must give,
> Else never can receive. The days gone by
> Return upon me almost from the dawn
> Of life: the hiding-places of man's power
> Open: I would approach them, but they close.
> I see by glimpses now; when age comes on,
> May scarcely see at all. . . .

The Prelude, like its sequels in Coleridge's *Biographia Literaria*
(1817), Carlyle's *Sartor Resartus* (1833–4) and John Ruskin's
Praeterita (1885–9) maps the developing personality not
through the events of public life, but through intellectual and
emotional shifts. It is necessarily related to the *Confessions* of
Jean-Jacques Rousseau, though Wordsworth is implicitly
critical of his predecessor. He gives little emphasis to sexual
love (his complimentary poems are rebukes to the genre and
stress the fellow-humanity of women) and he regards
education as a private matter between nature, the child, and a
few books, rather than the elaborate practical experiment
outlined in *Emile* (1762). George Meredith's novel *The Ordeal of
Richard Feverel* (1859) was to be a dramatised battle between the
father's Rousseauism and the son's Wordsworthian naturalism.
Wordsworth's Romantic autobiography also grew out of a
native strain; the spiritual testament, with its finest early
expression in *Grace Abounding* (1666) by John Bunyan (1628–
88), and a new surge of growth with the rise of Evangelical
Christianity from the middle of the eighteenth century. The
spiritual autobiographers were frank about the backslidings
and inadequacies of their lives since these were a means of self-
discovery on the journey towards a triumphant reconciliation
with God; the middle sections of *The Prelude* trace with equal
candour those periods of self-conceit that turned the poet's
heart 'out of Nature's way'. Wordsworth could afford such
openness; his patient, exalted vision of his task as the
uncommon common man reconciling his fellows to great
permanent truths, took periods of latency or despair in its

stride, just as the heart (that favourite Romantic metaphor) had its rhythms of expansion and contraction. Coleridge, on the other hand, found his times of poetic drought insupportably terrible, and his *Dejection: An Ode*, contemporary with Wordsworth's *Immortality Ode*, is a cry from the depths. Wordsworth gravely mourns the change in himself, but holds himself in expectant readiness for a fresh perception of nature and an answering development in his art; nature, he believed, had endless 'renovating' powers.

The Prelude, epic in scope and heroic in its view of man, and lyrical in its summoning of the famous 'spots of time' (those intimate recollections of harmony with nature which save the individual from the dulling effect of daily living or a pride of intellect divorced from experience or affection), enlarges themes present from the beginning of Wordsworth's career when they were expressed with a riddling brevity. In many of these lyrics Wordsworth fused in a single poem the paradox of innocence and experience that another Romantic forerunner, William Blake (1757–1827) had separated dramatically. Wordsworth's chosen role as 'Prophet of Nature' informs the eloquent and impassioned Preface of 1800, with its recall of poetry to the serious duty of proclaiming permanent moral truths to readers seduced by triviality, political upheaval, or a materialistic science. Wordsworth is not anti-intellectual, but makes a stronger claim for the holiness of the heart's affections, and prefers instinct to formal learning:

> One impulse from a vernal wood
> May teach you more of man,
> Of moral evil and of good
> Than all the sages can.

The 'impulse' is a term culled from the empirical philosopher John Locke (1632–1704), who provided much of the intellectual background to Wordsworth's theories; in the poet's terms, it meant a moment of heightened awareness and instinctive sympathy with all of creation. Such 'impulses' and 'spots of time' formed the imaginative expectations of the literature of the nineteenth century; poems and novels are studded with moments of vision and illumination, and Wordsworth's discovery is the psychological basis for the supernatural clarity, stillness and emotional tension in the Pre-

Raphaelite art of the mid-century, as well as in the earlier, supernaturally charged interpretations of rural life in the etchings of Blake's disciples Samuel Palmer (1805–81) and Edward Calvert (1799–1883) and the poems of John Clare.

The shorter early poems of Wordsworth tend to knot conflicting emotions tightly together, so that the reader is educated by the process of disentangling them; the quality of feeling and immediacy of the situation is clearly conveyed, but the meaning emerges only gradually. Wordsworth was, like Blake, a specialist in comparative states of awareness. The essential difference between the instinctual animal creation and self-conscious man is poignantly dwelt upon in the exquisitely mournful joy of the opening to 'Resolution and Independence', where the beauty of the natural scene and man's alienation within it lays the foundations for the poetry of Tennyson and Arnold later in the century. 'Anecdote for Fathers' counterpoints the child's integrity of being and knowing with the adult's barren desire to compare and reject experience; 'The Two April Mornings' shows apparently incompatible states of joy and grief existing in one mind in the same moment.

While Wordsworth celebrates growth and change, and has an heroic sense of the permanent consolations of nature, symbolised most powerfully in the image of Mount Snowdon towering over the last book of *The Prelude*, he is also grievingly aware of the irreplaceability of the individual human personality. This is the theme of the 'Lucy' poems; 'Lucy' herself bears notable affinities to his sister Dorothy, but is heightened into the perfection of responsive humanity, female in the sense that she complements the poet's personality, and because women were allowed to retain a greater share of 'wise passiveness' untampered with by formal education. The sequence of poems varies markedly in tone, as Wordsworth explores the question of whether individual personality can survive the immensity of nature throughout the gamut of his poetic sensibility. He uses the preternaturally acute imagery of Coleridge ('Strange fits of passion have I known . . .'), the lyrically rhapsodic vein ('Three years she grew . . .'), and, in the most striking poem of all, the minimalist 'A Slumber did my spirit seal . . .', he fuses grief at personal loss and the infinite context of that death into a completely new emotion.

Wordsworth's poetry earns its moral force by the self-critical honesty of each feeling and observation; it is a kind of mountaineering exercise in which each vantage point is carefully tested and perilously earned. His egotism does not separate him from humanity and he turns without condescension to 'men as they are men within themselves', apart from the accidents of class and education; the outcasts who people much of his poetry present a true humanity in the very extremity of their case. He uses language with the integrity possible to one who believes that 'words are but under-agents', enlarging and interpreting feeling, but not an end in themselves.

Henry James (1843–1916), that adjectivally lavish appreciator of the men and women of his century, described Samuel Taylor Coleridge (1772–1834) as that 'rare, anomalous, magnificent, interesting, curious, tremendously suggestive character, vices and all, with all its imperfections on its head'. The reference to *Hamlet* was almost inevitable; Coleridge, like Shakespeare's prince, was a self-advertised procrastinator, left unfitted for action by the habits of German philosophy. His personality, unlike that of the austere Wordsworth, was miraculously charming: 'his great and dear spirit haunts me still', mourned his former school-fellow, the essayist Charles Lamb, and after the bitter rift of 1810, when Coleridge had sunk into opium addiction, matrimonial strife and 'disease of the volition', Wordsworth could still admit that 'his mind has been habitually present with me', and pay awed tribute to those magnificent but short-lived poetic gifts in the 'Extempore Effusion on the Death of James Hogg':

> Nor has the rolling year twice measured,
> From sign to sign, its steadfast course,
> Since every mortal power of Coleridge
> Was frozen at its marvellous source; . . . .

John Keats left a vivid account of the perplexed delight of an early morning conversational walk with Coleridge, on which assorted subjects were seized upon with unflagging zest, but the social philosopher Thomas Carlyle, spokesman for a younger generation's belief that intellectual effort should produce practical results, left a less flattering portrait of the speculative sage in his *Life of John Sterling* (1851). The sixty-year-old '*Magus*, girt in mystery and enigma . . . heavy-laden, high aspiring and surely much-suffering man' was sealed off in a hopeless if eloquent sermon, where 'balmy, sunny islets, islets of the blest and the intelligible' would occasionally rise out of the mists of transcendental philosophy and associative thought. It was to take Carlyle's own disciple, the critic of art and society John Ruskin, to unite Carlyle's social prescription and Coleridge's inclusiveness of thought and random play of mind.

Coleridge as a poet flourished briefly but magnificently during his mutually inspiring friendship with Wordsworth, which waned from 1802 and was broken off in 1810. Like Wordsworth in his headstrong early commitment to republicanism, his later, deeper-rooted conservatism, and his sense of the vast unity of nature, Coleridge was temperamentally dissimilar. His unpremeditated career, need of supportive friends and his extravagant emotions contrasted with Wordsworth's prudent management of his poetic capital and practical life: the inevitable quarrel between the early collaborators foreshadowed that between Sigmund Freud (1856–1939) and Carl Jung (1875–1961). The man with the austere and ennobling sense that maturity involves the relinquishing of early hopes and that our most shaping experiences are laid down in childhood, detached himself from the more visionary intelligence with its speculative interest in the primitive and the magical, finding in the myths of mankind pathways to a new intuition of life.

Coleridge's life showed a genius for mismanagement; the precocious 'inspired charity-boy' of the spartan but intellectually invigorating Christ's Hospital School lost his way at Cambridge, romantically enlisted as a soldier, got caught up in Robert Southey's mad scheme for a republican commonwealth in America, married an impossible woman (sister to Southey's own wife), fell in love with Wordsworth's sister-in-law, ruined himself with opium and gave up his poetic career by 1802, yet failed to realise his ambitions as a philosopher. His neurotic habits of procrastination and plagiarism, odd in one so richly gifted, were legendary.

In the famous collaboration on *Lyrical Ballads*, Wordsworth reserved to himself 'subjects chosen from ordinary life', but presented by 'a meditative and feeling mind'. Coleridge agreed to treat 'persons and characters supernatural, or at least romantic, yet so as to transfer from our inward nature a human interest and a semblance of truth sufficient to procure for these shadows of imagination that willing suspension of disbelief for the moment, which constitutes poetic faith'. The end result of either method would be identical: the mind would be awakened from 'the lethargy of custom' and taught to see anew 'the loveliness and wonders of the world before us', too often dulled by 'the film of familiarity and selfish solicitude'.

The Rime of the Ancient Mariner and the unfinished *Christabel* (written between 1797 and 1800) are the most disturbing elaborations of this 'supernatural' genre. The Mariner, with his legendary antecedents in the Flying Dutchman and the Wandering Jew, is a scapegoat detached from humanity by an accursed act, and compelled to wander in search not of forgiveness but human empathy; the killing of the albatross, punishment through frost, heat and loneliness, the ghostly crew that sails the vessel home and the 'woful agony' that drives the Mariner to find hearers for his story, are all familiar in outline but remain mysterious in their mingling of the commonplace and the supernatural. The Mariner endures an ultimate desolation 'alone on a wide, wide sea', that the Hermit, that exponent of Wordsworthian closeness to nature, cannot comprehend; the mind's central 'inviolate retirement' is very frightening to Coleridge, and 'the hiding-places of man's power' are dangerous visions.

Christabel, a richly suggestive and highly-worked tale of the displacement of an innocent child in her father's affections by a lovely but corrupt woman found in the depths of the forest, has echoes of the folk tale and the modish additions of German Romanticism, with a new addition of psychological under-standing. Good and evil are inextricably mixed in Coleridge's universe, and nowhere so intertwined as in the human heart; the purest emotions are tinged with jealousy, sexual ambition and self-hatred, and the vignette with which the poem breaks off, the joyous child harshly rebuked by the normally adoring parent, reveals the deeper meaning of the poem in a dreadfully familiar form.

> A little child, a limber elf,
> Singing, dancing to itself,
> A fairy thing with red round cheeks,
> That always finds and never seeks,
> Makes such a vision to the sight
> As fills a father's eyes with light;
> And pleasures flow in so thick and fast
> Upon his heart, that he at last
> Must needs express his love's excess
> With words of unmeant bitterness.
> Perhaps 'tis pretty to force together
> Thoughts so all unlike each other;
> To mutter and mock a broken charm,
> To dally with wrong that does no harm.
> Perhaps 'tis tender too and pretty
> At each wild word to feel within
> A sweet recoil of love and pity.
> And what, if in a world of sin
> (O sorrow and shame should this be true!)
> Such giddiness of heart and brain
> Comes seldom save from rage and pain,
> So talks as it's most used to do.

'Kubla Khan', written around 1797–8, with its graceful patterning and relentless inner logic that came easily to Coleridge as a poet, illustrates those principles of simultaneous destruction and creation in nature, mirrored in the inspired creativity of art; the poem suggests the vortices and dissolving lights in the paintings of J. M. W. Turner (1775–1851), the foremost of the English Romantic painters.

While Coleridge's common fame rests on the 'supernatural' poems, each with its strange genesis, his 'conversational' masterpieces are supremely revealing acts of self-portraiture, and crystallise ideas about the poet's nature and social role that continue to be argued throughout the century. If Wordsworth presented his readers with considered answers, Coleridge asked unanswerable questions. ' The Aeolian Harp' (1795) is a poem of subdued mournfulness; the poet's subtly dramatised instinctual sense of that 'intellectual breeze' that fills the world and his own mind is chastened by that orthodoxy which he knew prevented his mind from disintegrating. In no other poem is the mystical aspect of Romanticism, a sense of all life as a dynamic, fountain-like unity in which all distinctions dissolve, so rapturously conveyed:

O! the one Life within us and abroad,
Which meets all motion and becomes its soul,
A light in sound, a sound-like power in light,
Rhythm in all thought, and joyaunce everywhere –

'Reflections on Having Left a Place of Retirement' of the same year is also a desperate renunciation of a private vision of joy in favour of social commitment. However 'This Lime Tree Bower My Prison' (1797) is a poised and calm reflection in which the relaxed mind of the poet controls his guilts and dissatisfactions; the finely apprehended imagery of light and shade, rock and water, dramatises the equally precise fluctuations of emotion and experience in the individual life, and Coleridge reaches into a wider world not by a forced declaration, but through a delicate empathy with his friend Charles Lamb. The landscape guides the moral argument, in its progress from the 'still roaring dell' to the distant vistas, its permanent forms graced with superficial movement. In 1854, on a far less happy occasion, the painter J. E. Millais (1829–96) was to produce a similar synthesis of a character-study, a self-portrait and an exact rendering of visible nature, in his portrait of Ruskin at Glenfinlas.

'The Nightingale' (1798) is an education in the genuine appreciation of nature and the true quality of poetry; its Gothic elements show the power of nature reasserting itself over the works of man, and a mysterious holiness – 'something more than Nature' – brooding over the visible world. 'Fears in Solitude' of the same productive year is a painfully honest and uneven poem, where the pressure of thought is keen, the social indignation sharp but controlled, the humanity large and wise, and the careful accuracy of the natural description proof of a general desire for truth.

The 'stateliest' of these 'dances of thought' is the celebrated 'Frost at Midnight' (1798), deeply Romantic in its union of a precisely realised vision of the natural world and a meditation on childhood. The rhetorical effect of deliberate repetition suggests the slow accretion of frost crystals and the gradual acquiring of experience, and the images have the Keatsian distinction of existing for themselves, with little symbolic undertow. There is a Wordsworthian optimism in the contrasting of past and present states of mind, and the glad prediction of the sleeping infant's future. The grave simplicity of Coleridge's fantasy makes the poem the obvious forerunner of the late-Romantic W. B. Yeats's 'Prayer for my Daughter' (1921), and Yeats was to coin the description 'excited reverie' for that inward yet generous self-communing which Coleridge had developed from its tentative beginnings in the musings of William Cowper.

'Dejection: An Ode' (1802), originally addressed to Wordsworth and reworked with a hopeless love in mind, is a bleak farewell to Coleridge's poetic gifts, the more telling for its borrowings from the earlier meditative poems, to suggest an inertia which is despairing rather than a 'wise passiveness'. The poem grows out of a tradition of winter pastoral, including such magnificent confessions of spiritual drought as 'The Nocturnall: Upon St Lucy's Day' and 'Twicknam Garden' of John Donne (1572–1631). There is no conscious pathos; the poem is controlled throughout by the hopeless fixity of the poet's state of mind, with the fountains of inspiration permanently sealed. Nor is there the sense, present in Wordsworth's Immortality Ode, that the unity and variety of nature exists in spite of the poet's stricken state: Coleridge chose the more perilous belief that nature was merely an outward form, an 'inanimate cold world' that takes life and beauty from the 'light' and 'glory' of the perceiving mind. He believes, unlike Wordsworth, that reason and duty have an incomplete control over the deeper processes of life and feeling and that nature itself is often anarchic and unfathomable.

The work that most vividly illustrates the strengths and weaknesses of Coleridge's highly personal and intellectually chaotic manner is his *Biographia Literaria*, published in 1817 when he was forty-four, and a philosopher rather than a poet. It is an autobiography as much as a seminal work of literary theory; emotional and intellectual dilemmas are grappled with as a means of self-analysis. The work grew out of a long brooding on the break with Wordsworth, as a justification of the 'radical difference in our theoretical opinions respecting poetry', which meant Wordsworth's emphasis on the language of poetry and Coleridge's preoccupation with the imagination which repeats the process of divine creation as the poet dissolves and reshapes his universe into fresh unities. The study introduced the concepts of irony and paradox, and the idea of organic form by which a work answers to innate laws of its own being rather than to imposed theories of composition; all of these were quantum leaps in literary criticism, and for the first time the genius of Shakespeare, so especially precious to Romanticism, could be accounted for without puzzlement or apology. The *Biographia Literaria*, 'the best piece of literary criticism in English, and the most annoying book in any language', as it has been pertly called, may be vast, craggy, opinionated and riddled with a philosopher's jargon, but it is Coleridge's most enduring contribution to the literature of his century and after.

Robert Southey (1774–1843) remains the forgotten Romantic poet, apparently beyond the reach of critical rehabilitation, remembered only as the innocently evil genius who involved Coleridge in the mad scheme of 'Pantisocracy', and the butt of Byron's devastating *Vision of Judgement* (1822), where Southey the unworthy poet laureate is the flatterer of a king almost too imbecilic to be contemptible. Like the painter John Martin (1789–1854) who enjoyed an equivalent fleeting public esteem, Southey felt it the duty of an artist to choose large canvases and achieve what Byron yawningly called 'yearly epics': Martin's *The Plains of Heaven* and *Nebuchadnezzar's Feast* have their equivalents in Southey's apotheosis of George III. The taste of the time, of which Wordsworth and Coleridge fastidiously gave no hint, ran to what art historians have called 'florid waywardness, misjudged contrasts and exotic hints', a cultivation of 'ingenuity' and absurd eclectisism, that took full advantage of a European taste liberated by revolution from all decorum, and was brilliantly expressed in the wonderful eccentricities of the Brighton Pavilion, built for the pleasures of the Prince Regent.

Southey never found his voice in poetry as surely as he did in his genuinely admirable prose. His poetry smacks of pastiche: Wordsworth sounds faintly in 'The Cross Roads' and 'Brough Bells', and the tough-minded George Crabbe is timorously reproduced in the *Eclogues* of England and Botany Bay, where Goldsmith is brought up to date with a dash of Coleridgean social criticism. The effortfully picturesque Eastern epics, *Thalaba the Destroyer* (1801) and *The Curse of Kehama* (1810) have none of Byron's satirical skill in comparing oriental nastiness with the homegrown variety, and they are emasculated by Southey's genuine distaste for the exotic (he noted the 'singular absurdity' of the 'Hindoo religion' while researching for *Kehama*). Even the pieces which still find their way into anthologies are exercises in genres better handled by others: 'My days among the dead are passed . . .' is a graceful lyric in the deceptively trivial style of Charles Lamb, but Southey's retreat to a controllable world of literature is handled without the shrewd psychological understanding of the ironic essayist. 'The Battle of Blenheim' and 'God's Judgement Upon a Wicked Bishop' are more assured works of controlled moral mayhem that the masters of grand guignol, the comic poets Thomas Hood and Richard Barham were to bring to perfection in the 1830s. A tenuous line stretches from Southey to Robert Browning through such individualistic Romantics; humanitarian feeling mingled with obsessive grotesquerie. 'The Soldier's Wife' is Romantic social indignation at its most compelling; a timely remainder of the sufferings of a large proportion of the population in these years, with Southey's usually barren metrical virtuosity throwing the picture of the woman and her starving children into stark relief.

The inflated subjects and strained utterance of most of the poems can be forgotten in the forceful ease of Southey's prose. Most Romantic essayists turned to the ornate models of the sixteenth and seventeenth centuries; Southey favoured the unemphatic and flexible styles of Jonathan Swift (1667–1745) and Daniel Defoe (1660–1731), preferring deftness and solid construction over elaborate fancy. His biographies of Nelson (1813), Wesley (1820) and Cowper (1833–7) helped prepare public taste for Carlyle's gallery of 'heroes', and many of the social topics casually referred to as 'Victorian' were located and discussed by Southey in his *Colloquies on the Progress and Prospects of Society* (1829), a work justly valued by social historians and hardly approached by general readers. The *Portuguese Journal* (1807) is compact, sardonic, brilliantly selective and surprisingly similar to the admired, impressionistic prose style of Byron, Southey's famous detractor. The 'safe dexterity' of his formal prose, so utilitarian that quotations cannot be drawn from it, was a happy influence on writers like Thomas Macaulay and John

Stuart Mill, who had been protected from Romanticism by their parents' creeds.

If Southey's youthful advocacy of revolution waned, like that of Wordsworth and Coleridge, he remained a passionate humanitarian. He deserves to be remembered for more than his tale of *The Three Bears* which usually earns him a snide literary footnote; he provided, among other things, a concise definition of how the visionary Romantic was modified into the Victorian gentleman:

Neither to solicit public offices, nor to shun them, but when they are conferred to execute their duties diligently, conscientiously, and fearlessly: . . . to be the liberal encourager of literature and the arts; to seek for true and permanent enjoyment by the practice of the household virtues; . . . behold the fair ideal of human happiness.

Percy Bysshe Shelley (1792–1882) inhabits a rather more attractive critical no-man's-land; still ranked among the 'great' Romantic poets because of his close association with Byron and Keats, and admitted to possess an overwhelming creative energy that fired a number of later generations including Robert Browning, but not unreservedly admired by any current theory of poetry. He still suffers from the purification of his character by prudent editors and biographers in the nineteenth century; the atheist apostle of political revolution and free love was redesigned as Matthew Arnold's 'beautiful and ineffectual angel', and Francis Thompson's 'child' peeping through 'the wild mask of revolutionary metaphysics'. The novelist George Eliot, a nice discriminator among the Romantic poets, sardonically captured this trivialisation of a dangerous intellect when an obtuse character in her *Middlemarch* (1871–2) fatuously describes an impetuous young man as 'a kind of Shelley, you know . . . I don't mean anything objectionable – laxities or atheism or anything of that kind. . . . But he has the same sort of enthusiasm for liberty, freedom, emancipation – a fine thing, under guidance'. By the end of the century the Romantic Lucifer had become so innocuous that George Bernard Shaw, who had an accurate sense of Shelley's challenge to orthodoxy, satirically proposed that the suggested memorial to the poet should include Shelley in top hat, escorting his wife and children demurely to church. The traducing of Shelley's poetic achievement was worse than the weakening of his personality by legend; under his widow's zealous editorship and understandable need for money, the lyric poems he had hardly bothered to work into finished form were thrown into prominence and his long, thorny metaphysical works shaded into oblivion.

Shelley's life was brief but volcanic. 'Baited like a maddened bull' at his first school, consoling himself with private scientific experiments like his wife's Frankenstein at Eton (Shelley was to run counter to the 'confusion to the memory of Newton' attitude of most Romantics in his belief that science could reconcile man and nature), and the runaway spouse of the first of several women he was to see as the victims of society, Shelley became attached to the circle of the materialist philosopher William Godwin (1756–1836) after his atheist pamphlet got him sent down from Oxford. Following the notorious suicide of Shelley's wife, marriage to Godwin's daughter, with whom he had been living, scarcely repaired his reputation; he lost custody of his children, felt confirmed in his hatred of authority, and embarked on the emotionally strenuous years of travel in Italy. These included a productive friendship with Byron, the deaths of two children through the stresses of bohemian life, love affairs with various Platonic flames, attempts to pacify his sister-in-law, Byron's mistress, and his drowning en route to meet Leigh Hunt, who was planning a journal that would feature the work of English poets in exile on the Continent. The cremation of the recovered body in a ceremony witnessed by Byron (who retired to his carriage to get drunk) and recorded by the unreliable but unforgettably dramatic Edward Trelawney (1798–1881), is a high point of the Romantic macabre. Yet Shelley's daily life was less offensive to moralists than that of his friend Byron: 'tea, Greek, and pedestrianism', and exhibited a thoroughly serious attitude towards his craft. Shelley's *Letters*, though less vivacious than Byron's, and less intellectually elaborate than Keats's, form an invaluable self-portrait of 'a high spirit and a failing heart', unexpectedly brisk and practical, forthright and displaying an extraordinary pleasure in exercising his critical faculty.

Much of Shelley's work is daunting to the casual reader, and must be left to experts adept at disentangling its knotty metaphysics. The Odes, and the confident sweep of *Adonais* (1821), his threnody on the death of John Keats in Rome, give a truer sense of his prodigal energies, and works like *Julian and Maddalo* (written 1818, published in *Posthumous Poems*, 1824), with its canny investigation of character and invigorating sense of landscape, show how Shelley came to strengthen his volatility with Byron's tough worldliness. 'Ozymandias' (1818), the one poem of Shelley's that the common reader is bound to know, is strangely uncharacteristic of his style, in its stubborn rigidity and conventional form.

Shelley prided himself on the creative chaos of his method; when Trelawney exclaimed in amazement over an illegible first draft that looked more like a water-colour sketch than a poem, his friend explained:

> When my brain gets heated with thought, it soon boils, and throws off images and words faster than I can skim them off. In the morning, when cooled down, out of the rude sketch, as you justly call it, I shall attempt a drawing.

Nothing could be further from the meticulous discipline of Wordsworth's 'emotion recollected in tranquillity'. Shelley's method was closer to the fervour and vividness of the sketches of Constable and Turner, often more passionate than the finished, more conventional oils. He shared Turner's obsession with dissolving or coalescing sources of light that are alternatively whirlpools of energy or vortices of destruction. As the 'Letter to Maria Gisborne' (written in 1820, published in *Posthumous Poems*) suggests, Shelley saw himself as an alchemist of words, transmuting emotion and experience into new forms.

> The spider spreads her webs, whether she be
> In poet's tower, cellar, or barn, or tree;
> The silk-worm in the dark green mulberry leaves
> His winding-sheet and cradle ever weaves;
> So I, a thing whom moralists call a worm,
> Sit spinning still round this decaying form,
> From the fine threads of rare and subtle thought –
> No net of words in garish colours wrought
> To catch the idle buzzers of the say –
> But a soft cell, where when that fades away,
> Memory may clothe in wings my living name
> And feed it with the asphodels of fame,

Which in those hearts which must remember me
Grow, making love and immortality.

Shelley's poetry, like Byron's, has the appearance of
negligence, though Byron's *sprezzatura* actually throws his
extreme technical agility and severe moral judgements into
relief. Shelley's formal carelessness arose out of the technical
problem of how to dramatise the processes of change in the
mind of man and the world of nature. The imagery of 'The
Cloud' (1820) seems to lack coherence, but only because it
describes nature working through a state of flux to final
harmony. This seething change within nature is in constant,
unresolved tension with Shelley's idealism, yet in the best of
his poetry, like *Adonais*, grand and permanent images of rest
and acceptance emerge from the fragmentary expressions of
rage and sensory experience.

Shelley's poetic voice is significantly more varied than that
of the other Romantics. He moves confidently from the lyric
dramas of *Prometheus* (1820) and *Hellas* to political balladry (*The
Mark of Anarchy*) and burlesque (*Swell-foot the Tyrant*), through
riddling myth-making ('The Cloud') to a personal
development of the classical elegy (*Adonais*). He invents
graceful lyrics in the style of Byron and of Thomas Moore, and
created the one drama of the period that is still taken seriously.
The Cenci (1819) had a scandalous success as a closet-drama, a
tragedy of incest in the manner of the great Jacobean
playwrights, though Shelley's play suffers somewhat from its
indignant decorum. The crime against Beatrice is an
undeniably powerful metaphor for the way in which traditional
forces corrupted youthful idealism, in Shelley's view.

Shelley's most underrated works are the indirectly self-
revealing lyrics; not the enervate vaguenesses of anthology
pieces like 'Lines: "When the lamp is shattered" ', but the
well-muscled 'Ariel to Miranda' and the tense 'Aziola', which
explores simultaneously the poet's tangled relationships with
the natural world and the women in his circle.

The life of John Keats (1795–1821) was even more brief and
urgent than that of Shelley, and his influence was more
immediate and as extensive. Keats set out to convey, with
lavish and scrupulous detail, the exact quality of his

apprehension of a seductive and unstable world, and his philosophic attitude emerges from the way he recreates this experience in his poems; his thought must be quarried from his imagery. At the same time, his vivid, argumentative and profound letters, with their convivial spirit, unforgettable phrase-making and impatience of strict logic, develop an intuitive and complex aesthetic. Like Coleridge and Shelley, Keats probes the curious union of opposites in the human mind; the melancholy that informs delight, the sense of mortality that whets passion, the drift to pure sensation countered by the appeal of philosophic speculation, and the guilty conflict between the poet's obligation to be receptive to all experience and his awareness of his social role.

Keats was, despite the Victorian legend of the doomed young poet killed by savage reviews, an intense, sociable and unsentimental individual, whose daily life during his poetical apprenticeship took him from the grisliness of operating theatres in the days before chloroform (with sights that the naturalist Charles Darwin and others were unable to stomach) to a private circle of friends who amused him and furthered the education of the young apothecary. He had the flair of the self-taught man (that Romantic archetype) for finding suitable influences; the lightweight Leigh Hunt, whose example taught him the delights of a free flow of imagery and a frank sensual pleasure through which his thought was to be conveyed; the painters Benjamin Haydon and Joseph Severn (1793–1879) who sharpened his exquisite visual sense and introduced him to 'Grecian' beauty through the newly acquired Elgin Marbles; and the critic William Hazlitt whose passion for Shakespearean drama underlies Keats's central doctrine of 'Negative Capability', which Shakespeare in his unmoralised inhabiting of a series of fictional characters was supposed to have possessed. Yet all such influences, like the women to whom Keats was passionately attached, were intelligently chosen and rationed in their control over him; Keats knew that he needed an 'unfettered scope', as he put it, in which 'the Genius of Poetry' could work itself out in him. While Wordsworth produced his Preface, Coleridge the *Biographia Literaria*, and Shelley his admirable *Defence of Poetry* (1821), Keats left no single critical document, nor did he work out a deliberate doctrine in his poetry. His intuitions develop themselves in his letters to his brothers and close friends; an artistic output in prose not much inferior to the poems themselves, and the product of the few fallow years of a brief but intense life.

The sonnet 'On First Looking into Chapman's Homer' (1816) is an assured, well-paced expression of the pride of a mind whose education has not come ready-made; Keats, who regarded Wordsworth as greater than Milton, has described a 'spot of time', a moment in which he stands on the brink of the possible, that was to occur again and again in his poetry. *Endymion* (1817) is a richly embellished, semi-allegorical narrative, its symbolism as usual only half-disinterred from the imagery. In his mature poetry Keats was to become one of those intellects admired by Goethe who could rest content with the vision of pure phenomena, unlike lesser souls who 'peep in a mirror and then turn it round to see what is on the other side'. *Endymion*, which Keats was later to reject ('there is not a fiercer hell than the failure in a great object') is a kind of intellectual diary, classifying and organising varieties of happiness, from the simple sensory response to beauty, to the workings of the poetic imagination, union with other human beings, and so on. The ample, lucid introduction to the poem shows that poetry is for Keats what nature is to Wordsworth; a kindler of amity, that binds men to the earth by protecting their powers of recollection. Already, private feelings are Keats's favourite milieu, and a 'brooding ardency' his characteristic tone.

In 'In a drear-nighted December' of the same year, Keats produced his own version of a Wordsworthian creed that man is marked by his capacity, alone in the world of nature, to remember and regret, and to feel contradictory emotions in the same instant. *St Agnes' Eve*, written in 1819 during the wonderful flowering of Keats's powers, is a superb evocation of sensory experience at its most intense, set within as much narrative as Keats's essentially static and pictorial art could manage. The Romeo and Juliet story set in the Romantic mediaeval past is a brief celebration of youth, love and sexual delight, which the poet's art conjures up from icy cold and chaos, and must regretfully allow to be swallowed up by the storm of time at the end; poetry heightens feeling, but cannot prolong it. *Lamia*, of the same year, is a fascinating experiment, not as adroit and poignant as 'La Belle Dame Sans Merci', that lyrical allegory of the limitations of imagination. *Lamia* loses its balance, falling into that vulgarity and absurdity that Keats was always willing to risk, but the psychological core of the poem, with its hero torn between philosophic rigour and his love for a serpent-woman, looks forward to those novels later in the century which analyse the death of love, where an unacknowledged flaw in the relationship constrains characters to perform increasingly destructive acts in an atmosphere of sterile artificiality. George Eliot's *Daniel Deronda* (1876) makes frequent references to *Lamia*. *Isabella, or The Pot of Basil* (1819) dramatises the perils of those emotions of love and desire through which the great lessons of the imagination must be learned.

The five Odes of the great volume of 1820 explore Keats's growing belief that the poet must imaginatively become the thing he contemplates; the initiatory 'Psyche' harks back to *Endymion*, where the loving union of god and mortal and the symbol of the poet as priest (learned from Wordsworth) lead to the creation of a vast inner landscape and the promise of universal reconciliation. 'Ode on a Grecian Urn' is a formally perfect but enigmatic study, contrasting the fictitious permanency of art and the humiliations and failures of human beings beset by time. 'Ode to a Nightingale' is a long meditation on the poet's typical loss of identity in his absorption in the physical experience offered him; opiates, wine and death are metaphors for his dissolving consciousness, as the bird, that Romantic symbol of the poet's art, frees him from the prison of his 'sole self' and offers the possibility of living other lives imaginatively. 'Ode on Melancholy' contains the most robust imagery and audacious thought in Keats, arguing that the richest humanity lies in a capacity for experiencing strong and conflicting emotion: a counter to the suave and lovely 'Grecian Urn'. 'To Autumn' is the fitting climax to what must be seen as a sequence; purged of argument, and simply transmitting flawlessly ordered imagery whose symbolism is simply that inherent in the natural world. The grandiose and commonplace live side by side, and the poignant sense of death and decay is balanced by the typically Keatsian sense of something about to happen: 'And gathering swallows twitter in the skies'. It is a poem whose pleasures can be enjoyed by the least sophisticated intellect, and whose profundities can never be exhausted.

The essential Keats is revealed in 'This Living Hand', whose eight lines are an angry cry against a common mortality, as vivid as anything John Donne wrote, and more agonising than the Gothic fantasy Keats exploited so tellingly in *Isabella*.

> This living hand, now warm and capable
> Of earnest grasping, would, if it were cold
> And in the icy silence of the tomb,
> So haunt thy days and chill thy dreaming nights
> That thou wouldst wish thine own heart dry of blood
> So in my veins red life might stream again,
> And thou be conscience-calm'd --see here it is --
> I hold it towards you.

George Gordon, Lord Byron (1788–1824) is only grudgingly admitted to the status of a Romantic poet, and it is not entirely clear that he would have sought it. An aristocrat in a generation of middle-class poets, and lacking the typical insular temperament (he took some trouble to travel to the Levant at a time when most Englishmen took grateful advantage of the wars with France to dispense with the Grand Tour, and he was rapidly off to Europe again after the peace), Byron was a net exporter of influence to the Continent, and Alfred de Musset (1810–57) in France and Alexandr Pushkin (1799–1837) in Russia were his disciples. But, as usual with English Romantic poetry, the novel reaped the richest rewards in the long run, and *le beau ténébreux* of *byronisme* translated itself into the heroes of Stendhal – the pseudonym of Henri Beyle (1783–1842). In an even more curious passage of literary history, Byron's success with oriental subjects now regarded as faddish, caused Sir Walter Scott ('Scotch Fielding! as well as great English poet – wonderful man! I long to get drunk with him . . .') to turn from his own colourfully banal narrative poems to his marvellous enrichment of the novel. That Byron was influential is beyond question; in what sense he was a Romantic, and to what degree he may be granted to be 'good' are more intractable problems.

Byron, 'an actor who devoted immense trouble to *becoming* a role that he adopted' according to his notable detractor T. S.

Eliot (1888–1965), led a crucial movement within the century of self-created literary figures: the familiar essayists with their assumed personae so lovingly dwelt on in all their crotchets, the notorious flamboyance of the privately prudent Disraeli, Dickens, with his larger than life personality and confident vulgarity, Tennyson, with his bohemian dress and disdain for timid decorum, and finally the literary dandies Oscar Wilde and 'Jimmy' Whistler (1834–1903), who sprang complete from their own conceptions of themselves. 'Vulgar' is a word perpetually flung at Byron: T. S. Eliot continued by demonstrating how

> . . . his own vices seem to have twin virtues that closely resemble them. With his charlatanism, he has also unnatural frankness; with his pose, he is also a *poète contumace* in a solemn country; with his humbug and self-deception he has also a reckless raffish honesty; he is at once a vulgar patrician and a dignified toss-pot; with all his bogus diabolism and his vanity of pretending to disreputability, he is genuinely superstitious and disreputable.

Byron's problem, until *Beppo* (1818) and *Don Juan* swam into critical focus and established him as something that could be called a satirist, was that he was only a Romantic in the vulgar sense, and a self-confessed Augustan in the works that really mattered. *Childe Harold* (1812–18) proved that he was a Romantic egotist, but not in the wholesome, didactic sense of Wordsworth, or with the discomposing candour of Coleridge.

> There is a pleasure in the pathless woods,
> There is a rapture in the lonely shore,
> There is society where none intrudes,
> By the deep sea, and music in its roar:
> I love not Man the less, but Nature more,
> From these our interviews, in which I steal
> From all I may be, or have been before,
> To mingle with the Universe, and feel
> What I can ne'er express, yet can not all conceal.

His Eastern tales, with heroes who share the traits of the Gothic villain, the hero of sensibility and the noble outlaw, are now the merest literary curiosities, an aberration of taste that nineteenth-century novelists soon deplored; Jane Austen pokes delicate fun at Byron in *Persuasion* (1818), George Eliot's Felix Holt objects to heroines whose hair weighs more than their brains, and Anthony Trollope shows how Lizzie Eustace's Byronism feeds her awesome self-delusion.

At a more serious level, Byron blasphemes shockingly against the central tenets of Romanticism. Whereas for Wordsworth the poet 'binds together by passion and knowledge the vast empire of human society, as it is spread over the whole earth and over all time', Byron claimed that:

> I by no means rank poetry or poets high in the scale of intellect. This may look like affectation, but it is my real opinion. . . . I prefer the talents of action.

He steered an uneasy course between 'the postscript of the Augustans', which included one poet he did admire, George Crabbe, and 'all of us youth' who ride the 'Pegasus' of the new poetry: 'we keep the saddle, because we broke the rascal, and can ride. But though easy to mount, he is the devil to guide; and the next fellows must go back to the riding school'. Byron was the complete Augustan in his irritating view that his main business was to amuse with what his inheritor W. H. Auden (1907–73) called the mastery 'of the airy manner':

> Art, if it doesn't start there, at least ends,
>   Whether aesthetics like the thought or not,
> In an attempt to entertain our friends.

In a later generation, Byron would probably have been a novelist and poetry would have lost a singular talent; he always saw the human being in his social milieu as the only possible subject.

The somewhat premature first volume, *Hours of Idleness* (1807) shows the Byronic persona already in full dress; a rationalist with a hankering after melancholy, a sentimental nostalgia and a taste for destruction; sexually experienced, but with an impossible idealism leading to bouts of revulsion. The lyrics have not worn well in their lush emotionalism, and Byron's friend Thomas Moore remains an Irish influence he cannot match, except in the plangent 'So we'll go no more a-roving', in which Byron calls on his Scottish roots. The 'Epistle to Augusta', his notorious half-sister, rumours of whose affair with Byron helped drive him from England, is the most gripping of the early poems, a curious equivalent to

Wordsworth's *Tintern Abbey*, and a portrait of the less protected milieu of a man of the world:

> Kingdoms and empires in my little day
> I have outlived, and yet I am not old.

The Waltz (1813), a neglected but robustly funny satire, indicates Byron's essential puritanism masquerading as worldly wisdom. *The Vision of Judgement* (1822) is an incomparably deft burlesque with affinities to Pope's *Rape of the Lock* (1714) and Milton's cosmic manner, using Byron's famous technique of elaborate digression as the central characters shuffle and sidle in all their inadequacy and malevolence while Byron struts. *Don Juan*, which occupied the last ten years of the poet's life and remained unfinished, and its overture, *Beppo*, are the achievements on which his reputation rests. 'It may be profligate, but is it not *life*, is it not the *thing*?' wrote Byron triumphantly to a friend. He had no very optimistic view of human nature, though it did not always take the morbid expression of 'Darkness', his blank-verse description of the end of all human life. In *Childe Harold* he mapped out

> . . . the moral of all human tales;
> 'Tis but the same rehearsal of the past,
> First Freedom, and then Glory, -- when that fails,
> Wealth, vice, corruption, -- Barbarism at last.

The desolate world-view of Carlyle and Ruskin is already in place with Byron; history is a spiral downwards, unless it can be checked by the efforts of the moralist.

Don Juan, that apparent impromptu ('For I write this reeling, / Having got drunk exceedingly today') moves adroitly from contrast to contrast, all leaps of plot engineered by predatory women competing for Juan, that Candide of sex. The ebullience of the plot, with its sheer love of movement and vitality, that inspired so many canvases of Ferdinand Delacroix (1798–1863) and J.-L. Géricault (1791–1824), balances a belief that the only constant fact of life is '*man himself*, who always has been, and always will be, an unlucky rascal. The infinite variety of lives conduct but to death, and the infinity of wishes lead but to disappointment'. What intrigued Byron was 'the controlless core / Of human hearts', that endless capacity for self-deception, the goad of sex, and the love of violence that makes his rare visions of innocence (notably in the idyll of Juan and Haidee and his strange tropical pastoral *The Island*) poignant rather than sentimental.

Byron's prose has for many readers as high a reputation as his poetry; vital, bawdy, ordering a flood of experience in an impressionistic manner, sometimes amounting to miniature novels, and always full of an audacious wit. Byron despised consistency, and the consolation of the human condition in his view was the free exercise of whatever talents he possessed.

'Phenomena of nature': the Romantic prose-writers

Leigh Hunt (1784–1859) was a literary impresario whose acknowledged forte was 'the admiration of genius in others'; the forerunner of a group of men of excellent critical judgements and not quite first-class talents, who acted as a link between the severe truths of Romantic poetry and public interest in the new sensibility. Hunt began his career of literary pollination by a volume of *Juvenilia* which inspired Byron to publish his own *Hours of Idleness*, and then flung himself into the periodical literature which flourished at a time when government was repressive and yet there was a consciousness that reform could not be far off. The exuberant *Examiner* (1808-21) drew on itself a series of law suits, culminating in the successful prosecution of the editors for their relishable attack on that 'fat Adonis of fifty', the debauched Prince Regent. 'The wit in the dungeon', as Byron patronisingly called his protegé, made a salon of his wallpapered prison cell for two years, but was not changed into a political theorist

> except inasmuch as all writing nowadays must involve something to that effect, the connection between politics and all subjects of interest to mankind having been discovered, never again to be done away with.

Hunt's whole-hearted association with periodicals was of enormous benefit to the writers of the period. Hazlitt made his reputation in *The Examiner*, Lamb perfected his style in *The Reflector*, while W. S. Landor wrote for *The Monthly Repository*.

Keats and Shelley were brought before the public by this Pandarus of the arts, though Keats was notoriously humiliated by his association with Hunt's flaccid and mildly indecorous verse in J. G. Lockhart's (1794–1854) attack in 1817 on 'The Cockney School of Poetry' in *Blackwood's*. The masterpiece among his journals, *The Liberal*, ran for four magnificent issues, providing a forum for the self-exiled Romantic poets on the Continent, though with Hunt's typically malicious luck it was the proximate cause of Shelley's drowning. When Byron tired of the slatternly Hunt ménage ('a Hottentot kraal') and their drains on his purse, and sailed for Greece, Hunt was left destitute. He revenged himself in the injudicious *Lord Byron and Some of His Contemporaries* (1825), and until his *Autobiography* of 1850 (which reveals less of him than Hazlitt's portrait in *The Spirit of the Age* in 1825), supported himself precariously through essays and anthologies.

Hunt's poetry is now hardly read, except for the curiosity 'The Fish, the Man and the Spirit', and the delicious rondeau 'Jenny kiss'd me', written, surprisingly, to the fearsomely acid-tongued Jane Carlyle. *The Story of Rimini* (1816) is a pallid and highly-wrought retelling of the doomed love of Paolo and Francesca; Hunt admired eroticism and constantly bewailed the puritanical spirit of the time. His closest imaginative affinities are with the academician William Etty (1787–1849), the only English artist to specialise in the nude, and despite his voluptuous reputation, a devout Yorkshireman.

Hunt's own best skills lay in his mastery of the familiar essay, that prose development of the Romantic lyric; intuitive, personal, and apparently random in its development, and 'memorandums for verse' as Hunt said. He based his ingratiating style on that of the 'unaffected' Oliver Goldsmith (1730?–74), and abandoned the eighteenth-century pose of detachment: 'I speak all in my own name, and at my own risk'. He developed an urban subject-matter, stuffing a few hundred words with visual plums and taut character sketches; Dickens was to take his method still further in his apprenticeship to the novel in *Sketches by Boz* (1836). By coincidence, Hunt had been the writer first considered to provide the text for the sporting illustrations that ultimately became *The Pickwick Papers* (1836–7), and even more ironically, he is best remembered today as the original of

Dickens's improvidently flighty and casually cruel Skimpole in *Bleak House* (1853).

In an age hungry for self-improvement, Hunt entered with compassionate enthusiasm into making knowledge 'accessible and attractive to the many'. He was an editor valuable for his pungent convictions, interest in many subjects and faith in his talents, and is especially remarkable for his services to the drama in a century when plays were poor ('bloated farces of mercenary writers') but the actors were great, and the profession of critic honourably filled by Hazlitt, G. H. Lewes (1817–78), William Archer (1854–1924) and George Bernard Shaw. Hunt inaugurated the new reign of critical impartiality in the theatre (before the advent of 'that damned boy' actors had usually purchased their reviews) and he kept the classical repertory firmly before the public mind in spite of a popular taste for spectacle and comedy. Like Shaw, his ultimate inheritor, he regarded music as part of his critical mandate, and was the first notable English critic to take Wolfgang Amadeus Mozart (1756–91) seriously.

Henry James wrote of the greatest of the familiar essayists

> To be light is not necessarily a damning limitation. Who was lighter than Charles Lamb, for instance, and yet who was wiser for our immediate needs?

Charles Lamb (1775–1834) lived in accordance with a deliberately undertaken obligation morally and materially to support his periodically insane but deeply loved sister Mary, who had in a 'day of horrors' murdered their mother. His writings have been neglected in the twentieth century but possess a permanent intrinsic value; they are wholly autobiographical in nature, including the tender, graceful and eloquent essay with sturdy roots in actuality and self-mockery, letters of great wit and moving self-revelation to his carefully tended circle of friends, and his lyric poems.

In his middle years, Lamb became a master of the essay form begun in the sixteenth century by Michel de Montaigne (1533–92), and the personality he reveals through layers of complex artifice is ultimately more 'real' and more moving than any act of simple confession could have made it. He remains the eighteenth-century man of sentiment, quick to feel a subtly expressed sympathy for the weak and suffering, but also the idiosyncratic Romantic with his 'imperfect sympathies' and moments of wild melancholy, prankishness and a leaven of malice, laying before the public his unconcealed flaws like that smoking and drinking to excess which allayed the stammer used to devastating effect in conversation.

The character of 'Elia', a name he abstracted from a clerk in his second place of employment, was as artificial as the neo-Elizabethan style of his language which paradoxically enhanced his Romantic insistence on testing the truth of every emotion he felt. There is a tense balance between his apparent frivolity and the restrained melancholy which is the concealed subject of every essay. In 'Old China', one of the most highly worked Elian pieces, the subject is mortality, and the occasion, Lamb's own love of oriental porcelain, that passion of nineteenth-century men of taste. He creates a domesticated version of Keats's noble 'Ode on a Grecian Urn', through the teacup's miniature 'world before perspective' which leads into the extraordinary soliloquy of Elia's alter ego Bridget (actually Mary), that rapidly reviews the ordinary but tender pleasures of the couple, the past blending with the present and hinting at that old age and dreaded bereavement that must come. The carefully judged rhetorical excesses, the delicate blend of pathos and comedy, and the sense of enchanted privilege accorded to the reader so deftly admitted to these mysteries of another personality, add up to something greater than the apparent sum of the parts. The essay, like its earlier models, presents the reader with an ostensible moral ('We could never have been what we are to each other, if we had always had the sufficiency which you now complain of'). But the real subject is the intricate dissatisfactions of the human condition, which Keats had dramatised more augustly but no more tellingly in his Ode.

Lamb's life was as well-managed as his *Essays*. He travelled scarcely at all, once to the Lakes and once to Paris, and moving house (often made necessary by Mary's instability) seemed to him a species of death. Tenacious of friendship, punctilious in filling his folios for East India House; routine and attachment to an unchangeable past sustained him against an uncertain future and his own mental disequilibrium. His literary productions outside his essays were extensive and mostly now forgotten: *John Woodvil: A Tragedy* (1802) and *Mr H—: A Farce in Two Acts* (1806) met the common fate of plays by Romantic artists in quest of money. He produced with Mary a series of soberly attractive moral books for children to meet the rational educative taste of the time, and that classic of proven value, the *Tales From Shakespeare* (1807). He was by temperament a voracious but discriminating reader, a finely sympathetic commentator on Shakespeare and his contemporaries (*Specimens of English Dramatic Poets*, 1808), and a drily reserved appreciator of his friends Wordsworth and Coleridge.

William Hazlitt (1778–1830) was born into a combative family tradition of radicalism, and began that career on his own account at the age of thirteen in defence of the scientist Joseph Priestley (1733–1804) who had injudiciously celebrated the fall of the Bastille. It ended in 1830 with the completion of a four-volume *Life of Bonaparte*, and Hazlitt had lived to see his former associates in liberalism defect. His perpetual sense of holding a beleaguered intellectual position coloured his literary style, and his vulnerable, surly temperament ('brow-hanging, shoe-contemplative, strange', as Coleridge described it), was a general matter for mirthful discussion.

Hazlitt was long in finding his profession, though he was invisibly laying the foundation of his essays: he studied philosophy greedily, worked as a portrait painter, got up economic theory, entered journalism as a parliamentary reporter, took up theatre criticism in 1813 and was soon, with Coleridge, the most influential literary critic of the day. He lectured on Shakespeare and the Elizabethan drama, while *The Spirit of the Age* (1825), first delivered as a series of lectures in 1818, gives an opinionated and invaluably contemporary view of Romantic poetry. Hazlitt had a great respect for anecdotal actuality and an ability to state his central ideas trenchantly; he bears a strong resemblance to his twentieth-century successor George Orwell (1903–50), seeing a man's political stance as defining his nature and achievements and while radical in his social and political views, aware of a gulf between the cultured man and the uneducated that cannot be bridged by goodwill.

Hazlitt's familiar essay, very different from the ornate form perfected by Lamb, was written with a copious fluency and no pauses for checking the quotations that poured from a well-stocked mind, nor for giving considered shape to what was written. In a revealing image, Hazlitt saw an essay as endless ripples radiating from the original topic. However, the negligent air of his essays is as contrived in its way as the 'assumed manner' Hazlitt so admired in Lamb; his rhetorical effects, involving the absurdist belittling of grand events or the puffing up of trivial glories, shuttle the reader bewilderingly between Lilliput and Brobdingnag in the hope of knocking sense into him. He relies on a code-like vocabulary – 'force', 'honesty', 'justice', 'originality', 'gusto' – which is laid on with cumulative effect. Literature appeared to Hazlitt as a kind of gladiatorial combat, suggested by his personal heroes the prize-fighters, the best of whom 'could either outwit his antagonist by finesse, or beat him by main strength'. Hazlitt has the absurdist writer's sense of the puniness of endeavour which must nevertheless be pursued according to fixed rules for its own sake, and his distrust of Romantic optimism – 'there is that secret affinity, a *hankering* after evil in the human mind' – makes him a cautious forerunner of Joseph Conrad and the Russian Fyodor Dostoevsky (1821–81).

The *Liber Amoris* (1823), half autobiography, half novel, is an uncomfortably fascinating example of Romantic self-revelation as it details the author's obsession with an amateur prostitute of the servant class; a deliberately degraded version of Richardson's famous *Pamela* (1740–1) or a backstairs version of Prévost's *Manon Lescaut* (1732). It has close contemporary resemblances to the painter Henry Fuseli (1741-1825) in his clinically appalled self-portrait and his scientifically prurient studies of emotionally cold women in erotic postures and their carapaces of fashionable clothing.

Thomas De Quincey (1785–1859) is the most quirkish and experimental of the Romantic essayists, and the one whose influence stretches most demonstrably into the twentieth century through his egocentric, impressionistic and heavily artificial prose. John Ruskin, Marcel Proust (1871–1922), James Joyce (1882–1941) and Virginia Woolf drew from his example their techniques of exploring a changing inner consciousness. De Quincey was notoriously indifferent to external logic, and regarded his vast, autobiographical fictions as dreamlike architectural structures in the manner of Giovanni Piranesi (1720–78), the Italian engraver who had specialised in mysterious prisons and ruined vistas. Works such as *The Confessions of An English Opium Eater* were also presented as musical fugues that joined sense impressions and solemn if imprecise emotions in an hallucinatory suspension of reason.

> Everlasting layers of ideas, images, feelings, have fallen upon your brain softly as light. Each succession has seemed to bury all that went before. And yet, in reality, not one has been extinguished. . . . But by the hour of death, but by fever, but by the searchings of opium, all these can revive in strength. They are not dead, but sleeping.

De Quincey idolised Wordsworth, choosing to become his friend and neighbour, and identifying painfully with the poet's family. His aesthetic theories became a hectic parody of the sober use of childhood visions in *The Prelude*; while Wordsworth calmly allowed these unsought insights to recede into the remembered past, De Quincey used opium to prolong and enhance the sensations and memories out of which he began spinning his *Confessions* in 1821. The fantastic and protean aspects of the mind which Coleridge had already begun to explore engrossed De Quincey; for him, as for Sigmund Freud later, dreams were the royal road to the unconscious and more revealing of the self than the awakened intelligence.

Certain human figures blend and blur through De Quincey's grandiose yet slipshod hallucinatory reminiscences; his dead sister, by whose bedside he had kept vigil one sunny afternoon, the forlorn young prostitute who may have taken care of him in London, and other outcasts and angels. Wordsworth's imaginative interest in those who were forced by poverty or idiocy to live outside normal society is exaggerated by De Quincey into a passionate Romantic identification with the pariahs of the world.

De Quincey's most habitual trait is that of amplification, as simple sensations transform themselves into vast symbols; a childhood recollection of his dying father being brought home along country lanes in a carriage radiates into the 'dream-fugues' of *The English Mail-Coach*, a trance-like meditation on terror, destruction and deliverance. His latinate style, recondite vocabulary, strange parenthetical asides and dense imagery suggest the masters of seventeenth-century prose such as John Donne and Sir Thomas Browne (1605–82) and their own sense of the interconnectedness of all things. The visible world exists for De Quincey, as it had for the Romantic poets Coleridge and Shelley, as a mirror of his own creative mind.

De Quincey's experiments in prose were especially useful to later nineteenth-century novelists; Charlotte Brontë created an absorbing pastiche of his torments and opium visions in both *Jane Eyre* and *Villette,* and Dickens, who used the plain approach of Leigh Hunt for his early narratives, reached into the trance-like prose of De Quincey for the poetic rhetoric of the novels after *Bleak House* (1853).

De Quincey was not only a stylist, but a sophisticated if unsystematic literary critic in his famous and characteristically perverse 'On the Knocking at the Gate in Macbeth'. His long essay 'On Murder Considered as One of the Fine Arts' inaugurates one of the obsessions of the nineteenth century; the sympathetic understanding of the criminal mind in fiction.

Thomas Love Peacock (1785–1866) was the Romantic unbeliever, an intimate of Shelley who nevertheless coolly and kindly anatomised the public image of the Romantic poets and their prodigious subjectivity of mind in a series of inimitable conversational novels. A disconcerting and gently subversive writer, with his roots in the *contes philosophiques* of Denis Diderot (1713–84) and Voltaire (1694–1778), he felt out of touch with the world of his more illustrious contemporaries, in which poetry was given the status of a religion and a morality. His detached comic presence in his fiction illustrates Voltaire's maxim that while doubt may be inconvenient, certainty is absurd. Peacock's habit is to get a group of characters with 'crotchets' or intellectual foibles linking them to the notable thinkers of the day into the pleasant surroundings of a country house with an inappropriately Gothic name, and to allow them to run on unimpeded. The distinct flavour of his comedy comes from their absolute inability to impinge at all on one another's consciousness, and resolution only comes, as a delighted contemporary put it, 'at the sound of the dinner-bell'. This chastening of intellectual pride and mild ridicule of metaphysics is softened by Peacock's epicurean insistence on the rational enjoyment of pleasure; he provides a bevy of handsome, spirited and witty heroines to add allure to his fiction and believes in the value of a good table as reconciling man to society.

Peacock managed the arts of living almost heartlessly well. He supplemented a private income with a salaried office at East India House that gave him the opportunity to enjoy London's music and theatres, and he used his leisure in the country for writing. He lived up to Goethe's maxim that the greatest of the arts is that of self-limitation; he conserved his energies wisely. The famous comment on his professional examination for entry to East India House had been 'Nothing superfluous; nothing wanting', and it stands as a fit praise of his literary style as well. His temperament was formal, ironic and retiring; George Meredith, who made an unsuccessful marriage to Peacock's daughter, left a double-edged portrait of him in the Dr Middleton of *The Egoist*, ever ready to sacrifice a child for a superior wine cellar.

Headlong Hall (1816), *Melincourt* (1817) and *Nightmare Abbey* (1818) grew out of Peacock's genuine regard for Shelley; when they read Greek together, it was significant that Shelley sought out Plato (427?–347 BC) while Peacock preferred the comic dramatist Aristophanes (c 448–after 388 BC). Despite the ingenuity and topicality of Peacock's satire, his style came to influence a broad range of English comic writing. Meredith counterpointed social and intellectual systems and undeniable human instinct in a very similar way; Bernard Shaw was Peacock's closest disciple in his formal yet dazzling displays of conversational wit, and *Heartbreak House* appears to echo the typical Peacockian title. Aldous Huxley (1894–1963) attempted modern versions of Peacock's *jeux d'esprit* and defined the country house comedy of ideas versus appetites as a world where 'we are all parallel straight lines' but in which some characters 'are a little more parallel than most'.

Peacock believed that art should liberate men into scepticism. His *Four Ages of Poetry* (1820) provoked Shelley's famous reply in his *Defence of Poetry*, securing his art against utilitarian objections. Peacock survives for two reasons; his own satisfying and witty prose, and his whimsical upholding of a rational, eighteenth-century tradition that forced the Romantics into a systematic defence of their attitudes.

The restraining judgement

What a life mine has been! -- half educated, almost wholly neglected or left to myself, stuffing my head with the most nonsensical trash, and undervalued in society for a time by most of my companions . . . getting forward and held a bold and clever fellow contrary to the opinion of all who thought me a mere dreamer – Broken-hearted for two years – my heart handsomely pieced again – but the crack will remain to my dying day. Rich and poor four or five times, once at the very verge of ruin, yet opened new sources of wealth almost overflowing – . . . And what is to be the end of it? God knows.

Sir Walter Scott (1771–1832) was a complex but not Byronically divided man in his fortunate blend of Romantic intuition and Augustan prudence. The first of the literary titans of the century, paving the way not only for Dickens, Thackeray and Trollope but for Honoré de Balzac (1799–1850) and Hugo as well, he single-handedly transformed the novel from the history of one central character to the dynamic account of the forces at work shaping a whole society. His influence spread rapidly throughout Europe because he could satisfy the needs of a public wild for its own history after the excitements of revolution and war, and his zesty narratives were easily imitated at a superficial level. His Scottish heritage gave him an advantage that no purely English novelist could possess: his ambiguous, often sympathetic understanding of the Jacobite rebellion against the English crown brought him into imaginative contact with the milieu of Stendhal and Balzac, where the Romantic heroism and individualism of the Napoleonic years are dwelt on nostalgically.

Scott's life shows his unexampled flair for putting to good use all the experience that came his way: 'he was makin' himsell a' the time', as an observer put it. Through his private version of the 'negative capability' of the Romantic artist he was able to allow disruptive emotion and a tranquil judgement to co-exist within him, and loved the challenge of hard work at several professions at once: the security and sobriety of a law practice, the lucrative mystery of his anonymous authorship of the Waverley Novels, and the vigorous arts of business. His romantic desire to found a feudal estate on the banks of the Tweed involved him in a series of financial close calls until the printing firm in which he was a partner went bankrupt; even then, he set to work to extricate himself by his own efforts, and after prodigious labours of composition, died happy in his family and public fame, with the posthumous sale of his copyrights paying off his debts.

A voracious reader and a passionate antiquarian with a retentive memory, Scott began his literary career with that occupation of his leisure hours, the three-volume *Minstrelsy of the Scottish Border* (1802–3). He supplied his own interpolations where the originals failed, and this success lured him into original composition. *The Lay of the Last Minstrel*, *Marmion* and *The Lady of the Lake* gave much pleasure to the average reader, for Scott popularised the Romantic sensibility, making its imagery and range of feeling available to a wide audience (as Jane Austen's characters so often testify). Wordsworth and Coleridge were austerely disapproving; Wordsworth rebuked Scott for his triviality, and Coleridge, who felt that the world of *Christabel* had been plundered for gain, wrote contemptuously that Scott's verses were no more than a well-sounding collection of rhyming place-names, castles, armour and nunneries. Scott is not entirely negligible as a poet; the songs from the novels, the piercing eeriness of 'Proud Maisie' and the avowal of genuine Romantic feeling in 'The Dreary Change' all attest to a genuine gift too freely watered down.

Fortunately, Scott's success as a narrative poet faltered after 1813 with the publication of Byron's 'pretty poems never known to fail', those rattling 'samples of the finest orientalism . . . mixed with western sentimentalism', like *The Corsair* and *The Giaour*, and the alluring heroism of *Childe Harold*. Pride forced Scott into a new form of authorship, suggested by the sudden emergence of the regional novel in Ireland. Maria Edgeworth (1767–1849) combined a lively use of the vernacular and the display of custom and folklore with an astringent analysis of Irish history at this period of transition. Her outstanding first novel, *Castle Rackrent* (1800), is a tragi-comic treatment of the dilemmas of landlordism; *Ennui* (1809), *The Absentee* (1812) and *Ormond* (1817) attest to her lifelong practical involvement in education by using romantic comedy and mildly picaresque adventure to show the central character's advance towards self-knowledge in the midst of initially unfamiliar Irish scenes. Her intelligent exploration of national mores and discontents, at once intuitively sympathetic and deeply critical, established the tone of the nineteenth-century regional novel throughout Europe; the genre was brought to perfection by Ivan Turgenev (1818–83), who acknowledged his debt to Maria Edgeworth, and returned the influence to the Irish novel through his disciple George Moore.

If Scott developed his analysis of Scottish manners and his theme of the moral education of the individual from the sober art of Maria Edgeworth, his more flamboyant and immediately appealing traits were drawn from the early and brilliant success of the prolific Lady Morgan (Sydney Owenson) (1776–1859). *The Wild Irish Girl* (1806) became a European cult with its extravagant emotions, welter of local colour supplemented by copious footnotes, and Romantic primitivism. Much of its dashing glamour is imported into *Waverley*, where Lady Morgan's sense of a Catholic Gaelic past imaginatively challenging the Protestant Ascendancy is transformed into Scott's deliberative weighing of Jacobite and Hanoverian attitudes.

Waverley (1814), was described by Goethe as 'one of the best things that have been written in the world', and the tale of a young Englishman caught up in the Jacobite rebellion of 1745 was the first in a long series of novels that were to explore the relations between Scotland and England: a theme as broad in its sweep and suggestive in its implications as the history plays of Shakespeare, who remained Scott's deepest influence. *Waverley* is the story of a young man's moral, imaginative and political education, and so belongs to a genre developed by Rousseau, Goethe and Wordsworth, but Scott adds a broad understanding of the background against which his hero moves; Highland Jacobite against Lowland Hanoverian, with the old feudal loyalties undermined by the mercantile and parliamentary ambitions of the rising class. Waverley can detach himself from the spurious glamour of the Prince's entourage only by his own growing self-awareness, and at length he is safely installed within 'the quiet circle of domestic happiness, lettered indolence, and elegant enjoyments'. The good life in its outward form is still what it had been in the polite literature of the eighteenth century, but its tranquil moderation is enriched by a secret imaginativeness, through the hero's experience of the perils and delights of romantic infatuation and chivalrous sacrifice. The novel becomes an intelligent and often melancholy weighing of the gains and losses of maturity.

What David Daiches, the eminent modern Scottish critic, has called Scott's 'negligent genius' did not produce novels of consistent quality. Critics are divided about what must be admitted to the core of his achievement: some works, like *Ivanhoe* (1820), once enjoyed a huge popularity but are now ignored, and others, like *The Bride of Lammermoor* (1819), are alternately condemned as trivial melodramas or hailed as acerbic allegories. *Guy Mannering* (1815) explores a theme central to Romanticism; the growing indifference to social bonds. Village tradition is brutally set aside in the name of progress, and a crude enforcement of the law supplants the delicate balance between tenant and laird. *The Antiquary* (1816) initiates another theme; the self-consciousness of the present age and its relation to the past, and the dangers of weakening such a precious and necessary connection by sentimentality or empty erudition. The scholars are drily mocked by the existence of Edie the beggar, a news-carrier, a minstrel, and so the true historian of the district. Scott has Wordsworth's reliance on the uncompromised integrity of peasants and outcasts.

Old Mortality (1816), the favourite novel of the materialist social philosopher Karl Marx (1818–83), is a bold risk, set for the first time beyond the range of living memory, and balancing extreme and frequently unsympathetic elements within Scottish society at a convulsive and murderous period. The Royalists' idealism has degenerated into a defensive greed, while the Covenanters are a fanatical, ruthless and volatile amalgam of selfish interests. It is a remarkable performance; Scott's own cool judgement arbitrates between the repellent factions.

Rob Roy (1817) fills in another piece in the puzzle of national history by describing the decline of the clan system before 1745. Scott realises that a tribal society must of its own nature evolve into a less personal culture, and the example of England must infiltrate Scotland. In his own quiet way, and from a strictly capitalist standpoint, he is as great a believer in economic determinism as Marx himself. The modern Lowlander of 1715, Nicol Jarvie ('Honour is a homicide and a bloodspiller, that gangs about making frays in the street; but

Credit is a decent honest man, that sits at hame and makes the pat play') is lured deeper and deeper into the Highland territory of his primitive brigand-kinsman, and Scott concentrates on the grudging friendship that develops, transcending apparently irreconcilable differences of attitude.

The Heart of Midlothian (1818) is Scott's most ambitious and perplexing novel. It no longer weighs clearly defined alternatives, but offers a disenchanted view of human society. The opening chapters describe a public execution and a riot, and the main plot centres upon Effie Deans, condemned to death for the murder of a child she cannot be proved to have borne, and her sister Jeannie's heroic journey to beg a pardon from the English court after she refused to tell a lie to prevent the sentence. Scotland is suffering from thwarted national pride and rule by an absentee monarch, its subjects aridly preoccupied with law without justice, or the anachronistic principles of a rigid religion. Jeannie Deans's stubborn integrity and compassion, melodramatically set at odds, become Scott's Romantic vindication of humanity in his temporarily pessimistic belief that freedom, justice and dignity must be the possessions of individuals rather than whole societies.

The coolly-received *Redgauntlet* (1824) also makes extraordinary demands upon the reader, and looks forward to Joseph Conrad in its intricate teasing-out of the emotions that underlie political philosophies. Darsie Latimer is drawn like Waverley into a Jacobite plot, this time to restore the Pretender forty years after his defeat. The conspirators are not allowed the conditional heroism of the earlier novel; they are 'discontented fools', jealous even of their monarch, and eventually dismissed with suave contempt by the emissary of George III. Scott's view of history is a pragmatic one; the glamour of the past must be a refreshment to the spirit rather than a call to action in irrevocably changed times. Scott is the Darwin of the political process, and Scotland his Galapagos, where some species thrive and others become extinct according to immutable laws.

There is a still deeper reason for him to welcome the new age of politics. The mysterious Redgauntlet declares with tragic fatalism that 'the privilege of free action belongs to no mortal: we are tied down by fetters of duty, our moral path is limited by the regulations of honour; our most indifferent actions are but the meshes of a web of destiny by which we are surrounded'. The determinist attitudes of feudalism held out no opportunities for the novelist interested in the growth of character and the results of conscious choice, and when Darsie in reply demanded 'the privilege of acting for myself', he was rejecting a faded if glorious world, and claiming a Romantic autonomy for himself and his creator.

Scott, the great man of his generation, was a generous critic, and left a handsome tribute in his *Journal* to Jane Austen, that contemporary analyst of the social contract on a smaller but no less adequate scale.

> The Big Bow-wow style I can do myself like any now going, but the exquisite touch which renders ordinary commonplace things and characters interesting from the truth of the description and the sentiment is denied to me.

Jane Austen (1775–1817) was a Romantic in that she could present everyday sights and actions in a way that offers a fresh sense of human experience, building on the novels of young female consciousness invented by Fanny Burney as surely as Scott had done on the Irish novel. Coleridge himself had 'a high opinion of her merits', and at times her acute piacing of figures in a moralised and carefully described landscape echoes the manner of his conversation poems. The famous remark in *Emma* that 'a mind lively and at ease can do with seeing nothing, and can see nothing that does not answer' suggests a Romantic self-sufficiency, and Emma's mind, 'delighted with its own ideas', sums up a Romantic joy in creation. As a subdued Romantic, Jane Austen values integrity, a fresh and candid response to nature, pure emotions, and a treasuring up of past associations: the implicit values of *Mansfield Park* make the novel a long gloss on the Preface to *Lyrical Ballads*.

Jane Austen lived a life of retirement within a congenial family, and was so confident of her powers that she could avoid the literary world and turn away an ill-advised commission from the Prince Regent himself. If her uneventful life had its dark passages, they remain concealed; her letters give a complete picture of the frugal comforts and gentle pleasures of a young woman of the upper middle class, spiced with occasional deep malice or genuine pious reflection, for she took religion as seriously as her literary mentors, Samuel Johnson and William Cowper. She composed her fiction in a very sociable environment, sharing the progress of her work with her family, 'great Novel-readers, and . . . not ashamed of being so'.

Her creative life falls into her early writing for pleasure, which grew out of a childhood habit of creating plays and drolleries, a fallow period, during the move to uncongenial Bath, and the years of public authorship and high critical standards after 1809. Her letters give ironic accounts of her creative methods, including her celebrated depreciatory reference to 'the little bit (two Inches wide) of Ivory, on which I work with so fine a brush, as produces little effect after much labour', and her fastidious dislike of exotic settings, colloquialisms, and social classes beyond or beneath her notice. She wrote to a niece who was trying her hand at novel-writing:

> You are now collecting your People delightfully, getting them exactly into such a spot as is the very delight of my life; – 3 or 4 Families in a Country Village is the very thing to work on.

Jane Austen's novels fall easily into two groups: *Pride and Prejudice, Sense and Sensibility* and *Northanger Abbey* are attempts to balance and reconcile contrasting qualities within the developing personality, while the more sophisticated *Mansfield Park, Emma* and *Persuasion* show the process by which men and women form societies, deal with the threats of duplicity and selfishness, and reaffirm their values. Jane Austen is by temperament a conservative, but she recognises the need to admit change and her novels are comedies of reinvigoration.

Pride and Prejudice (1813, but the dates of publication are no guide to the order of composition or revision) was for a time the 'darling child' of its author, though she came to consider it 'too light, bright and sparkling'. It is perennially appealing but somewhat superficial; Jane Austen takes little trouble over her heroine's inner life, and the deepest interests of the later novels are treated here with a smart perfunctoriness. *Sense and Sensibility* (1811) is darker in its implications, and happiness is a matter of luck rather than desert in a world of debt, duels, broken vows and illness. Marianne Dashwood is a disconcerting study in tragic realism that Jane Austen chose not to develop; her agonised response to her lover's perfidy is very similar to Natasha's reaction to her failed elopement in Tolstoy's *War and Peace* (1865–9). Such violent feeling, fully comprehended by the novelist even as she disallows it, contradicts Charlotte Brontë's impetuously Romantic indictment of Jane Austen's art.

> What sees keenly, speaks aptly, moves flexibly, it suits her to study; but what throbs fast and full, though hidden, what the blood rushes through, what is the unseen heart of life and the sentient target of death – this Miss Austen ignores.

Northanger Abbey (1818) is often given less than its due because of its interest to literary historians; it is in part a very lively parody of the Gothic novels of Ann Radcliffe (1764–1823) and others, with a heroine who, in the manner of the American Charlotte Lennox's *Female Quixote* (1752), has the disquieting habit of importing the conventions of fiction into ordinary life. The charmingly naïve Catherine Morland has the essential innocence of Scott's Waverley as she uses her vivid imagination to come to a fuller understanding of the life actually within her grasp, and she deepens her emotions through their exercise in a thoroughly Romantic way. Her intuitions rebuke the sophistication of more experienced people.

Emma (1816) is a novel of awesome formal perfection. It develops a Romantic subject – the human need to create – though Emma has only human personalities as the medium for her talent. The novel is about firm but unspoken social covenants, which is why the secret engagement of two characters is so devastating a breach of trust; it is about language, and the manifold puns, word-games and slips of the tongue emphasise a Romantic belief that expression must be fitted scrupulously to perceived truth.

> Mystery – finesse – how they pervert the understanding! My Emma, does not everything serve to prove more and more the beauty of truth and sincerity in all our dealings with each other?

Like Wordsworth's early poetry, *Emma* takes the workaday world as its subject, or landscape well known but suddenly suffused with a shock of delight or sense of harmony; Donwell Abbey calls up sensations familiar from Tintern Abbey itself. Nor does *Emma* confine itself to the emotions of leisure hours, for in it men and women farm, go to law or bear children, and Jane Austen's later admirers, George Eliot and Anthony Trollope, develop her discreet insistence on the role of work in forming personality. When *Emma* appeared that same year in France, it was delightfully entitled *La Nouvelle Emma, ou Les caractères anglais du siècle*; a deft encapsulation of its roots in Rousseau's Romanticism and its proud insularism ('English verdure, English culture, English comfort'). Most significantly, *Emma* predicts the development of the novel form later in the century: when Mr Knightley muses, 'There is an anxiety, a curiosity in what one feels for Emma. I wonder what will become of her', he is speaking prophetically of her literary descendants, the heroines of Trollope, George Eliot, George Meredith and Henry James, similarly 'affronting their destinies'.

Mansfield Park (1814) goes right to the heart of such Romantic topics as the education of the young mind, the influence of landscape on the moral life, and that 'selfishness more or less disguised' that must be overcome by the imagination. The unexamined decorum of the eighteenth century at Mansfield Park is invaded by the metropolitan wit and rapacity of the Crawfords, and the best aspects of the old dignity are preserved by the Romantic integrity of the thoughtful, feeling and introspective Fanny and Edmund. Genuine emotion and cultivated intelligence are valued over egotistical displays of wit and the counterfeit passions of amateur theatricals; rural stability over the heartless allegiances of London. Jane Austen's apparent puritanism is really Wordsworth's own selectivity; a careful discrimination between genuine culture and superficiality.

Persuasion (1818) is another sophisticated version of her favourite Cinderella plot, in which hidden merit is recognised and rewarded. Despite its occasional acerbities, it is a sentimental and autumnal novel, its felicities of expression and the wrenching loveliness of its conclusion offset by a sketchiness of plot. It makes use of a broader social background; an England invigorated by a new class of man enriched by his own merits and assuming a position of leadership left vacant by that landed gentry that Carlyle was to take bitterly to task in the 1840s, and that Disraeli was to try to inspire in his Young England movement.

The minor works and fragments have an interest of their own. *Lady Susan* is an early fling at the epistolary novel in the style of Samuel Richardson (1689–1761) and Fanny Burney. *The Watsons* in its unfinished state marks out territory fully charted in the mid-century by Charlotte Brontë and Elizabeth Gaskell; the difficulties of an unmarried woman's life. Her sex's need to marry was as neutral a fact for Jane Austen as an officer's need for promotion, though she is intermittently candid in her letters about its disadvantages (the lack of privacy, continual child-bearing, and loss of a 'delicious play of mind'). *Sanditon*, by contrast, is an alert and optimistic treatment of the human love of change and fashion: witty, bracing, and marking out new artistic departures just before Jane Austen's relatively early death.

No less than Scott, Jane Austen dramatises the tension between the claims of feeling and imagination in the individual, and the need for men and women to live together by systems of elaborate compromise. Her Romanticism is qualified by the empiricism of the eighteenth century, but it is surprisingly pure.

Jane Austen once declared mischievously that 'if she ever married at all, she could fancy being Mrs Crabbe'. The actual George Crabbe (1754–1832) was probably unlike the figure of her imagination, and very like the spiritually negligent *bon viveur* Dr Grant in *Mansfield Park*, but his work closely resembles hers in its incisive depiction of family relationships, provincial life, and characters damned through small insincerities and a faulty moral education. Like Jane Austen, Crabbe had the Augustan habit of letting the reader see in practical terms the result of an imbalance of passion, and like her he was a Romantic in that his characters' worst faults are failures in sympathy.

Wordsworth, that most exclusive of critics, refused to see any good in Crabbe's deliberately reactionary couplets, particularly when the subject-matter poached on his preserves: 'Nineteen out of 20 of Crabbe's Pictures are mere matters of fact; with which the Muses have just about as much to do as they have with a collection of medical reports or of law Cases'. Crabbe's world, unlike Wordsworth's, was a dourly implacable one which could not be transcended by visionary insights, and its characters are brought up hard against circumstance; his murderous Peter Grimes

> nursed the feelings these dull scenes produce,
> And loved to stop beside the opening sluice;
> Where the small stream, confined in narrow bound,
> Ran with a dull, unvaried, sadd'ning sound;
> Where all, presented to the eye or ear,
> Oppress'd the soul with misery, grief, and fear.

Byron had a sardonic admiration for 'Nature's sternest painter, yet her best', and claimed that 'Crabbe's the man', despite his 'coarse and impracticable subject'.

Crabbe was the creature of a single place, the 'poor and wretched' Aldeburgh of the eighteenth century; son of an unsympathetic father, negligently apprenticed to a surgeon, Crabbe managed to secure the influential statesman and political writer Edmund Burke (1729–97) as his patron, prudently became ordained as a chaplain to the nobility, and set out on his adult course as an active friend to the establishment. *The Village* (1783) was followed much later by *The Parish Register* (1807), which had gone into four editions by 1809, the year of Wordsworth's first independent volume. *The Borough* (1810) and *Tales of the Hall* (1812) were solid successes, and the death of Crabbe's mentally disturbed wife in 1813 allowed him to lead a life of 'tempered exuberance'.

Crabbe's characters are as fascinating, rebarbative and melancholy as the maritime landscapes he described with such morbid fidelity. In his overlapping series of tales he dramatises the way in which compassion is eroded by greed, snobbery and resentment; despite the titles of his volumes, Crabbe's world has little sense of community, and indeed his villagers are depressingly slow to resent Grimes's murdering of his apprentices. The outcasts of his world are not Wordsworth's symbols of resilient humanity, but barely recognisable as members of the species.

Crabbe's poetic vision is, though severe, not lugubrious. A significant body of his verse argues, in a Chaucerian manner, the right basis for married happiness. Such verse tales develop from the eighteenth-century exemplary essay in the *Spectator,* the *Rambler* and the *Idler*, though Crabbe subtly indicates his approval of those who cannot conform; 'The Confidant' and

'The Frank Courtship' show sympathy for the woman with a past and the overimaginative girl. In a similar way, Crabbe's fluent couplets are used not to ensure consensus and point the general moral in the Augustan manner, but to achieve striking feats of characterisation and to suggest volubility of speech; Crabbe works best when he works against the grain.

The Irish poet Thomas Moore (1779–1852) represents a more brilliantly popular mode of Regency verse. This accomplished singer of his own delightful lyrics based on Irish melodies and sentiment, who assiduously cultivated the friendship of Byron and championed the deceased poet against the attacks of Leigh Hunt, was not, as he disarmingly put it, among 'the great guns of modern Parnassus'. Yet he was responsible for the tone of the age; melodiously sentimental, yet rakish, satirical and politically inquisitive, but in love with high life and its opportunities. The gifted son of a Dublin grocer, he rose by his musical creations to become minstrel to the Whig aristocracy in England, and the winning apologist for those fashionably libertine attitudes which Jane Austen treats with such severity in *Mansfield Park*. But while Moore knew that his power to please depended on his amorous lyrics, he also dwelt with tactful vehemence on the tragic history of his native land:

> Then blame not the bard, if in pleasure's soft dream
>   He should try to forget what he never can heal;
> Oh! give but a hope – let a vista but gleam
>   Through the gloom of his country, and mark how he'll feel
>   Every passion it nursed, every bliss it adored, ...

His fulsome offer of the Prince Regent as Ireland's sympathetic saviour did not endear him to his radical acquaintance Hazlitt, who objected sardonically that 'Mr Moore converts the wild harp of Erin into a musical snuffbox'.

Moore's early success with verse of an oddly decorous licentiousness was the inspiration of the younger Byron, who claimed facetiously to have been corrupted by it in 1803; certainly Moore's reputation rested on 'Thomas Little's' propensity to kiss and tell.

Farewell! and when some future lover
  Shall claim the heart which I resign
And in exulting joys discover
  All the charms that once were mine:

I think I should be sweetly blest
  If, in a soft imperfect sigh
You'd say, while to his bosom prest,
  He loves not half so well as I.

The magisterial Francis Jeffrey of the *Edinburgh Review* had handled these poems with a fine puritanical scorn for their coy suggestiveness ('a tissue of sickly and fantastical conceits, equally remote from truth and respectability') despite their undeniable 'singular sweetness and melody of versification'. Moore and his reviewer met for a duel, in one of literary history's more curious anecdotes, but the pistols were providentially unloaded, and Jeffrey fell victim not to a bullet but to Moore's engaging manner ('an innocent, good-hearted, idle fellow'). Moore's life was to be filled with such sudden capitulations to his charm.

Moore was as outspoken a devotee of sexual love as his northern counterpart Robert Burns (1759–96), though his verse was (in a formal sense only) more sophisticated, tampering with native idioms to admit the suave indelicacies of the Earl of Rochester (1647–80). The immense popularity of *Epistles, Odes and Other Poems* made the more enduring *Irish Melodies* (1807–34) possible, not to mention Byron's clever, affecting, but not quite flawless imitations of Moore's style in his *Hebrew Melodies*.

Moore was paid £500 a year by his publishers to present his songs in the drawing-rooms of men and women of fashion and influence. He was an ardent nationalist in music: 'Our National Music has never been properly collected, . . . while the Composers of the Continent have enriched their Operas and Sonatas with melodies borrowed from Ireland'. He knew that his verses owed their singularity to 'that rapid fluctuation of spirits, that unaccountable mixture of gloom and levity, which composes the character of my countrymen, and has deeply tinged their music'. The lyrics, inseparable in the memory from their music, mix a heady sentimentality with a delicate ruefulness at the power of sexual attraction or national feeling to overcome the judgement:

The time I've lost in wooing,
In watching and pursuing
　The light that lies
　In woman's eyes,
Has been my heart's undoing.

Though Wisdom oft has sought me,
I scorn'd the lore she brought me,
　My only books
　Were women's looks,
And folly's all they've taught me.

Moore's influence would have surprised the moralists, or even those readers who noted that the perennial popularity of the *Irish Melodies* could not conceal Byron's ascendancy: *The Fudge Family in Paris* (1818) is delightful in its way, but far outstripped by the satire of *Beppo* and *Don Juan*, and *Lalla Rookh* (1817) is a mediocre version of Byron's orientalism. The American author Edgar Allan Poe (1809–49) was to make Moore's musicality the basis for his intense and morbid Romanticism in a perverse blend of matter and style. Moore's nationalism and his belief in the revelatory nature of sexual love was to be echoed more profoundly in the poetry of Wilfrid Scawen Blunt, while James Joyce the Irish novelist was an enthusiast for Moore in his letters, and apparently chose the uncanny lyric 'O ye Dead' as the motif for the focal story of *Dubliners* (1914).

Moore's achievements in prose were substantial. He was offered the editorships of considerable journals of his day, and wrote a four-volume history of Ireland, as well as biographies of the Irishmen Lord Edward Fitzgerald and Robert Brinsley Sheridan. His memoir of Byron was a valuable early study of the poet, and Moore was an appealing letter-writer and diarist; like the familiar essayists with whom he was acquainted, he gave free rein to his whimsicality, exploring the texture of daily life and eagerly on the lookout for those chance events and quirkish inconsistencies which made life endurable.

The very different Walter Savage Landor (1775–1864) is one of the most unfairly neglected of writers; though a few short poems are known and rather frigidly admired for their austere elegance, his habit of constraining Romantic passion within the outlines of a classical spareness excludes him from most critical traditions. A self-conscious artist, for whom style was the outward manifestation of the moral life, he was some time in finding his distinctive voice. It is unfortunate that he superficially resembles Walter Pater and the Aesthetes and the Decadents, as he set himself resolutely against the separation of art from life: his own style was, as he said, 'select and sparing in the use of metaphors: that man sees badly who sees everything double', and paradox, that basic rhetorical figure of the *fin de siècle*, 'bears the appearance of originality, but is usually the talent of the superficial, the perverse, and the obstinate'. Content mattered more than style: 'It is better to find the object of our researches in ill condition than not to find it at all'.

Landor sought in his poetry and his equally distinctive prose the aesthetic equivalent of his idiosyncratic philosophy of living; a blend of epicureanism and stoicism that consoled him for the disappointments of an embattled life, and which is best described in 'There is delight in singing, though none hear' written to his friend Robert Browning. Ancient Athens was his 'only grand example of social government and of the polished life', and he is a forerunner of Matthew Arnold, whose gravely tender 'Strew on her roses, roses', shares the humanity latent in even the most glacial quatrain of Landor's; their classicism is not a retreat to an art that does not need to forge standards, but a stirring call to measure the present against a more demanding set of values.

Landor collected enemies, and poured a considerable fortune into idealistic enterprises; a volunteer force against Bonaparte, a model estate in Wales, and marriage to a hopelessly unfaithful penniless beauty. The early poems of his long creative life were in a strenuously Romantic mode: *Gébir*, published in the same year as *Lyrical Ballads*, and *Chrysaor* (1808) are well-handled epics in the manner of paintings by Claude Lorrain (1600–82), vast in scale, well-designed, and enlivened with pleasing touches of human emotion. They are completely unlikely to revive in popularity. *Count Julian* (1812) was a drama on a more human scale, in which Landor recognised his 'instinctive horror of declamation'. The elegy or poetic compliment, pared down to four lines, or the frieze-like 'Hellenic' or 'Idyllium', coolly describing moments in classical legend, and the deliberately restrained *Imaginary*

Conversations (1824–9 and 1853) all expressed his desire to reflect upon emotion in order to master it. His poetry 'soothes but to afflict'; the strong feeling that prompts it calls attention to itself by the meticulous planing away of sentiment.

> Past ruin'd Ilion Helen lives,
>   Alcestis rises from the shades;
> Verse calls them forth; 'tis verse that gives
>   Immortal youth to mortal maids.
>
> Soon shall Oblivion's deepening veil
>   Hide all the peopled hills you see,
> The gay, the proud, while lovers hail
>   These many summers you and me.
>
> The tear for fading beauty check,
>   For passing glory cease to sigh;
> One form shall rise above the wreck,
>   One name, Ianthe, shall not die.

Diffuse verse forms had no appeal for Landor; even the sonnet was 'tossing shuttles to and fro', and imagery, though he could show an attentive sensitivity to natural beauty, seemed to him a vulgarism.

Isaac d'Israeli (1766–1848), father of Benjamin Disraeli and the author of the intellectually whimsical and most attractive *Curiosities of Literature* remarked that Landor had written either a century too early or a century too late. The *Imaginary Conversations* do not appeal to the average palate, but they are a highly refined form of Romantic autobiography. Browning and Swinburne deeply admired Landor, and Matthew Arnold sought but never attained his poise. In painting, the French J.-A. Ingres (1780–1867) mirrors his development in an endless search for 'the probity of art', and that interplay of intensity and detachment, the abstract and the physical, which suggests the modern world in all its ferment and complexity measured against the calm austerity of Hellenism. Within England itself the artists Albert Moore (1841–93) and Lawrence Alma-Tadema (1836–1912) shared Landor's elegantly abstract classicism that discreetly promoted the good life.

If Landor represents a Parnassian strain in Romanticism, John Keble (1792–1866) delved back to its devotional roots. His famous sermon on 'National Apostasy' in 1833

inaugurated the Oxford Movement, through which Romanticism infiltrated the established Church, and he produced a
long-lived classic of religious verse that remained in print
from the first neat edition of 1827 to the florid gilt parlour
volumes of the end of the century. In what rapidly became
an essential adjunct to the Book of Common Prayer and
the Bible itself, this ardent clerical follower of Wordsworth
produced a Christian approximation to *Lyrical Ballads*, using
the Romantic apprehension of nature to draw man closer to
God. *The Christian Year*, in its delicate probing of newly
recognised emotions of disenchantment with self and joy in the
natural world, which is 'God's glorious gospel', purges
Wordsworth of his obscure pantheism, and is the essential link
between early English Romanticism and Tennyson's *In
Memoriam*, anticipating its cadences in

> I cannot paint to Memory's eye
> The scene, the glance I dearest love –
> Unchang'd themselves, in me they die,
> Or faint, or false, their shadows prove.

'Seeing is believing': the private vision

Dorothy Wordsworth (1771–1855) is gradually acquiring an
independent status as a Romantic artist. The housekeeper,
secretary and confidante of her brother William, she recorded
the precise daily texture of their lives together with an
unconscious lyricism. Her emphases owe something to the
delicate natural observations of Gilbert White of Selbourne
(1720–93) or to the etchings of Thomas Bewick (1753–1828).
She shares Coleridge's deep belief in the imaginative efficacy
of making accurate descriptions of minute sensory
impressions, and the practical events of daily living – making
pies, washing linen, fetching the mail – are touched with a
reverent gravity that finds the marvellous in the mundane.

> William had slept badly – he got up at 9 o'clock, but before he rose he had
> finished the Beggar Boy – and while we were at breakfast that is (for I had
> breakfasted) he, with his basin of broth before him untouched, and a little
> plate of bread and butter he wrote the Poem to a Butterfly!

She has in addition the ability to convey highly charged

scenes which hover on the brink of profound symbolism; a child catching hailstones, or the vagrant poor moving despairingly over Cumberland. There is a natural eye for perspective – that revolution in aesthetic judgement which gave so much pleasure to connoisseurs of landscape and helped pave the way for the Romantic attitude to nature – and for placing her figures in emotionally eloquent surroundings, while her attention to focus, lighting and the animating element of sound is exquisite. Her landscapes lit by moonlight and charged with expectation and satisfaction are close to the slightly later woodcuts of Edward Calvert ('visions of little dells, and nooks, and corners of Paradise; models of the exquisitest pitch of intense poetry') and Samuel Palmer, with his brief visionary ardour. All together, they share William Blake's passionate truth to nature and the individual revelation. But Dorothy Wordsworth also hints at the later preoccupations of Emily Brontë, that most idiosyncratic of Romantics. Their characters move in a landscape which is both anthropomorphised and aloof, and they share a powerful nostalgia.

> William heard me breathing, and rustling now and then, but we both lay still and unseen by one another. He thought it would be sweet thus to lie in the grave, to hear the peaceful sounds of the earth, and just to know that our dear friends were near.

Emily Brontë's *Wuthering Heights* (1847) was to link two opposite manifestations of the Romantic spirit: the calm visions of Dorothy Wordsworth and the hectic, epoch-making fable *Frankenstein* (1818), the master-work of the nineteen-year-old Mary Shelley (1797–1851), daughter of the social iconoclast William Godwin and the feminist Mary Wollstonecraft (1759–97), and wife to the poet.

Luxuriant myths have grown up about the genesis of this story of the conscience-stricken scientist who gives life to a monster assembled from fragments of corpses. It is an inexhaustibly suggestive archetype that mingles notions of good and evil, creation and destruction in the manner of her husband's poetry, and echoes the legends of Faust and Prometheus. The paradoxes and vivid imagery recall *The Rime of the Ancient Mariner*, and the novel throws out motifs which are woven into fiction throughout the century. Victor, the tormented creator, shares the knowledge of a guilty act that divides him from humanity with Arthur Dimmesdale in Hawthorne's *The Scarlet Letter* (1850) and Raskolnikov in Dostoevsky's *Crime and Punishment* (1866); the Monster, in his longing for acceptance, foreshadows the mysteriously born and unwillingly nurtured Heathcliff of *Wuthering Heights*, who also rends with demoniacal energy that domestic happiness from which he is excluded.

All Mary Shelley's fiction, and *Frankenstein* in particular, has a strong autobiographical bias enforced by her guilt and loneliness. Like her Monster, she had been the agent of one parent's death, and had sought unsuccessfully to win the love of her brilliant father. But these raw energies within the novel are subordinated to the tight plotting and a careful, endlessly refracting structure by which events are reflected through a succession of sceptical minds: Edgar Allan Poe learned from this example how Gothic elements could be rigidly controlled to increase psychological disturbance.

The Monster soon became an indispensable metaphor for the century's first perilous steps towards democracy. 'Reform Bill's First Steps Among His Political Frankensteins' was a success in 1833, and no less apposite when Sir John Tenniel drew the creature as a vote-wielding navvy in 1866, or as the Irish extremists who perpetrated the Phoenix Park murders in 1882, which hardened English opinion against Home Rule.

Mary Shelley wrote five other novels between 1823 and 1837, none of them memorable, but serving to provide for her son until he came into his father's inheritance, along with her editorial work, encyclopaedia entries, travel books, and tales for popular 'albums', those gift books of the period ridiculed so trenchantly when they appear in the Vincy home in George Eliot's *Middlemarch*. Nevertheless, those sugary compendiums helped the short story into existence, and Mary Shelley's show a bewildered talent, able to announce but not to develop a striking idea. Her obsession with the theme of loneliness, etched deeper by the deaths of children and husband, disables her later fiction. 'The Parvenue' is a revealing study of a daughter who cannot shake off a nightmarishly importunate family; 'The Bride of Modern Italy', an immensely entertaining satire on continental manners, developed around Shelley's infatuation with the deceitful Emilia Viviani; like

Charlotte Brontë's *Villette* (1853) it is a lively reworking of events that had humiliated the author in real life. Mary Shelley, a Romantic misfit in the rationalist Godwin household, then a victim like her Monster of Romantic experiment, finally settled down to the sober, productive and industrious life of a Victorian woman of letters.

John Clare (1793–1864) the peasant poet, was the son of a thresher, village wrestler and ballad singer. His sensitive, introspective and nostalgic evocation of a vanishing countryside grew out of an intermingling of the folk verse of his parents and polite literature in the form of a chance-met copy of Thomson's *The Seasons* (1726–30), which set his heart 'a-twitter with joy', and further acquaintance with the 'marvellous boy', the Romantic literary forger and suicide Thomas Chatterton (1752–70), an ominous alter ego. Family poverty forced Clare to hire himself out as a labourer and then as a perilously insubordinate soldier; his first love rejected him, and he married the woman who became 'Patty of the Vale' in his private mythology. He was obsessed with recapturing in his imagination the innocence of childhood: 'There is nothing of poetry about manhood but the reflection and remembrance of what has been nothing more', he wrote, in that deliberately ungrammatical style which removed him from that formal literary culture from which he felt excluded.

> I am generally understood tho I do not use that awkward squad of pointing called commas colons semicolons etc and for the very reason that altho they are drilled hourly daily and weekly by every boarding school miss who pretends to gossip in correspondence they do not know their proper exercise for they ever set grammarians at loggerheads.

Keats's publisher, John Taylor, published Clare's *Poems Descriptive of Rural Life and Fancy* in 1820, and he enjoyed a brief vogue. His creative life was inextricably linked to his native Helpston in Northamptonshire:

> Strange scenes mere shadows are to me
> Vague unpersonifying things
> I love with my old hants to be
> By quiet woods and gravel springs.

Intense, unmoralised observations from nature, or an equally charged mysticism in which a shepherd boy could become the young David, a beanfield Araby, Moses with his rod could appear in a sunset, and Eden in the local fields, have their forebears in the unquestioned visions of William Blake, whose sexual primitivism Clare shared. Like Robert Burns, another dialect poet, and W. B. Yeats much later, Clare used folk idioms in praise of the poet's enlivening appreciation of female beauty:

> . . . when she with garments flowing
> Went talking with me down the lane.
>
> She passed me like a stranger; I think I see her still:
> I could not tell my own true love in such a dishabille.

Clare's modest success was short-lived; by 1827 his publisher was warning him that 'the time has passed away in which poetry will answer', and tried to mould Clare's work into a more saleable form while providing him with a modest annuity. *The Village Minstrel* of 1821 had sold poorly, as did *The Shepherd's Calendar* and *The Rural Muse* of 1835, a reworking of his beloved manuscript 'The Midsummer Cushion', alluding to the country custom of taking plaited wildflowers into the house, had to be seen through the press privately. Failure, poverty, a mass of dependents, marital discord and a move to a new cottage were too much for Clare, and John Taylor arranged for the poet to be taken to a private asylum. Clare escaped after four years, making an agonised pilgrimage on foot, his *Journey out of Essex*:

> The man whose daughter is the queen of England is now sitting on a stone heap in the highway to bugden without a farthing in his pocket and without eating a bit of food since yesterday morning . . . .

The poems written during the years of insanity are exceptionally fine. Clare uses Byron as his persona: the inviolate aristocrat and satirist, untroubled by the sexual guilt and social inferiority which ravaged Clare himself. He believed that his madness had come upon him through his zeal to tell the truth to a world mired in a conspiracy of falsehood; his background of 'greasy-thumbed wenches and chubby clowns' mocked him, and language gave him no more delight. Poetry, he told the sympathetic superintendent of the asylum, came to him 'whilst walking in the fields; he kicked it out of the clods'.

Clare wrote feelingly of the difficulty of preserving an emotional purity in an increasingly sophisticated age. Enclosure – the impounding of land meant for common use in the interests of more efficient farming and profit-taking – became his symbol of the destruction of man's natural impulses. 'Remembrances' shows how memory is desecrated when nature is destroyed: 'Inclosure like a bonaparte let not a thing remain'. The natural world became for Clare a refuge from the hypocrisies and compromises of human society, a kingdom peopled by compliant and innocent women, bathed in a visionary splendour, where the troubled mind of the poet dissolves into the consoling minuteness of grass and flower. This becomes in time the microscopically enlarged universe of Richard Dadd (1817–87) that other asylum-artist who used his imprisonment after murdering his father to produce fantasy paintings that are both chilling and beguiling, including the obsessively detailed *The Fairy Feller's Master Stroke* (1855–64). Christina Rossetti's intensely evoked ceremonies of personal extinction also belong to the evasive tradition of Clare and Thomas Beddoes.

Thomas Lovell Beddoes (1803–49) takes two aspects of English Romanticism to their extremes; a passion for the language of Renaissance drama, and a graveyard-haunting morbidity. A sullen, impetuous intellectual, germanophile and anatomist, an expatriate dedicated to European revolution, he ignored his Romantic peers except for Shelley, whom he helped to see published, and devoted himself to resurrecting the sensibility of Shakespeare's contemporaries.

Beddoes published his first work, *The Improvisatore*, in 1820 and later destroyed every copy he could find; *The Bride's Tragedy* came out in 1822 to very favourable reviews, but was the last work to appear in his lifetime. He developed a strong dislike of England, left the country, and began to study medicine in Europe while writing the first version of his magnum opus, *Death's Jest-Book*, and searching with avidity for 'every shadow of a proof of a probability of an after-existence, both in the material and immaterial nature of man'. His English friends found his finished manuscript baffling, incoherent and unpublishable. The first of his suicide attempts led to his expulsion from university and rootless wanderings over Europe, a bitter return to England, more grotesquely unsuccessful attempts to kill himself, and the bizarre conclusion to his long flirtation with death. 'I ought to have been among other things a good poet', he declared in the will which disposed of his manuscripts and provided champagne for his mourners.

In Beddoes's eccentric and neurotic poetry, life is a mere ghostly prelude to the more significant state of death. The dramas of John Webster (1580?–1625?) are the most obvious influence, along with the graveyard sentiments of Edward Young (1683–1765), but Beddoes has incorporated Shelley's Romantic obsession with dissolution, energy turned against itself, and new forms springing from the putrefaction of tyrannous custom. Beddoes is purely Romantic in his search for a pure and uncorrupted form of feeling; in *Death's Jest-Book* 'the dead are ever good and innocent / And love the living', and remain 'the newborn of mankind . . . in grace and patient love and spotless beauty'. His murder, which left the ghostly hero musing by his corpse like one 'gazing upon a house he was burned out of', has given him the chance to ponder 'a grave-deep question':

> Dead and living, which are which? A Question
> Not easy to be solved. Are you alone,
> Men, as you're called, monopolists of life?
> Or is all being, living?

Beddoes interspersed his plot with lyrics that have a characteristically evasive charm: 'We have bathed where none have seen us', and 'If there were dreams to sell . . .'. His grotesqueries, on the other hand, similar in their self-conscious repugnancies to the drawings of that other Romantic expatriate, Henry Fuseli, have the verve of Robert Browning and his experimental dislocation of syntax to match moral confusion:

> Squats on a toad-stool under a tree
> A bodiless childfull of life in the gloom,
> Crying with frog-voice 'What shall I be? . . . .'

Beddoes is not in control of his vast drama, and the pleasures come from the frequent chance delights of pregnant imagery and the metaphysical wit of his endless meditation on death: 'world-sanded eternity', 'cool as an ice-drop in a dead man's eye', 'damnation's iron egg, my tomb', and 'transparent as a glass of poison'd water / Through which the drinker sees his murderer smiling'. Beddoes's singular and macabre talent for seeing the skull beneath the skin, his crisp imagery, and his heroes who drift half-realised between the dissatisfactions of life and the beckonings of the imagination, mark his affinities with T. S. Eliot:

> The crevice 'twixt two after-dinner minutes,
> The crack between a pair of syllables
> May sometimes be a grave as deep as 'tis
> From noon to midnight in the hoop of time.

The Irish poet George Darley (1795–1846) has never had the general recognition he deserves. His absorbed cultivation of the personality of the Romantic malcontent of rare and delicate imagination, longing to be dissolved into that natural world that offers more truth and sympathy than human relationships, places him squarely between Beddoes and John Clare, and his tenderly wistful treatment of fairy legend makes him a forerunner of his compatriot William Allingham (1824–89). Despite his deliberate decision to live away from Ireland where he would have been condemned to be 'one of those useless appendages to the living world', a poor relation, he was indelibly Irish in his faith in a supernatural element in nature and in the nurturing power of the past: 'I have been to "la belle France", and to "bella Italia", yet the brightest sun which ever shone upon me broke over Ballybetagh mountains'.

Darley's neglected childhood left him unable to trust human affection (despite the potent charm of his 'blackbird's eye'), and he often doubted his own unusual gift; many of his poems show him musing, like Beddoes's heroes, on his grave while helplessly recalling the past or mocked by his capricious talent:

> Wherefore, unlaurelled Boy!
>   Whom the contemptuous Muse will not inspire,
> With a sad kind of joy
>   Still sing'st thou to thy solitary lyre?

This typical despondency is balanced by the lovely clarity of
his invented worlds (his 'leaf-light' fairies leave footprints on
the 'frosted dews' and his unicorn 'feeding on the wind' has a
pelt of 'tissue adust, dun-yellow and dry, / Compact of living
sands') and an ecstatic version of himself as a visionary. His
'Walter the Witless' dances with the ghosts in the churchyard
in festive ghoulishness, or hangs high in the steeple, observing
'huts plain as hives' and 'streams like bright threads' far
below, in a spirited blend of Shelleyan imaginative energy and
Tom o' Bedlam folklore. Darley, a poet's poet, created the
extra-human world of mermaids and imaginative longing so
tellingly exploited by T. S. Eliot in 'The Love-Song of J. Alfred
Prufrock' in 1917; Eliot's closing lines are a fine pastiche of
Darley's *The Sea-Bride*, and Darley in his turn had created his
own uncanny versions of sixteenth-century poetry with the
exquisite 'It is not beautie I demand' and 'With a Lampe for
mie Ladie Faire'. The later critic George Saintsbury (1845–
1933) called him a 'magician' of prosody, who anticipated the
fine and apparently original effects of Matthew Arnold and
George Meredith. It was this discriminating ear, along with
his 'picture-mad' visual imagination, that must have made
Tennyson offer to bring out a collected volume in the 1830s.
Darley refused, out of his stubborn sense of independence, but
scraped up enough money in his review-writing, lodging-
house existence to see his major narrative poem *Nepenthe*
privately printed in a villainous and tiny edition in 1832; a bid
for posthumous fame at least. He grieved over his scanty
reputation, as his single poems found print only in ephemeral
magazines: 'I had as soon be ranked among piping
bullfinches'. A collection of nervous ailments, including
migraine and an exaggerated stammer, made him unfit for
much society, though Carlyle wrote approvingly of his
acquaintance as 'a mathematician, considerable actually, and
also poet, an amiable, modest, veracious, intelligent man;
much loved here'.

Darley's imaginative worlds were not escapist ends in
themselves, but, as he explained them in a letter to a friend, 'a
promontory of thought from which to spring': a means of
freeing himself from his disappointments to a Romantic
liberation of the intellect and the emotions. His grave in
Kensal Green cemetery was discovered in 1973, and he has

been excellently served by a discriminating editor, Anne Ridler; his long-deferred fame cannot be far away.

In addition to his work as a poet, Darley was an accomplished art critic, with an early interest in the Italian Primitives who were to become the new touchstone in English taste with the theories of Ruskin and Dante Gabriel Rossetti. Benjamin Haydon (1786–1846) was similarly fascinated by the need to translate the visible world into forms on paper and canvas, and tragically convinced of his mission to paint vast historical subjects that would rival the French and American achievements of Delacroix and Benjamin West (1738–1820). In devoting his life to this end, he had mistaken the drift of his countrymen's sensibility: Romanticism in England developed on the one hand into the grandiose fantasy of John Martin, and on the other into the tenderly humble subjects of William Mulready (1786–1863) and Sir David Wilkie (1785–1841), and thus into the Victorian mania for genre paintings. The great retrospective exhibition mounted to save Haydon from penury was ignominiously deserted by the crowds when the American showman P. T. Barnum displayed the dwarf 'Tom Thumb' in an adjoining room; in despair, Haydon took his own life.

He left behind an *Autobiography* and twenty-six folio volumes of *Journals*, an invaluable and fascinating compendium of anecdotes and impressions of the great figures of the age; 'fervid and coarse at once, with personal references blood-dyed at every page', according to his unwilling executrix, Elizabeth Barrett. The compositional values and sense of drama which eluded the painter are splendidly present in the raconteur, who gives a vivid sense of occasion when Wilkie argues in execrable French with a print-seller, Wordsworth hisses Canova's nude statue of Cupid embracing Psyche, Hazlitt fails to find a parson to christen his child, and the roll-call of Romantics takes place at the 'immortal dinner' of 28 December 1817, when Keats met Wordsworth.

Haydon explores, like the great novelists of the century, the positive value of illusion; in his finest moments, he has the power of Dickens or Leo Tolstoy (1828–1910) to suggest a sudden reanimation of the past, or presentiment of the future, such as his falling in love with his wife over the deathbed of her first husband, or the grotesquely moving reunion of his aged mother with the deaf suitor of her youth. His wretched, still-born and devouring talent as a painter becomes an obsession which crystallises his imagination, like the amorous infatuations in the fictions of Dickens, Flaubert (1821–80) and Proust.

Haydon's tragically mistaken sense of his abilities – his furious desire to be a painter when his gifts were verbal – emphasises the lure of the visual imagination in the nineteenth century. Hazlitt, Thackeray and Charlotte Brontë all made false starts as painters, and even the writers who were not also artists were deeply touched by this new passion for describing the visible world.

Haydon died just before the revolution in English painting which he had sought to bring about emerged as the Pre-Raphaelite Brotherhood, with its mutual inspiration from the image and the printed word, and the ideal of making 'art in its higher range a delightful mode of moral elevation', as Haydon had predicted rapturously. If he had failed to make Wordsworth lurking behind a pillar in *Christ's Entry into Jerusalem* (1820) in the least ennobling, he had nevertheless discovered the principle that was to bring past and present into a jolting unity in Millais's genuinely revolutionary *Christ in the House of His Parents* (1849).

A much quieter talent, Mary Russell Mitford (1787–1855), author of *Our Village* (1824–32) and *Belford Regis* (1835) besides many forgotten poems and aristocratic melodramas, tapped the vein of Mulready and Wilkie, and is the earliest of a notable nineteenth-century sisterhood; women who wrote to support their families after the male providers had failed. Fanny Trollope (1780–1863) made good the inadequacies of her gentleman-farmer husband with her novels and travel books, despite her belief that the grandeur of Niagara ought to defeat the pen of a gentlewoman. Harriet Martineau (1802–76) gave up needlework and tea-making when her family 'lost their gentility' and she made a reputation and a modest fortune with her able and oddly endearing popularisations of Malthus in her *Illustrations of Political Economy* (1832). Felicia Hemans (1793–1835), deserted with her five children, ransacked history for instances of juvenile heroism and maternal tenderness to be done into inoffensive verse, only the parodies of which ('The boy stood on the burning deck . . .' and 'The stately homes of England . . .') remain current today.

Perhaps the most remarkable woman of this type was Fanny Burney (1752–1840), who lived on into the early years of Victoria's reign as a relic of Dr Johnson's circle. Her style and taste eventually hardened into a grotesque parody of eighteenth-century sensibility (in her journals) and Johnsonian orotundity (in her cruelly-received 1832 biography of her father); she possessed illimitable courage and resolution, but was not adaptable, and not sympathetic to the world of her old age. Fanny Burney had enjoyed eight years of public fame as the author of the spirited novels *Evelina* (1778) and *Camilla* (1781) before sacrificing her talent to her family's ambition by becoming Mistress of the Robes at the unimaginative and parsimonious court of George III; the journals of these years of dreary servitude have a high, stylish comedy in their indirect criticism of the cold selfishness of the royal couple and the antic scandals of their children, but she paid a high price for her inevitable reserve, in the loss of what her direct successor Jane Austen called a 'delicious play of mind'. Fanny Burney married an emigré aristocrat, and as Madame d'Arblay was trapped on the Continent during the Napoleonic wars. Her journals of the period give an outstanding picture of the lives of private citizens during the upheavals of the decade, and her account of Waterloo anticipates the fictional blend of pathos and the unromantically commonplace in the famous central chapters of Thackeray's *Vanity Fair* (1847).

Mary Mitford was the daughter of loving but improvident parents, and her father's passion for gambling and disinclination for his own profession of medicine soon ran through her fortune and her mother's. Fortunately the young woman discovered a style and a subject that would sell: an amalgam of Jane Austen's finely observed rural families, and 'one of the most fascinating books ever written', Gilbert White's *Natural History of Selbourne* (1789). *Our Village*, a delightful precursor of the more reflective *Cranford* (1853) of Elizabeth Gaskell, shows a very acute gauging of the reader, whose intelligence is flattered by Mary Mitford's shrewdness, while nostalgia is satisfied by the discreet expurgation of subject matter. The detailed scenes are left unmoralised; no awkwardness intrudes, and certainly no social commentary. Her tone is that of the female letter-writer with time to amplify and the obligation to amuse, and her flexible syntax generously accommodates her observational powers. An attentive irony towards her own presentation of herself stops her natural optimism before it becomes banal.

The pugnacious and ebullient William Cobbett (1762–1835) could not have been more unlike the discreet and conscientiously charming Mary Mitford. He does, however, share her nostalgia for a vanishing rural England, vigorously articulated in the *Rural Rides* of 1830, where he relishes good housekeeping on a national scale: '*plain manners* and *plentiful living*'. He was the first of his century's Romantic socialists; 'the pattern John Bull of his century', wrote his admirer Carlyle, and 'one of the cheerfullest sights . . . in the sickliest of recorded ages, when British literature lay all puking and sprawling in Werterism, Byronism and other sentimentalism . . .'. Carlyle, Ruskin and William Morris were all to share Cobbett's desire to retrieve a phantom world of mediaeval harmony, presided over not by the 'white-washed and dry-rotten shell on the hill, called the "gentleman's house" ', but by great nurturing monasteries.

Born into that nine-tenths of the population who 'gain our livelihood by the sweat of our brow', Cobbett remained an ardent believer in self-help, spelled out in his opinionated and immensely likeable *Advice to Young Men* (1829): literature was one of the applied arts, in his view, and his family had book-learning thrust upon them to keep their farm going while Cobbett himself was in prison for an article that had protested against flogging in the army. A good hating man, he loathed the universities for 'the drones they contain and the wasps they send forth', and imaginative literature as well:

> An empty coxcomb, that wastes his time in dressing, strutting, or strolling about, and picking his teeth, is certainly a most despicable creature, but scarcely less so than a mere reader of books, who is, generally, conceited, thinks himself wiser than other men, in proportion to the number of leaves that he has turned over.

Cobbett wrote vigorous, Swiftian prose, and if he was slow in getting his political bearings, he was endearingly articulate about these intellectual shifts: in fact, his capricious blending of conservative and radical positions was the hallmark of the English social Romantic. The lampooner of the French Revolution became the friend of Bonaparte; the Tory whose windows were broken by the American mob later returned to bring back the bones of the revolutionary Tom Paine (1737–1809) for burial in England. Hazlitt, who shared Cobbett's aggressiveness and his susceptibility to criticism, wrote sympathetically of his unaffected egotism, his 'outrageous inconsistency', and 'headstrong fickleness', and also praised his undeniable raising of political journalism into 'a kind of *fourth estate* in the politics of the country'.

Cobbett's strength lies in his Carlylean enjoyment of his own achieved moral and intellectual position. He can, like the Romantic poets he affected to despise, involve the reader sympathetically in his world by the vivacious recall of key moments in his life; shared emotions that make all men kin. 'It makes a part of my happiness', he wrote, 'that I have the means of calling on so many just and merciful men to rejoice along with me.'

2
'Excitement of every kind':
1830–50

By 1830, the first generation of Romantic writers with their serious attitude to the powers of the imagination and the wider obligations of the poet had died or become inert; Keats, Shelley and Byron were gone, Wordsworth and Coleridge had become remote sages, and the death of Scott in 1832 would leave English fiction to ineffective regents until the emergence of Dickens with *The Pickwick Papers* in 1836. A void existed to be filled; the golden age was over, and the heirs to Romanticism were to make hay with the legacy of imaginative freedom. The 1830s was a time of extravagance, experiment and a lively crudity; Thackeray, who laid down the pattern of his robust art during these years, praised the 'philosophy of exaggeration' that prevailed, and wished that more writers and painters would 'work for the galleries'. Eventually, the crowd-pleasing fictions that dealt in fantastic criminal prowess and an impossibly luxurious aristocracy (the 'Newgate' and 'silver fork' novels) were sobered into narratives that projected remedies for poverty, disease, and the evident lack of mutuality in a newly industrialised society. As political reform proceeded without disaster and the threat of revolution receded by the late 1840s, fiction was transformed from lurid projections of crime, insurrection and suspicion into a detailed and sympathetic depiction of the actual lives of a working class that was destined to play an increasing part in the politics of the century.

If the 1830s were a time of 'much leisure and unbounded curiosity, when excitement of every kind is sought after with a morbid eagerness' (according to the religious reformer John Keble), there was a satisfying sense of real progress and achievement in politics, economics, science, technology and spiritual feeling. It seemed to many that the millennium had arrived with the Reform Act of 1832 that increased the electorate by 50 per cent, and the social and economic reforms that were suggested by the Utilitarians, the *laissez-faire* economists of the 'Manchester School', and the post-Romantic social philosopher Thomas Carlyle promised to remedy all ills with simple formulae: 'the greatest good for the greatest number', and 'Do the Duty which lies nearest Thee'. In 1872 George Eliot was to write nostalgically in *Middlemarch*, her great novel of Romantic feeling percolating through English society at the time of the 1832 Act, of 'those times when reforms were begun with a large young hopefulness of immediate good which has been much checked in our days'.

The 1830s and 1840s are notorious for the miseries which natural disasters and an imperfectly regulated economy visited on the poor. The Corn Laws, imposed in 1804 to suit an electorate of land-owners, had kept the price of wheat artificially high, and the Anti-Corn-Law League of 1839 became a focus for reformist agitation, with its articulate leaders and astute manipulation of public opinion through monster rallies and the use of the penny post. The repeal of the Corn Laws in 1846 was a significant victory for reform. The Poor Law Amendment Act of 1834 was a less happy solution to the problem of poverty, typical of the formulaic answers of the period. Old systems of relief had begun to fail in a time of a mobile and increasingly urban working population, liable to be thrown into want by the vagaries of industrial supply and demand, and the burden of care was transferred to local boards under centralised control; the workhouses provided as a grudging reprieve from starvation were designed as 'uninviting places of wholesome restraint', where inmates were humiliated and their families torn apart. The implication was that the very poor had created their own misery by reckless breeding and improvidence, and this Malthusian attitude to poverty was attacked indignantly by writers throughout the century. The squalid system of dubious relief existed until 1929 despite the fear and loathing it caused; in 1883 a compassionate clergyman wrote in *The Bitter Cry of Outcast London* that one Londoner in eight died in the workhouse. No doubt these places, by allowing paupers and their families to barter liberty for life, prevented outbreaks of violence similar to those of 1816, and damped down that civil insurrection so feared before 1848. The nineteenth-century Poor Law became the prototype of the new bureaucracy (a word that had to be explained to Queen Victoria), and the administration of relief to paupers provided the model for those local boards of public health which eventually did away with the scourge of cholera.

The decisive imaginative event of the decade came with Keble's 1833 sermon on 'National Apostasy' that awakened a latent mystical and Romantic strain within the Church of England. In 1830 Dr Arnold, headmaster of Rugby School, had felt that 'no human power' could save 'the Church as it now stands', referring not to its admitted spiritual torpor but to the undermining of its legislative and economic privileges through secular reform. The Oxford Movement of Keble and his colleagues was ecstatic, introspective and authoritarian, and it made a stand against the liberalising and scientific trend of the age until 1845, when irresistibly worldly and empirical impulses broke its power.

1830–50 is a time of preparation and experiment, in which minor figures now hardly read marked out opportunities for more able writers, and poets and novelists whose greatest achievements came after the mid-century explored the possibilities before them. Public taste was equally uncertain, and swung between a hankering after Byronic or Shelleyan Romanticism and a new practical absorption in invention, reform and commerce, that would be welded together in the late 1840s as a realism touched with poetic insight, of which Dickens's *Dombey and Son* is the finest example.

'A LARGE YOUNG HOPEFULNESS': THE 1830s

The free play of talent: novelists of the 1830s

The novelist and prime minister Benjamin Disraeli, later Lord Beaconsfield (1804–81) was the most successful literary opportunist of this experimental age; his uncanny ability to exploit a trend at exactly the right moment came from his inner compulsion to dramatise the possibilities that lay before him in his own life. The Byronic heroes in his early novels were discreetly made to conform to the standards of a traditional community, and for all his emphasis on style and wit, the political health of England remains the greatest good throughout his novels. There is a bedrock seriousness, a lifelong search for permanent principles, that draws him close to such apparently antipathetic serious writers as Anthony Trollope and George Eliot. The exotic, precocious dandy of the 1820s gradually became the self-controlled, patient statesman of the Millais portrait of 1881, and it was significant that he chose to be painted by a man similarly muted by time. Disraeli created his political identity by the controlled experiments of his novels which projected fantasies of his ambitious self in a way that could not compromise his pragmatic career; he only wrote when held back from action. 'My books are a history of my life – I don't mean a vulgar photograph of incidents, but the psychological development of my character', he explained in 1875.

The first set of novels, *Vivian Grey* (1826–7), *The Young Duke* (1831), *Contarini Fleming* (1832) and *Alroy* (1833) are examples of the 'silver fork' school of fiction, with all its vulgar opulence of setting and heady emotionalism that survives only in the parodies of Dickens's *Nicholas Nickleby* (1839) and Thackeray's *Novels by Eminent Hands*, where Disraeli is guyed in 'Codlingsby'. These early novels are consoling fantasies, notes towards the construction of a public personality that Disraeli always treated ironically. From the beginning, the discovery of self is achieved by the interplay of the handsome and gifted alter ego, the powerful, enigmatic and often Jewish mentor, and a beautiful, spiritually alert woman. *Henrietta Temple* (1836) and *Venetia* (1837) are an emotional clearing of the decks; full-blooded episodes of romantic love and poetry and the aristocratic sense of *noblesse oblige* with which Disraeli the commoner and outsider always identified, that left him purged of impractical idealism and ready for a political career and a notably successful marriage of convenience.

Coningsby (1844), *Sybil* (1845) and *Tancred* (1847) are also written during a period in the political wilderness; the first is a messianic bravura piece, a manifesto of 'Young England' reviving 'a crown robbed of its prerogative, a church extended to a commission, and an aristocracy that does not lead'. Carlyle, who called Disraeli an absurd monkey dancing on John Bull's chest, had obviously been picked up and used to good purpose. In *Sybil* Disraeli coined the still-current term 'The Two Nations' to describe the threatening gulf between rich and poor in England, slipping effortlessly into the novel of social exploration at the right moment. *Tancred* painted a broader picture of spiritual aridity as his high-born hero left his privileged surroundings to make a journey of self-discovery in the Holy Land; Disraeli had already shaken into place the elements of George Eliot's extraordinary *Daniel Deronda* (1876), with its own sense of society as a living organism and the need for the individual to find a higher purpose. The last two novels had to wait until the fall of Disraeli's Conservative government: *Lothair* (1868) had a hero who asked the pertinent Victorian question 'What I ought to DO and what I ought to BELIEVE', and *Endymion* (1880) is an experimental gallery of psychological portraits in the manner of Browning.

Disraeli's novels have an amplitude of scale, strong visual sense and stylish wit that ought to have ensured them greater popularity. He can bring the inner and outer worlds into an exhilarating tension, manipulating the balance between psychological and social realism. Disraeli's combination of a respect for the world's judgement and his inherited sense of values which despises outward success in the spirit of Ecclesiastes fills his novels with a high, ironic comedy.

Edward George Bulwer Lytton (1803–73) was far less poised; a blasphemer against Romanticism who was privately 'overcome with the sense of his own identity' and who lived intensely in an 'imagination kept rigidly from the world', even as he sat in Parliament as the representative of Benthamite radicalism and claimed that the modern writer 'must find an audience in Manchester and Liverpool' where 'the people at large . . . are the best judges of music and of poetry'. He detached himself obsessively from his early love of Byron: 'the aristocratic gloom, the lordly misanthropy, that Byron represented, have perished amid the action, the vividness, the *life* of these times'. This sense of estrangement between the man who was a 'popular' writer by theoretical conviction and the secretly guilty Romantic made writers of a happier integrity uneasy about his slippery style: Joseph Conrad referred to his 'polished and so curiously insincere sentences', and Thackeray, an enemy who wrote *Catherine* (1839) as a satire clarifying his obscure hatred of his colleague, explained that 'there are big words which make me furious, and a pretentious fine writing against which I can't help rebelling'.

Bulwer Lytton's habit of following his market in a surpassingly vulgar age ensured his quick passage to oblivion. *Falkland* (1827) was a deliberately Byronic novel, an attempt to translate Goethe's own *Werther* (1774) into English terms. *Pelham* (1828) was an outstanding success, an obsessively heartless novel which takes as its motto 'Nothing is superficial to a deep observer', and it shows men and women who can only exist on the stage of the fashionable world. The characters are seduced by the glamour of high life without having the inner complexity and private standards of de Rastignac and his associates in Balzac's *The Human Comedy* of the 1830s and 1840s. Thackeray's *Vanity Fair* (1847–8) may be an attempt to make good the deficiencies of *Pelham*, by showing the genuinely seductive nature of wealth and fashion in the context of mortality and disappointment.

Bulwer Lytton then turned to the most controversial form the novel was to take in this experimental period. *Paul Clifford* (1830), *Eugene Aram* (1832) and *Devereux* (1829) invented the hero who is idealistic and intelligent, but compelled by circumstances to become a criminal: the novelist was fascinated by 'a world of dark and troubled secrets in the breast of every one who hurries by you!' These works grew out of a period of depression, and remain deeply troubling because Bulwer Lytton's authorial direction is so slight; his criminals have a ruthless amorality and final exhaustion which anticipates Heathcliff in *Wuthering Heights*.

As Bulwer Lytton's personal unhappiness increased with the notorious failure of his marriage and political ambitions, he redoubled his efforts as writer and editor: *The Lady of Lyons* (1838) and *Money* (1840) are, along with the pleasant dramas of the Irishman Dion Boucicault (1822?–1890), some of the very few worthy plays from the 'winter solstice' of the British drama.

'Great crime', Bulwer Lytton decided, 'is the highest province of fiction . . . . It is moral, and of the most impressive and epic order of morals, to arouse and sustain interest for the criminal.' His two novels set during the Terror probably influenced Dickens's *A Tale of Two Cities* (1859) – a novel which does not sit easily in the Dickens canon – and the sympathetic presentation of the criminal is explored with a wealth of intelligence in *Great Expectations* (1860–1). Bulwer Lytton's highwaymen and murderous ushers had made *Oliver Twist* possible in 1838, and Bulwer had also anticipated Dickens in creating that quintessentially Victorian figure of law and order, the fictional detective (in *Night and Morning* in 1841). If Disraeli coined the phrase 'the two nations', Bulwer Lytton provided the even more invaluable 'the haves and the have-nots' in *Lucretia* (1846).

The influence of this unstable artist on his colleagues was profound. Disraeli modelled his early social manner on *Pelham*, and the older novelist managed Disraeli's political début and introduced him to his future wife. Bulwer Lytton maintained a long friendship with Dickens, suggesting by his blundering and bold experiments lines that Dickens could explore with greater assurance.

The genres in which Bulwer Lytton wrote are either vanished or transmuted beyond recognition by greater artists. He remains both the impresario and the victim of the 1830s.

The chastening of Romanticism

'The genius of this time', according to Bulwer Lytton, was 'wholly anti-poetic.'

> When Byron passed away, the feeling that he had represented craved utterance no more. With a sigh we turned to the actual and practical career of life: we awoke from the morbid, the passionate, the dreaming.

Even so, this hectic involvement in public life and the literature of social prescription – what the philosopher J. S. Mill (1806–73), writing of Carlyle, called 'the anti-self-consciousness theory' – was prompted by an essentially Romantic fulness of feeling. Carlyle was the arch-foe of introspective feebleness but nevertheless claimed the intuitive powers of the poet: 'the characteristic of right performance is a certain spontaneity, and unconsciousness' and 'the healthy know not of their health, but only the sick'. Most writers kept up a covert, animating connection with Romantic modes of thought which stimulated their powers of discovery, and none expressed this with more openness than J. S. Mill. He was the supremely gifted and influential reformist of the century, author of the *Essay on Liberty* (1859), the *System of Logic* (1843), *Principles of Political Economy* (1848), *Utilitarianism* (1863) and a strangely melancholy document, his *Autobiography* of 1873. As a boy he had been the subject of a notorious and outwardly successful experiment in enforced precocious education by his father, a colleague of Jeremy Bentham (1748–1832), the inventor of the concept that the central criterion of human morality was 'the greatest good for the greatest number'. J. S. Mill, reading Bentham in young adulthood, 'felt taken up to an eminence from which I could survey a vast mental domain, and see stretching out into the distance intellectual results beyond all computation'. Bentham's Utilitarianism, which was to be so violently attacked by Dickens in *Dombey and Son* (1848) and *Hard Times* (1854), was in its best aspects 'the commencement of a new era in thought', as crucial to nineteenth-century material progress as Coleridge's theories had been to spiritual development. Yet Mill himself, while not repudiating his rationalist training, came to feel 'a dry heavy dejection' in 'the melancholy winter of 1826–7' and described his feelings in the exact terms of Coleridge's own Ode. He was saved from the destructive effects of prolonged depression when he discovered Wordsworth's poetry, which taught him to blend a generous humanitarianism and a reverence for the self with utilitarian theory. The poems

> seemed to be the very culture of the feelings, which I was in quest of. In them I seemed to draw from a source of inward joy, of sympathetic and imaginative pleasure, which could be shared in by all human beings; which had no connexion with struggle or imperfection, but which would be made richer by every improvement in the physical or social condition of man.

In retrospect it seems that the post-Romantics were ignoring the solution that Wordsworth had proposed in his Preface; that the poet was the most necessary of men, keeping alive the purest forms of feeling, memory, and a sense of brotherhood that did away with social injustice. Most of the great Romantic poets had, as a basic aesthetic task, described their progress from self-absorption to an identification with a wider world; Coleridge's conversation poems argue that man finds his greatest happiness only in a social context, Shelley merged his egotism in revolutionary fervour, and Byron became a critic of society. But as the world of the nineteenth century became more complex, more ruled by technological advance, which its literature found no way of incorporating, more urban and more prone to controversy, Romantic optimism and the constant reference back to nature as the test of integrity of thought and feeling became impossible. Wordsworth's 'Nature' became the 'long unlovely street' of Tennyson's *In Memoriam* and Arnold's introspective questionings, and city living mocked the Romantic sensibility in poetry. The post-Romantic aversion to the apparently narrow indulgence of private feeling became a powerful guilt that provides the drama of Victorian poetry, even while it disables it from the great achievements of Romantic verse.

Alfred Tennyson (1809–92) came from a background of brooding instability; his father, an unwilling clergyman, tutored his sons in a rectory in Lincolnshire whose flat, misty, threatening surroundings became the outward shapes of inner gloom in *Mariana* (1830) and *Morte d'Arthur* (1842). *Poems by Two Brothers* (1827) was followed by Tennyson's first independent volume in 1830, the product of his Cambridge experience and his friendship with the brilliant Arthur Hallam (1811–33), whose sudden death, followed by long years of hardship and the emotional strain of a long engagement, was the subject of the long elegy *In Memoriam*, after which Tennyson's life altered for the better, with marriage, the laureateship and public adulation. The period before 1850 was marked by hostile criticism, to which Tennyson affected indifference, and solid advances in technique. His success was to harm his reputation in the twentieth century; he gained the reputation of being an adroit flatterer of his audience, or 'the most punctual exponent of contemporary feeling', in G. M. Young's dismissive phrase. He is still in the process of being re-evaluated: 'the bower we shrined to Tennyson' was described by Thomas Hardy in 'An Ancient to Ancients' as a ruin of rubble and spiders' webs, and is still being cleared of débris.

'Supposed Confessions of a Second-Rate Sensitive Mind', of all titles the most defensive, is Tennyson's earliest exploration of that Romantic subjectivity so unacceptable to the mood of the 1830s; that 'damned vacillating state' of imaginative suspension which was so congenial to his gifts. 'The Kraken' (1830), with its monstrous, surging imagery suggests the vast and dangerous depths from which the conscious mind draws the material for its creative acts; a latter-day 'Kubla Khan', and like Coleridge, Tennyson worked best when symbolically exploring the sources of his art. *Mariana* is an awesomely efficient mood-piece, vague but potent in its evocation of a generalised sexual guilt that Dante Gabriel Rossetti was to develop as an obsession in poetry, in his own stricken landscapes and sense of enslavement to the past. A great many of the early poems stress Tennyson's interest in the isolated or imprisoned life, and none more so than 'The Lady of Shalott' (1842), with its dense, eloquently organised and highly coloured imagery, its Shelleyan enchantress, Coleridgean curse, and enigmatically Keatsian conclusion. It suggests how Tennyson will always divide the human personality into a masculine activity and idealism and female passiveness and creativity; the dramas of his inner life and his sense of social conflict present themselves in sexual terms.

Despite the languorous beauties of its verse, 'Oenone' (1832) is another work of self-admonishment; the nymph suggests the banished world of Romantic contemplation, and Paris must choose between allowable attitudes: the 'Honour and homage' of the public sphere as Herè advises, or the Arnoldian 'Self-reverence, self-knowledge, self-control' that Pallas urges. Nature no longer offers the old solace, as Oenone's pine-groves are felled like Gerard Manley Hopkins's Binsey poplars later in the century; the future is a world of war, and Troy in flames.

'The Palace of Art' (1832) underlines the vehemence of Tennyson's rejection of pure imagination, but is an unpleasing poem, since the Soul's decision to leave her 'lordly pleasure house' for a life of duty among men is based on a craven fear of horrors lurking within the individual mind rather than on a genuinely social instinct. 'The Lotus-Eaters' (1842), deliquescent, almost repulsive in its exaggerated musicality and lush imagery, is a preparation for the state of uncertainty and decay hungrily dramatised in 'Ulysses' and 'Tithonus'. *Morte d'Arthur*, like the other poems of this bridging period, finds its way out of the impasse of subjectivity by using an heroic central figure, a past of recollected vital action, and a puritanical rejection of 'the giddy pleasure of the eyes'; its imagery is intense but restricted. 'Ulysses' and 'Tithonus' share the same 'deep-chested music', a Wordsworthian orotundity that is used by Tennyson to present unresolved situations rather than absolute conclusions pondered over many years. These two poems were written in the shadow of Hallam's death, 'with the feeling of his loss more upon me than many poems in *In Memoriam*', and their paradoxes and ambiguities are more puzzling than those of the dramatic monologues of Robert Browning later, since Tennyson offers no guide to discrimination between the opposing attitudes within the poems. 'Break, break, break', Tennyson's finest short lyric, is purely Romantic in its definitive statement of the loss of an illuminating joy in nature, and finely democratic in its expression of this complex sentiment through a readily available experience.

> Break, break, break,
>   On thy cold grey stones, O Sea!
> And I would that my tongue could utter
>   The thoughts that arise in me.
>
> O, well for the fisherman's boy,
>   That he shouts with his sister at play!
> O, well for the sailor lad,
>   That he sings in his boat on the bay!
>
> And the stately ships go on
>   To their haven under the hill;
> But O for the touch of a vanished hand,
>   And the sound of a voice that is still!
>
> Break, break, break,
>   At the foot of thy crags, O Sea!
> But the tender grace of a day that is dead
>   Will never come back to me.

By 1842, Tennyson was winning back for poetry the respectability it had lost in the years when material and political progress had engrossed the public imagination. According to Richard Monckton Milnes (1809–85) of the *Westminster Review*, 'the large and intelligent middle class of this country' was now eager to purchase a poetry 'more respectable than it has ever been before . . .; more human, more true to the common heart of man'. The Christian Socialist Charles Kingsley praised the 'specifically democratic' tendency of Tennyson, and his working class hero Alton Locke found the 1842 volume 'the embodiment of thoughts about the earth around me which I had concealed, because I thought them peculiar to myself'. 'Locksley Hall' was urgently modern, violent and impatient of intellectual subtlety; a hymn to progress that dare not draw breath for fear of admitting doubt.

The Princess (1847) was a deserved success; the combination of apparent flattery of the age, a fairy-tale, and a love story, put the long narrative with its exquisite incidental songs through seventeen editions by 1877. It is a gigantic fruit-cake of a poem, rich and nutritious, piling up imagery, event and suggestion; a mixture of the lyrical, the 'mock-heroic gigantesque' and the 'true sublime'; a wilful farrago, and a Victorian Shakespearean comedy. The final message is a triumphant, Romantic valuing of instinct over theory, of simple, shared human experiences over the refining of the intellect and imagination. The careless, jumbled riches of the poem suggest that life must be lived in its own incoherent and deeply satisfying way, and the songs threaded through the bizarre narrative mark the common anniversaries of sexual awakening, responsive love, birth and death.

In Memoriam (1850) marks the end of the first half of Tennyson's creative life; a meditation on the death of Hallam, who had founded his career and from whose influence he needed to emancipate himself without doing violence to the memory of his friend. The poem combined the emotional truth of Romanticism with the egalitarian intellectual spirit of the time: 'All who have suffered will read it with delight', wrote the critic George Lewes, and Coventry Patmore, author of a later philosophic elegy *The Unknown Eros* (1877), praised its lack of 'self-consciousness'. Tennyson called his verse cycle 'a kind of Divina Commedia', and it is a precise mapping of the experience of loss and recovery. Powerful Romantic feeling is communicated not by the 'egotistical sublime', but through a diffident, exploratory tone that enlists the reader in a common search for truth, and the roots of the poem lie in popular devotional verse; the hymns of John Wesley (1703–91) which

Tennyson greatly admired, and Keble's *The Christian Year* (1827). 'In a good hymn', Tennyson explained, 'you have to be commonplace and poetical.' *In Memoriam*'s strengths lie in its exquisite, unhurried gradations of emotion, like those of the contemporary song cycle in Germany, where every lyric unfolds a single emotion and is also part of a careful formal arrangement which expresses a sense of growth and development.

Charles Tennyson Turner (1808–79), the brother of the laureate (he took his surname from an uncle who had made him his heir), is almost unknown today, a few anthologies doing scant justice to his subtle and crepuscular sonnets. He had the family failings of melancholy, slovenliness and morbid reserve, made worse by his addiction to opium, but he was also an indefatigably industrious clergyman who turned a barbarous, drunken and superstitious parish into a sober and healthy community. He had published with his brother in 1830 and kept back his work until 1864; his naturally morbid modesty shrank from comparison. However, his 342 sonnets are remarkably good reading and have been revived to some extent by the poet John Betjeman (1906–), a more recent commemorator of small emotions.

Like his forebear William Cowper, 'a soul too sad for trust and prayer', for whom he felt 'a rapture of pure sympathy', Tennyson Turner 'enforced his own solitude', and concentrated on developing an exquisitely original sensibility in which the commonplace illuminated by a sudden insight became proof of eternal existence. His poetry dwells on the uncertainty of human happiness and the ever-present nearness of death in a brooding sense of an after-life, and his poetry (like that of the later Thomas Hardy) often takes as its subject that which is not quite human but which has been touched by human qualities: a scarecrow left out in the fields, a skeleton, an agricultural machine, or a household pet. His art is one of indirections operating within a very formal context, a precise play of light and darkness, and fluid shifts of imagery; his vocabulary uncommonly pleasing for a minor poet, with the 'unbaffled grace' of a swallow, or the 'shuffling leafage' of autumn. He is no sentimentalist, despite his propensity to dwell on the children life denied him, or to juxtapose the great and small in nature. His thought is frequently toughly metaphysical, as when he concentrates on the face of an infant victim of smallpox, 'all-confluent now, and molten by disease'.

Tennyson Turner's death was the occasion for one of his brother's finest poems, the Catullan threnody that dedicates the 1880 collection; a pastiche of Tennyson Turner's own marked preference for shifting imagery of water, shadow and sound, developed in his greater brother's more robust tones.

> Midnight -- and joyless June gone by,
> And from the deluged park
> The cuckoo of a worse July
> Is calling thro' the dark:
>
> But thou art silent underground,
> And o'er thee streams the rain,
> True poet, surely to be found
> When Truth is found again.

Thomas Hood (1799–1845) found his own way of reconciling private feelings and the obligation to appeal to middle-class readers with works of general popularity and social relevance, by developing a strand of comedy latent in Romanticism into a passionate and tender grotesquerie. His comic verse has affinities with the *Trivia* of Keats; nimble, neat, self-consciously infantile, half self-portraiture and half deliberate concealment. He is even closer to his friend Charles Lamb in his shrewd awareness of the therapeutic value of laughter, his apologetic stammer and clerical appearance, his domestic loyalties, incurable punning and free association of ideas. Hood's comedy is based on insecurity, indignation and a fascinated fear of cruelty, easily transformed into the memorable ballads of moral outrage: 'The Song of the Shirt', 'The Workhouse Clock' and 'The Bridge of Sighs', that real-life Lady of Shalott.

> One more Unfortunate
> Weary of breath
> Rashly importunate,
> Gone to her death!
>
> Take her up tenderly,
> Lift her with care;
> Fashion'd so slenderly,
> Young, and so fair!

> Look at her garments
> Clinging like cerements;
> While the wave constantly
> Drips from her clothing;
> Take her up instantly,
> Loving, not loathing.

Ruskin, another possessor of a whimsically associative brain and a strong moral sense, praised Hood and his contemporary, the satirical illustrator George Cruikshank (1792–1878).

> When the powers of quaint fancy are associated . . . with stern understanding of the nature of evil, and tender human sympathy, there results a bitter or pathetic spirit of grotesque, to which mankind at the present day owe more through moral teaching than to any branch of art whatsoever.

Hood, a not very successful journalist, always short of money and reduced on one occasion to writing his comic pieces with the bailiffs lurking and his wife in childbed in the next room, was grimly aware of the incongruity of his life and his reputation as a humorist: 'no gentleman alive has written so much comic and spitten so much blood . . .'. Early Romantic pastiche in the manner of Keats ('The Plea of the Midsummer Fairies' reads like early Tennyson) was soon discarded in favour of comic verses, often with the cheerfully crude illustrations by the author. Leigh Hunt observed that Hood's comedy was based on obsession:

> His brain teems with humorous fancies, but he cannot afford to part with one. Every quip or crotchet which the train of associations suggests he insists on imparting to the public . . . . Once caught by a play on words, his course defies calculation.

Though Hood knew that his true subject-matter was 'things words cannot reach' – a profound melancholy and sense of disjointedness – he had an inexhaustible delight in language: the pun, revived by Lamb's researches into Elizabethan drama, and the argot of the streets and the sporting scene that developed out of Regency rakishness into Hazlitt's essay style and Pierce Egan (1772–1849) who wrote *Tom and Jerry: Or, Life in London* (1821). Hood's juxtaposition of different worlds and their codes develops into the bizarre masterpiece *Miss Kilmansegg and Her Precious Leg*, a satire on a society dehumanised by greed; the heiress with her golden artificial limb (so much more enticing than one of mere flesh) is beaten to death with the appendage by her gamester husband. It is the world of Dickens's *Our Mutual Friend* thirty years before its time; a mushroom society imaged forth in symbols of maimed bodies and useless property, in tones of defiant glee.

Another comic writer, Richard Harris Barham (1788–1845) was an eccentric who claimed that 'I am a man of regular habits, and unless I go to bed by four or five in the morning at latest, I am really fit for nothing next day'. He developed a peculiarly English talent for fantasticated family reminiscence during his convalescences after the many injuries of his accident-prone career. An antiquarian and a Tory of the deepest blue (condemning *Oliver Twist* for its 'radicalish tone'), he collected his fables and anecdotes in the *Ingoldsby Legends* of 1837, a volume free from all constraints of good taste.

Barham was a genuinely learned man, owing as much to the irreverent and scholarly inventions of Peacock as to the verbal flourishes of Hood. His vivacious language conquers by excess in its grab-bag of dog-Latin, legal and heraldic terms, slang and foreign languages; his supple verse is stiffened with a multitude of internal rhymes. Yet he is whimsically aware of the slipperiness of language, and most of his plots can be summed up as people betrayed by niceties of meaning:

> Remember Old Nick
> To take folks at their word is remarkably quick.

Barham's comic verse is distinguished by a ruthlessness that plays a prominent part in the comedy of the nineteenth century, from Miss Kilmansegg's fate, to Lewis Carroll's jokes about death in the *Alice* books, W. S. Gilbert's spirited renderings of executions and lampoons on faded beauties in his librettas for the Savoy operas and in the *Bab Ballads* and his passion for a crude poetic justice. Yet Barham could change tone abruptly, into the genuinely poignant lament 'As I Lay A-Thynkynge'. As a comic writer of ebullient invention and darker implications, he laid the foundations for those 'cult' figures of the twentieth century, Ronald Firbank (1886–1926), William Plomer (1903–73) and in particular, Mervyn Peake (1911–68).

While Tennyson willingly modified his imaginative powers to suit the new anti-self-consciousness of the 1830s and 1840s, a loosely associated group of neo-Romantic poets defiantly flaunted their Shelleyan idealism and a passionate sensitivity. The 'Spasmodics' have finished as a sad and slightly ridiculous footnote in literary history, doomed by their grandiose and anti-intellectual idea of poetry and killed by their sober reception of a malicious parody in 1854. There is no likelihood of Philip James Bailey's *Festus* (1839) and its successors regaining popularity, but some passages of Spasmodic verse should be salvaged from the wreck. The aspirations of the Spasmodics, to 'soar away toward illimitable heavens, unknown ecstasies, and the eternal mysteries of Divinity' were expressed with Promethean extravagance, but the yearning is that which Dickens dramatised more tactfully in *Dombey and Son*: to help the imagination to flourish in an age of materialism.

The Spasmodics were not privileged aesthetes; their gusty epics show English poetry trying to respond in kind to the power and wonder of the age of steam. They sought to be contemporary in setting and sensibility, and several of them were artisans who had fought their way to learning; one reason that their poetry has its shapeless form and self-absorbed manner. Ebenezer Jones (1820–60), whose *Studies of Sensation and Event* (1843) was 'full of vivid disorderly power', according to Rossetti, wrote in time snatched from a twelve-hour working day and paid for publication out of his earnings as a clerk; his employers warned him that 'pride of intellect' was 'one of Satan's peculiar snares'. His verse turns the imperturbable calm of Wordsworth chokingly against itself, but deals in the same large concepts, as in *A Development of Idiotcy*:

> He was a force-filled man,
> Whom the wise envy not; his passionate soul,
> Being mighty to detect life's secret beauty,
> Detecting, would display; and in his youth,
> When first visions unveiled before his gaze
> Their moral loveliness and physical grace,
> With the sweet melody of affectionate clamour
> He sang them to the world, and bade it worship:
> But the world unrecognised his visions of goodness,
> Or recognising, hated them and him.

Another self-taught man, Gerald Massey (1828–1907), defended the defiantly slapdash and impressionistic verse-forms of the Spasmodics: 'a poor man, fighting his battle for life, has little time for the rapture of repose which Poetry demands'. J. Westland Marston (1819–1890) hoped that his own verse would soothe the pains of the working class, and Ebenezer Elliott (1781–1849) who belonged to the Chartist Movement (1838–48) that sought universal manhood suffrage and rights for the working man, was one of the few poets to express an unambiguous awe at the energy of the industrial age. His 'Steam at Sheffield' is a powerful and eccentric poem in which a blind old man is led through scenes of terror and wonder which suggest Turner's railway paintings and Dickens's fascinated gusto for the locomotive in *Dombey and Son*.

The Spasmodics hardly formed a coherent group; their preference for intuition over intellect and their valuing of individual poetic revelation kept their association very loose. They were supported critically by the eminent Scot, George Gilfillan (1813–78), who took a liking to their energetic treatment of moral themes, and whose own 'opium style', according to the appreciative Carlyle, was 'full of fervour and crude, gloomy fire'.

The Spasmodic movement began with Bailey's epic *Festus* in 1839 and ended with Alexander Smith's *Life Drama* and Sydney Dobell's *Balder* in 1853. Then the celebrated parodist William Aytoun (1813–65), writing under the ineffably 'Spasmodic' name of 'T. Percy Jones' concocted an elaborate literary hoax; an anonymous antagonistic review of *Firmilian: A Spasmodic Tragedy* followed by the 'work' itself, with a self-justifying preface by 'Jones', which was in fact an admirable resumé of what theory the group possessed. Aytoun was even a little dismayed by how good some of *Firmilian* was. But it was burlesque, and serious Spasmodics welcomed it as their own and were swept away in a burst of ridicule.

There were two postscripts to the Spasmodic experiment. Elizabeth Barret Browning's *Aurora Leigh* came out in 1856, but it was a true poem of the 1840s when it was conceived; a fervent argument for the poet as the interpreter of a 'live, throbbing age', pulsating with strenuously cultivated emotion. 'It is no poem. No woman can write a poem', Dobell declared, somewhat ungratefully. Tennyson's *Maud* (1855) is often spoken of as clandestinely Spasmodic, with its monumentally egotistical hero in revolt against a world that drags him down, but Tennyson preserves his own detachment and crafts the verse with un-Spasmodic care.

The experiment gave Victorian verse a courage which it unhappily forfeited. Emily Brontë found her way to a Spasmodic independence of formal technique, and an impatient belief that strong emotion justifies itself. Matthew Arnold, the most intellectual of poets, combined emotionally eloquent metaphors and a dramatic flatness of expression in an unconsciously Spasmodic way. Browning flirted so violently with the group that his early reputation suffered. The experiments of the 1840s gave a brief hope that a Romantic sensibility would be fused with the 'heroic heat' of the industrial age, but before the decade was out the more successful revolutionaries of the Pre-Raphaelite Brotherhood had drawn Victorian poetry into a fabricated mediaeval past.

Robert Browning (1812–89) was slow to find a congenial form in which to express his idiosyncratic talent for the 'confidence and creation' of poetry; his ability to enter other consciousnesses was offset by a fastidious intellectual idealism and a fascinated interest in himself. It was not until the late 1840s that he learned to combine his taste for the magnificent and uncompromising with the pungent brevity of the dramatic monologue, in which he temporarily inhabited a character not his own, portrayed at a moment of crisis or self-doubt. His style was aggressive and experimental, hammering a conversational urgency into deceptively fluent verse in the tradition of John Donne, and like Donne he excelled in the lyric but did a complex intellect fuller justice in the extended poem of emotional argument. A passion for Shelley, which had led the fourteen-year-old Browning into a brief episode of vegetarianism and atheism, lasted all his life; the 'Sun-Treader's' idealism remains the basis of Browning's often obscure philosophy. He found all of Shelley's poetry 'a superb fragmentary essay', reconciling the universe to its creator, the natural world to the spiritual, and the actual to the ideal. His own poetry presented a total reality in suggestively splintered form, in a way anticipating the mature style of Ezra Pound (1885–1972).

Browning kept his inner life jealously guarded from the public gaze, despite his cultivation of friends in literary and government circles and his patronage of societies of admirers. Like W. B. Yeats he was preoccupied with the way in which the artist reveals himself in his work and with the masks that protect the deepest sources of his talent and through which he explores anti-social but liberating forms of being. He regarded his own life as his most important creation – 'R.B. – a poem' – and the real function of the poet as the reconciling of the outside world to the surpassingly interesting private self.

Browning's early life was extremely sheltered. His adoring father gave him a minimum of formal education but provided the use of an excellent library which whetted his appetite for obscure knowledge. Browning's first poem *Pauline* (1833) was well received; the plot had a Shelleyan or Spasmodic intensity, and the saving of the hero burdened with an oppressive self-consciousness by a virtuous, silent woman came to be parodied in his later, obsessively pathological 'Porphyria's Lover'. *Paracelsus* (1834) was the first example of an unhappy trend in Browning's poetry; the static drama in which the hero's spiritual development is charted through a series of conversations. The message that one must believe in the divine elements in one's own nature is more appetisingly dramatised in the later 'Fra Lippo Lippi', and the sense that failure is relative and even death cannot compromise the essential self comes through more persuasively in 'Childe Roland', 'A Patriot' and 'A Grammarian's Funeral'.

Sordello (1840) temporarily destroyed a reputation that had been growing in a flattering way. Wordsworth had praised *Paracelsus*; the tragic actor William Macready (1793–1873) wanted a play, and Browning visited Italy in preparation for a truly ambitious poem. Italy was to supplement his native rigour with a delicious sense of light, vivacity and moral freedom, captured in the poem 'De Gustibus': the Mediterranean was as essential to the full development of his art as it became to that of Turner and Ruskin.

> What I love best in all the world
> Is a castle, precipice-encurled,

In a gash of the wind-grieved Apennine
Or look for me, old fellow of mine,
(If I get my head from out the mouth
O' the grave, and loose my spirit's bands,
And come again to the land of lands) –
In a sea-side house to the farther South,
Where the baked cicala dies of drouth,
And one sharp tree – 'tis a cypress – stands,
By the many hundred years red-rusted,
Rough iron-spiked, ripe fruit o'ercrusted,
My sentinel to guard the sands
To the water's edge. For, what expands
Before the house, but the great opaque
Blue breadth of the sea without a break?

Sordello, when it came out, made the name of the young poet synonymous with obscurity, and established writers invented cruel witticisms against it. The plot is overelaborate; a sixty-year time span, the division of interest between father and son, and the unfamiliar background of mediaeval Italy, all tax the reader's concentration beyond hope of reward. Such complexity, as Tennyson and the Spasmodics had found, was only possible with a single consciousness at the centre of the poem. *Sordello* was an intriguing attempt to break free from Romantic introspection, but Browning was not to solve this puzzle of acquiring objectivity without losing dramatic force until his multifaceted presentation of events in *The Ring and the Book* (1868–9). The blow took some living down, though the brilliantly artificial and perversely presented character study 'My Last Duchess' was salvaged from material gathered for the disastrous enterprise.

Browning's ignominious failure as a dramatist appears surprising, given his eventual fame as the inventor of the dramatic monologue and his skill at characterisation. *Strafford* fastidiously ignored all questions of motivation, while *King Victor and King Charles* (1842) showed a similar aversion to anything happening on stage. By *The Return of the Druses* Macready had given up hope, and *A Blot on the Scutcheon*, in which Browning lowered himself to write of 'drabbing and stabbing', ended their friendship. *Colombe's Birthday* was published in sulky desperation in 1844: 'something I *must* print, or risk the hold, such as it is, I have at present on *my* public'. Browning's obsession with the theatre, and the discipline of writing in a fixed form, kept him free from a damaging association with the Spasmodics, and his awe at the power of the great actors of the period was reflected later in the monolithic personalities of the heroes of his dramatic monologues. In this fallow time of lost reputation, Browning developed a protective independence and a non-literary circle of friends; his remarkable and yearning poem 'Waring' (which should be read whenever one has the urge to use the term 'Victorian' loosely) expresses his fastidious moral solitude.

A series of poems paid for by his father helped to redeem his reputation. *Bells and Pomegranates* promised to unite 'the gay and the grave, the Poetry and the Prose, Singing and Sermonising'. Browning was beginning to find his special forte, where the need to play characters off against one another on stage is replaced by a fluid representation of the inner life of a central intelligence. *Pippa Passes* (1841) is ostensibly a play, but is not dramatic in any recognisable sense, though it is completely absorbing. Pippa's innocence and optimism as she moves through a world of lurid depravity is like that of Dickens's later Amy Dorrit, who brings a Romantic enlightenment to characters and readers who are merely experienced.

In A Gondola combines the structure of a drama and the urgency of a lyric, with a plot similar to that of Keats's *Isabella*, and the argument that a commitment to any impulse outside the self, including passionate sexual love, endows human beings with the power to transcend the limitations of mortality. A sacrifice of expediency to romantic love was the traditional test of moral stature in Browning's life and art, and the famous elopement with his poetic colleague Elizabeth Barrett from her parental home and her father's tyrannical jealousy in 1846 was the crucial event of his career. In a period when only continental pens were permitted to dwell on the guilt and misery of adultery, Browning used the symbol of flight from a cloying or barbarous marriage to a more responsive lover as a powerful suggestion of the liberated spirit, in 'The Flight of the Duchess' and the more resonant *The Ring and The Book*.

Bells and Pomegranates shows Browning working his way towards full development as a poet in *Men and Women* (1855). By the time of his *Dramatic Romances* (1845) he had invented the prototypes of the dramatic monologue, and in 'My Last

Duchess' and 'Soliloquy of the Spanish Cloister', what is natural and innocent asserts itself with Romantic vehemence, despite the sophisticated malevolence of the speaker.

'Seekers of light': the hero as man of letters

With the publication in 1836 of *The Pickwick Papers*, Charles Dickens (1812–70) became the natural successor to Sir Walter Scott. His undogmatic, exploratory art developed the novel into a timeless criticism of permanent wrongs within society, whereas the more conservative Scott had concerned himself with dramatising the forces that act within history.

Dickens was a man whose overwhelming personality acted like a gravitational field on those around him; his exuberant pleasure in acting and his endless gallery of fictional characters grew out of his sense of one life as too narrow for his spirit. He was a furious worker to the day of his death, as a writer for cheap serial publication needed to be, and beside his voluminous novels he kept up a flow of weekly journalism while finding time for amateur theatricals and public philanthropy. His frenzied sociability was balanced by a solitary, troubled inner life, in which he was a lonely night-walker in London, oppressed by a sense of his own solitude, brooding over wrongs done him in childhood, and drawn imaginatively to the criminal underworld and the fascinating processes of bodily corruption; an insomniac become the prey, like De Quincey or Bulwer Lytton, of his own fancy. His private life remained jealously hidden, while he gave a portion of himself unstintingly to a delighted public.

The children of John Dickens grew up in the shadow of insecurity; he was constitutionally unable to keep out of debt, and when he was finally imprisoned, Charles was removed from school at the age of twelve and set to work in a warehouse. The experience appears as something of an artistic outcrop in the semi-autobiographical *David Copperfield* (1850) and more lucidly and painfully in a fragment of autobiography written for his friend John Forster. The sudden descent from a precarious gentility into the hopelessness of the labouring classes had a permanent influence on his imagination; particularly his sense of the untrusting relationship between parents and children, and his grieving sense of the undependability of women in particular. His compulsive reliving of those miserable months may seen overindulgent to twentieth-century readers, but in Dickens's youth a station in the middle class meant self-respect, literacy, and the leisure to imagine; a 'caste' to be retained whatever the cost, as the nearly mortal privations of Charlotte Brontë's Jane Eyre make plain. Dickens never approves of the class basis of society, and his early sufferings made him an acute analyst of the way in which social discrimination warps personality; his narrow escape from oblivion gave him a special understanding of the despised and rejected.

Eventually, the boy was sent back to school, and managed his independent career astutely. He gained a reputation as a parliamentary reporter, and entered journalism at twenty-one with the captivating *Sketches by Boz*; the essay on Newgate Prison in particular ends with a hint of his future ability to inhabit alien states of mind and make them sympathetic even as he withholds final approval. The publishers Chapman and Hall then commissioned a text to go with some sporting prints they had purchased, and *Pickwick*, a success amounting to a cult, was born.

Dickens married a colleague's phlegmatic daughter, by whom he was to have ten children before their contrary temperaments drove him to seek a separation, and successive novels followed even more rapidly than Kate's pregnancies, which Dickens regarded with rueful detachment. A setback came with the disillusioning journey to his American public and the comparative failure of *Martin Chuzzlewit*, rapidly redressed by the perennially popular *A Christmas Carol* (1843), and Dickens travelled to Europe in a journey that appeared fruitless until it was brilliantly mined in *Little Dorrit*. He returned to England and an abortive attempt at editing a newspaper, and when he returned to the novel, it was with a new craftsmanship. *Dombey and Son* (1847–8) was not the first 'great' Dickens novel, but it was the first of the mature ones.

The Pickwick Papers (1836–7) is hardly a novel at all, 'merely a great book', as the later novelist George Gissing wrote. It begins as a shapeless narrative, trying out the tones of Fielding and his contemporaries, and padded out in the eighteenth-century manner with dubiously relevant digressions. The work gains assurance with the introduction of Sam Weller, a servant with Sancho Panza's loyalty and Figaro's resource, overcoming evil and hypocrisy with healthy ridicule. In the almost too powerful scenes in the Fleet Prison, Dickens discovered the heart of his mature fiction; the intractability of human misery, and the need to enter imaginatively into such suffering.

Oliver Twist (1837) is a less idyllic, more realistic novel, despite its occasional grim facetiousness, the coincidences of plot, and the mawkishness of the middle-class characters. Dickens had no love for Bulwer Lytton's 'Newgate' novel in which the hero might do murder but 'was afterwards so sorry for it that he ought to have been let off'. In *Oliver Twist* he is resolute in resisting the attractions of the criminal underworld, playing wantonly on the fear and loathing of the underclass that his readers had, yet insisting that they will tolerate social evil so long as it is kept at a distance: the novel illustrates J. S. Mill's observation a year earlier that 'the spectacle, and even the very idea of pain, is kept more and more out of sight of those classes who enjoy in their fulness the benefits of education'.

Nicholas Nickleby (1838-9) is the first 'typical' Dickens novel, loose-knit, rich with characters and changes of scene, bumptiously self-confident, and completely disarming. It dramatises almost of its own accord; Thackeray wrote a journalistic *tour de force* on a pirated stage version he had seen in Paris. However, the novel treats the problem of evil either too lightly (the gentlemanlike Nicholas is allowed only a brief dip into adversity before being taken up by the impossibly benevolent Cheeryble brothers) or too seriously for the texture of the novel; Smike and the wretched children of Dotheboys Hall seem to have strayed in from a novel like Dostoevsky's.

The Old Curiosity Shop (1840-1) has suffered greatly from critical abuse since its first rapturous reception on both sides of the Atlantic. The neglect into which it has fallen makes it easier for a modern reader to approach it without preconceptions, and in fact it is a fable that looks forward to Mark Twain (1835-1910), whose *Huckleberry Finn* (1884) shows another innocent child witnessing endless episodes of adult greed and depravity. At this stage Dickens is given to dramatising the forces of evil and mayhem more potently than images of good, and Nell, a sketch for the entirely successful

Amy Dorrit, moves through the novel like a ghost. In this autobiographical fairy-tale in which Dickens copes with a damaging bereavement in his own life, he argues the dangers of any obsessive love for the past, and the famous (or infamous) death of Nell is an impressively described exorcism.

In *Barnaby Rudge* (1841) Dickens makes use of the warnings of Carlyle, taking up the idea of revolution as the punishment for a merciless inhumanity in society. *Martin Chuzzlewit* (1843) shows Dickens embarrassed by the fluency of his invention, and the novel is splendid in incidentals and unwieldy as a whole. The graceful, mordantly funny *A Christmas Carol* of the same year develops the themes of *Chuzzlewit* with a strict economy. *Dombey and Son* (1848) repays all the labour that Dickens lavished on its preparation. It is a comprehensive but controlled view of England in the 1840s, a magnificent literary analogue to the exemplary painting *Work* (1852–63) by Ford Madox Brown (1821–93), with characters who are social types and potentials as well as intensely realised individuals. The novel warns of the possible results of unchecked Utilitarianism, with its disrespect for the tender emotions of children, and Dickens probes the perilously concealed inadequacies of Dombey himself until he achieves the insights of Matthew Arnold in his poetry. The railway, 'irresistibly powerful and manmade', contrasts in no crude way with the natural ebb and flow of the sea, that mysterious Romantic symbol of the imagination and shared sensitivity. After this eloquent celebration of the sanctity and resilience of the individual imagination, Dickens entered upon his mature career with the most autobiographical of his novels, *David Copperfield*.

Thomas Carlyle (1795–1881) also laid down the roots of his strongly emotional intellectual style in early childhood. His father was a Calvinist Scot and a peasant, who taught his children the necessity of spiritual and mental exertion:

> We were all particularly taught that work (temporal or spiritual) was the only thing we had to do, and incited always by precept or example to do it well. An inflexible element of authority surrounded us all. We felt from the first (a useful thing) that our own wish had often nothing to say in the matter.

Carlyle was to play the father with his readers, and the Romanticism which he distrusted in poetry found expression in his confident referral of all ideas to his own feelings. His years at school and university were spoiled by his social isolation and intellectual aloofness, and the rationalist tone of Edinburgh University, still dominated by the civilised scepticism of John Locke and David Hume (1711–76), gave the potential Romantic no imaginative sustenance. His parents hoped passionately that he would become a minister and he spent fruitless years as a schoolmaster while trying to pay for his studies in theology. Eventually he suffered a breakdown and returned home, depressed, sleepless, and unable to work; in the throes of that crisis of faith and direction endured by most Victorian thinkers at some time in their careers and explained by Wordsworth and Coleridge as a loss of 'joy'. Carlyle was partially liberated by a reading of the German Romantics, Goethe and Schiller, whom he translated and interpreted and whose emotional freedom filled him with – in a significant phrase – 'holy joy'. He gave up the narrow faith of his parents, though not his belief in God, nor his habit of measuring the most trivial acts of life by exacting standards. By 1824 he was able to support himself in his frugal life by writing, and in 1826 he made an amazing marriage to the heiress Jane Welsh who supported his genius until her death in 1866 and earned a substantial reputation as a wit in her ascetic salon in Cheyne Row, London.

Carlyle was the victim and beneficiary of a clash between rationalism and Romanticism, and he liked to think of himself as one who had made himself independent of the accident of his station in time. To Carlyle, history was a repeated series of 'soul-crises' in representative gifted men; talent and intelligence were nothing in themselves (and he attacked Burns and Scott for their triviality), since the business of the exceptional man was to discover the will of God, which could only be done by rooting out a Romantic self-consciousness. Yet Carlyle valued intuition over logic, as the Romantics had done, and shared the social conservatism of the mature Wordsworth and Coleridge. Men of a more liberal and thoroughly Romantic stamp – Dickens, Ruskin and William Morris – had no difficulty in appropriating large amounts of Carlyle's philosophy, particularly his stress on the organic nature of society and his choice of a mediaeval model for his ideal world.

For all its vehement insistence on order and obedience and the unforgiveable tirades against blacks and the Irish, the best of Carlyle's theory grows out of a sympathy for individuals, and a Romantic reverence for uniqueness. The essence of his art was biography:

> For as the highest Gospel was a Biography, so is the Life of every good man still an indubitable Gospel, and preaches to the eye and heart and whole man, so that Devils must believe and tremble, those gladdest tidings: 'Man is heaven-born'.

Biography and the history of which it forms a part are nothing until the 'seeing eye' of the biographer sorts the distracting material details into a version of the eternal drama of a spiritually promising individual discovering how to renounce his own self and the lures of personal ambition for a full sense of the divine order. Only the 'seeing eye' could discern this pattern, and the 'loving heart' of the ideal biographer submits itself as a disciple to the greater subject, interpreting the 'soul-crisis' with insightful tenderness. Carlyle praised the 'love and childlike Open-mindedness' of James Boswell (1740–95), Samuel Johnson's biographer, in positively Wordsworthian terms.

Carlyle's own great biography is his *Sartor Resartus* (1833–4), an attack on the materialism of the modern age, anti-scientific and allusive, cumbered with editorial paraphernalia and clotted with metaphor. The temptation to Romantic despair ('the Everlasting No') is rejected with stern joy, and the Everlasting Yea, with the centre of interest shifted outside the self, is an exultant identification with the historical process. The revitalised man sees society as a collection of exhausted forms but secretly providing herself with new garments. The superficial demands for electoral reform are a sham, since true freedom lies in conformity to the will of God and hero-worship is loyalty to that which is God-like in man.

Carlyle's prose style grew out of his idealism; his sense that the visible universe was merely symbolic of invisible truths and that language must match it in a feast of metaphor. His extravagant, flaming style, a mingling of the Bible, Shakespeare, Swift, Calvinist sermons, German Romanticism, Scots colloquialisms and pungent coinages, imposed itself by force on its readers. Just as the French Revolution had been God's chastisement of vanity and disorder, so Carlyle saw about him 'a time of literary, as other revolution, with Newspaper-Cockney and Scott's-Novel Scotch storming in on us'. It was no time for purism of style, but for the utmost violence of rhetoric; literature was a battlefront, with heroes like Johnson and Carlyle reproaching men like Voltaire who had given up the struggle to achieve faith. The subject of all writing must be 'gospel-tidings'; in an age when most writers worked to some extent as journalists, Carlyle swore that 'he'd as soon wash his face in a dirty puddle' or work as a road-sweeper, as write for the press.

Carlyle's Histories continue the drama of his biographies on a larger scale. *The French Revolution* (1837) is an elaborately severe illustration of cause and effect within history; moral disorder and spiritual indifference leading to mutual destruction. It was a clear warning to England, coming at a time when suffrage demands, labour unrest and hunger seemed to point to a similar revolt at home. *Heroes and Hero-Worship* (1841) is an early study of evolutionary process; 'the tools to him who can handle them' is Carlyle's formulation of Darwin's 'the survival of the fittest' in 1859. Carlyle's hero is intuitive, idealistic, unique, passionate and free from personal ambition, and a far cry from the vulgar dictator of the twentieth century who has been fathered upon him. *Past and Present* (1843) was a typically idiosyncratic approach to contemporary social problems, at a time when Karl Marx was already working towards the materialist solutions of the *Communist Manifesto* (1848). The evils of the 'cash nexus' that replaced the old sense of the brotherhood of man with a belief that people were expendable economic units is compared to the more equitable world of the twelfth century, theocratic and protective of its citizens, and Carlyle's forceful examples of modern indifference to squalor and disease become the nucleus for Dickens's great novels of social protest, beginning with *Bleak House* in 1853.

Carlyle produced his most lucid and personal work in the 1830s, out of his unlimited faith in a transcendental philosophy and the godlike nature of man; in the 1840s this Romanticism hardened into a prescription for social order, and illness and frustration forced him into sustained invective against the world in 'Shooting Niagara' and 'The Nigger Question' in *Latter-Day Pamphlets* (1850). But this venom is balanced by the fresh intuitiveness of *The Life of John Sterling* (1851), in which a superlative close observation shows that the 'loving heart' has asserted itself over the 'seeing eye'.

Carlyle gave to his century a shaping sense of identity and narrative, and an imperative awareness of duty and mutuality. He rises out of a tradition of Romantic puritanism begun by Wordsworth in England and Goethe in Germany, and in his turn he influenced Dickens and George Eliot in their chosen themes of the need to transcend egotism and to recognise the wholeness of the social fabric. His sweeping, Biblical denunciations of national guilt provided the pattern for Ruskin's ambitious moral fables of decline. The enemy of individual self-consciousness made his countrymen vividly self-conscious as a nation.

THE MOVE TO SOCIAL COMMITMENT: THE 1840s

'Hanging on to the skirts of history': novelists and the social context

Harrison Ainsworth (1805–82) had a sense of the past closer to the writers of Gothic fiction than to Carlyle's Old Testament dramas. He gave a growing public peppery novels with a strong didactic element, with plots that turned on illegitimacy, fake marriages, witches' covens, plague-pits, torture chambers and scaffolds, and where the tale of terror was mingled with the 'Newgate' novel's superficial admiration for the criminal. His fictional world is governed by monsters of depravity in search of absolute power who commit atrocities because they find scruples absurd. Such repellent instances of justice indistinguishable from the crime it pursues may have inspired Dickens's own deeply serious *Great Expectations* (1860–1), which has specific resemblances to Ainsworth's fiction.

Ainsworth's highly coloured historical romances repudiated his prosaic beginnings in Manchester, which he dealt with at last in *Mervyn Clitheroe* (1856). *Rookwood* (1834) established him in the salons of London, where he was briefly the heir of Scott before the arrival of Dickens in 1836; by the mid-1840s the vogue for crime and violence had given way to a taste for domestic realism and social consciousness, and Ainsworth, burned out with editing and reviewing, moved about England in a series of gloomy and impoverished peregrinations. It had been at one of his lavish entertainments following his initial success that his guest Dickens was introduced to his first publisher, his first illustrator, and his eventual biographer, John Forster. *Jack Sheppard* scored the singular success of having eight pirated stage versions produced, while *The Tower of London* (1840), *Guy Fawkes* (1840–1) and *Old St Paul's* (1841) appeared, like Dickens's novels, in the cheap serial format that built up a highly democratic audience at a time when only the rich could afford the thirty shillings for a three-volume novel, or two guineas for an annual library subscription.

William Makepeace Thackeray (1811–63) had an unsurpassed ability to create a fictional world with plane upon plane of alluring naturalistic detail, braced by his stern belief that human moral stature was limited while human suffering was not.

> It is better, with all one's sins upon one's head, to deem oneself in the hands of Fate than to think with our fierce passions and weak repentances, with our resolves so loud, so vain, so ludicrously, desperately weak and frail, with our dim, wavering, wretched conceits about virtue, and our irresistible propensity to wrong, that we are the workers of our future sorrow or happiness.

Thackeray's best novels dramatise the humiliating failure of human resolve and human love; whereas a key point in *Middlemarch* is made when the Wordsworthian George Eliot shows the wife of a ruined man supporting her husband, Thackeray the anti-Romantic had gone on in *Vanity Fair* to show the demoralising steps by which such idealism turns to petty bickering in cheap lodgings. *Vanity Fair* is deliberately 'A Novel without a Hero', in which possessions notoriously outlast their owners, and even the most obsessive love turns in the end to critical detachment. The profoundly selfish characters judge one another harshly but are rebuked in a tacit way by Thackeray's sense of finely mingled motive and his poignant awareness of the brevity of human life.

Thackeray's own life, in which his rueful talent for the

mismanagement of his emotional and financial affairs improved on appalling luck, furnished the material for his journalism and the novels which became more and more like memoirs. In his fiction, and in the addictively readable ephemera from the hard-working decade 1837–47, Thackeray undermines his pose of the clubbable, infinitely knowledgeable worldling by his constant reminders that this delightful existence to which he is so agreeable a guide is not worth anything in the long run; a state of mind brilliantly evoked in *Vanity Fair*:

> This, dear friends and companions, is my amiable object – to walk with you through the Fair, to examine the shops and the shows there; and that we should all come home after the flare, and the noise, and the gaiety, and be perfectly miserable in private.

Like Dickens, with whom he shared an armed truce that degenerated into open hostility, Thackeray was unsure of his real position in society, and for that reason an equally sophisticated analyst of the delicate gradations within the respectable classes. He had forfeited his birthright by gambling away a fortune, and despite his vaunted fondness for an adopted bohemian life ('the easiest, merriest, dirtiest existence possible') he resented the fact that a literary man was ranked 'below that class of gentry composed of the apothecary, the attorney, the wine-merchant'. The highly respectable novels of his later years, in which he descants on the idea of the gentleman, restored him to some of his lost privileges. Unlike 'Mr Dickens in geranium and ringlets' he took no interest in the labouring poor; nor did Dickens's connections with social reform impress a conservative for whom misery was an unavoidable part of our fallen condition; a man should not 'quarrel with the world and its ways' by which 'we live, love, marry, have children, educate them and endow them'. Dickens, for his part, disliked Thackeray's 'eternal guffaw at all things', though Thackeray privately declared that 'our profession seems to me to be as serious as the parson's own'. He saw himself as a serious moralist, and his *Book of Snobs* (1846–7) has affinities both to Henry Fielding (1707–54) and Carlyle.

Thackeray was never financially or emotionally secure. His mother's remarriage sent him home from an entrancing world of 'great saloons and people dancing in them, enormous idols and fireworks' in India, to miserable schooldays at the brutal Charterhouse, and he ran through a quarter of his fortune at Cambridge and was only prevented from losing the rest by the speculations of his stepfather. Intellectual excellence 'smelled a little of the shop' in his dandiacal code, and his wanderings as a painter through France and Germany were reverted to nostalgically in his later poetry and prose. An ill-advised marriage to a handsome Irishwoman ended with his caring for two surviving daughters and a hopelessly insane wife: 'Ladies', he exclaimed bitterly in *Vanity Fair*, 'what man's love is there that would stand a year's nursing of the object of his affections?' He turned his disasters into a defensive jocularity: the embarrassed gourmand taking the water-cure in Germany with his unhappy wife, the lamentable figure he cut as the platonic lover of his best friend's wife, the greed and corpulence of 'Our Fat Contributor' to *Punch*, the radical humorous magazine he had helped to respectability, and the flattened nose from forced battles at school. His poetry lyrically dramatised painful inadequacy and loneliness; the greedy nostalgia of the 'Ballad of the Bouillabaisse', and the mocking 'Peg of Limavaddy', with its wistful infantile humiliation. Thackeray vowed that he would not put on his spectacles to see Venus arising from the sea, but this defensive 'fogey' was one of the few English novelists of the century to see sex as a driving force in society.

His journalism has stood up to the passage of time almost unscathed, and is undergoing a critical revival at the expense of his later novels. 'Going to See a Man Hanged' from *Fraser's Magazine* in 1840 is not only an uncomfortably vivid account of the event, but a meditation on the power of fiction to sedate a true apprehension of reality; the essay's emotional versatility shows Thackeray's debt to Charles Lamb, whom he idolised. His deliberately provocative art criticism anticipated fashion; he admired Turner instinctively, and hated the 'simpering Madonnas' of Raphael years before Dante Gabriel Rossetti and his associates banded together under this shared prejudice. His novels are the work of a man with an unusually acute visual imagination, and a fine eye for placing figures under dramatic lighting, with copious detail intelligently deployed.

The travel books, including the *Irish Sketchbook* (1843) and

Notes of a Journey from Cornhill to Cairo (1846) are absorbing exercises in the boundless egotism of that *nil admirari* style later favoured by Mark Twain in *The Innocents Abroad* (1869). The *Irish Notes* are deeply troubling; the sceptical Thackeray refuses to sympathise with the starving tenantry pulling nettles in the hedgerows – not cadaverous enough to suit him – and within a few pages is complaining of an undercooked meal and a crumpled cloth at his inn. As a novelist, he took care to avoid scenes of gross suffering.

Vanity Fair (1847–8) grew out of the admirable journalism of the previous decade, as a whimsy on the 'silver fork' novels of the now forgotten Mrs Gore, whom Thackeray reviewed wittily and sharply:

> Supposing that Pall-mall were the world, and human life finished with the season, and Heaven were truffled turkeys and the Opera, and duty and ambition were bounded in dressing well . . . . [then] the world is the most hollow, heartless, vulgar, brazen world, and those are luckiest who are out of it.

The novel soon leaves its trivial genesis behind and becomes an English approximation to the *Lost Illusions* of Balzac; ability, initiative, the seductive power of high society and beautiful possessions are given their due, yet each novel is a study in mutability and failed heroism.

The change that occurred in Thackeray between *Vanity Fair* and *Pendennis* (1850) is difficult to explain. A sudden good-humour and reserve overtook him, and whereas *Vanity Fair* had demonstrated the impossibility of coming to simple conclusions about human nature, the novels set back in the seventeenth and eighteenth centuries cajole his readers into a bluff optimism. The novelist George Meredith referred to such a highly varnished dream world as 'an aspiration after some form of melodious gentlemanliness', and though *Pendennis*, *Henry Esmond* (1852), *The Newcomes* (1853–5) and *The Virginians* (1857–9) have their supporters, they are the work of a different man, providing himself with imaginary consolations for that loneliness and sense of futility expressed so astringently in his work up to 1848.

'The frontier of all accustomed respectabilities'

George Borrow (1803–81) was a larger than life literary man who inherited a love of wandering, delight in the Bible and an insatiable combativeness from his recruiting officer father. After a desultory schooling, he lived a hand-to-mouth existence, reporting on criminal trials and translating Gaelic and Scandinavian ballads; he later claimed to know more than thirty languages. His eccentric fictions were borrowed from the eighteenth century; he had Fielding's faith in dialogue as a revealer of hypocrisy, the stylistic inventiveness and deliberate illogicality of Laurence Sterne (1713–68), and, most of all, that exquisite understanding of the English middle class enjoyed by Daniel Defoe, who also knew how to dish up vice with a sermon, and whose heroes were masters of resource and compounds of egotism and godliness.

Borrow found his career by accident when the Bible Society sent him as an agent to St Petersburg and then to Portugal; *The Zincali or An Account of the Gypsies of Spain* (1841) and the more famous *The Bible in Spain* (1842) are idiosyncratic, ingenious and prejudiced travel books. Like the novelist Charles Kingsley he allowed his heroes to transgress everyday moral codes because of the evident wickedness of their enemies and their role as God's agents on earth. In 1843 Borrow astonishingly outsold Dickens; evangelical taste was flattered, and Borrow played the literary lion with childlike pleasure. *Lavengro: The Scholar, the Gypsy, the Priest* (1851) is an advance on *The Bible in Spain*; it conquers by its crisp vignettes, outrageous characters and curious perspective on the world, but it failed to impress the critics and the public, who were puzzled by its deliberately random organisation. *The Romany Rye* (1857) takes up at the exact moment that its predecessor left off, with the same cast of characters including the un-Victorian horsebreaker, Isopel Berners, whose idea of courtship involves learning Armenian from the narrator and sleeping with him in the open air. Borrow uses the Appendix to settle scores with his critics in the most vituperative way, and this book too fell dead.

Borrow mellowed as he grew older; *Wild Wales* (1862) was an account of a walking tour that reverted to the picturesque inconsequentialities of *The Bible in Spain*, but was sourly reviewed as 'the record of every glass of ale which Mr Borrow drank'. Borrow remains a genuinely independent figure who kept himself uncontaminated by a society unlikely to have accepted him at his own valuation; he was a real-life version of Browning's 'Waring' or Matthew Arnold's Scholar-Gipsy, and, as such, a Romantic survival.

Alexander William Kinglake (1809–91) was as independent as Borrow, but the rebelliousness of the author of *Eothen: Or Traces of Travel Brought Home from the East* (1844) was strictly rationed. His career progressed from a fondly remembered education at Eton and Cambridge to a seat in Parliament, and his *Invasions of the Crimea* (he was present at the battle of Alma) became a classic of military history.

Kinglake wrote in a holiday spirit of a brief escape from 'that poor, dear, middle-aged, deserving, accomplished, pedantic and painstaking governess, Europe', past 'the frontier of all accustomed respectabilities'. Civilisation waits to 'throw her lasso' over her not unwilling truant at the end of it all, but the 'pure wealth' of adventure that makes the epics of Homer seem to have come alive, sweetens the 'matter-of-fact-ridden world'. It is Kinglake's own version of the contemporary struggle between Byronism and Utilitarianism.

Eothen is a classic of subtle comedy, maintaining an exquisite poise in the face of privations and dangers described through elegantly managed extended similes, depreciatory hyperbole, and the terse rejection of any Romantic fancy or spiritual extravagance. Kinglake poses as Edward Gibbon (1737–94), author of the sceptical *Decline and Fall of the Roman Empire*, as he admits 'I felt hopelessly sane', and as a heavily qualified modern Byron, satirising European customs from the 'splendour and havoc of the East'. He creates a mirror world like that of Lewis Carroll, where one may be summarily put to death 'for not being a vagrant, for not being a robber, for not being armed and houseless'. He makes a stand, more successfully than Thackeray, against 'that nearly immutable law which compels a man with a pen in his hand to be uttering every now and then some sentiment not his own'. Yet he is no idle satirist; in the midst of his comedy he conveys that 'strong vertical light' of actuality he so admired in Homer:

No words are spoken, but your Arabs moan, your camels sigh, your skin glows, your shoulders ache, and for sight you see the pattern and the web of the silk that veils your eyes, and the glare of the outer light.

'The autobiographies of nations': individual views of history

The Times obituary notice of Thomas Babington Macaulay (1800–59) referred to him as 'the most powerful, popular and versatile writer of our time', and in his life the historian enjoyed a fame more common among novelists: anecdotes abound of mill-workers who had heard his five-volume *History of England* (1849–61) read aloud by their employers, writing to thank him for 'a history which working men can understand', and the celebrated young lady at the Zoo who exclaimed: 'Never mind the hippopotamus; there is Mr Macaulay!' He was an intimidatingly precocious child, who planned his first outline of world history when he was eight; the son of Zachary Macaulay, editor of the *Christian Observer* and one of the 'Saints' of the influential, politically reformist Clapham Sect of Evangelicals. Macaulay entered print with an anonymous defence of Fielding's novels, taking issue against his father who had referred to reading fiction at all as 'drinking drams in the morning'.

Success came easily to Macaulay, and stayed long, and he was to Victorian prose what the equally gifted and favoured Felix Mendelssohn (1809–47) was to the music of the period. He was too much an eighteenth-century rationalist by nature to share his father's evangelical sympathies, but he remained a convinced Whig, supporting the cause of reform even though it cost him the seat he had been presented with two years before. 'His opinions are quite liberal, and yet he is by no means a vulgar radical', wrote a satisfied contemporary.

The *Edinburgh Review* formed his intellectual and prose style, through its editor's scepticism, common sense and strong didactic spirit; in its 'tribunals' of criticism the views of the reviewer were always more significant than the work reviewed. Macaulay's style was essentially that of the public speaker; his *History*, and the *Critical and Historical Essays Contributed to the Edinburgh Review* (1843) are balanced by his parliamentary speeches, with their reformist concern for the spread of

education, minority rights, and his classic expositions of the
duties of the state towards its citizens; as Legal Adviser to the
Supreme Council of India he showed himself tolerant and
humane.

Macaulay was an amiable intellectual, an indefatigable
researcher, and a populariser by nature. His reputation has
suffered grievously from the attacks of Carlyle and Matthew
Arnold, who viewed him as a facile optimist blinded by the
material well-being of the middle classes whose aspirations he
flattered; it is more likely that he was a man who took a middle
course in an age of subjective extremism.

Like Carlyle, with whom he had otherwise nothing in
common, Macaulay had the instincts of a novelist which
blessed him as an historian. As a devotee of Scott, Macaulay
claimed that the best historical accounts are always 'those in
which a little of the exaggeration of fictitious narrative is
judiciously employed. Something is lost in accuracy, but much
is gained in effect'. Scott's generous realism taught Macaulay
the importance of showing 'ordinary men as they appear in
their ordinary business and their ordinary pleasures', and in
the decade of Chartism, when the likelihood of revolution was
constantly brought to mind by Carlyle, Dickens and others,
Macaulay made the moderate claim that:

> The circumstances which have the most influence on the happiness of
> mankind, the changes of manners and morals, the transition of
> communities from poverty to wealth . . . from ferocity to humanity –
> these are, for the most part, noiseless revolutions.

He countered the Romantic, Carlylean hero with the Whig
principle: 'how small a proportion of the good or evil effected
by a single statesman can bear to the good or evil of a great
social system'. His *History* was a deliberate artefact, dependent
on his 'management of perspective', never more than
relatively true, and relying on the dramatic tact of 'transitions'
and 'arrangements' to bring out the general truths latent in
events. His art concealed its art so effectively that only he was
aware of the difficulties of composition: 'What a labour it is to
make a tolerable book, and how little readers know how much
trouble the ordering of the parts has cost the writer!' There
is no sense, so explosively present in the histories of his
rival Carlyle, of the tortuous process by which the mind

delivers itself of its ideas, and though his inner life was evidently complex, he left no record like *Sartor* to explain its crises.

The irreverent biographer Lytton Strachey (1880–1932), whose *Eminent Victorians* (1919) was modelled, somewhat captiously, on Macaulay's artificialities, claimed facetiously that Macaulay's urbane yet simple style was 'one of the most remarkable products of the Industrial Revolution'. Strachey's further comment that Macaulay's writings were masterpieces of imagination rather than history holds good for Victorian historiography as a whole.

Like most post-Romantic writers, Macaulay interpreted his own age through a deep attachment to the past. He had Thackeray's fondness for the sceptical, wordly climate of the eighteenth century, and if he celebrated the material prosperity and legislative advance of his own day, he measured it against a sternly classical republican heroism: his *Lays of Ancient Rome* (1842) were some of the most popular and certainly the most democratic works of the century, setting the secrets of a gentleman's education to the swinging rhythms of street ballads, and founding the idiosyncratic, flexible and socially critical poetic art of Rudyard Kipling.

John Ruskin (1819–1900), the art critic and social theorist, was the greatest prose writer of his century and the last of the great Romantics, exploring man's apprehension of his relationship with the natural world through the art and architecture which had evolved as a symbol of that bond. 'You will never love art well', he admonished his readers, 'till you love what she mirrors better.' Bernard Shaw observed that few men have embodied our manifold nature more markedly than Ruskin; his perverse but humane theories of man, his art and his society are often contradictory in expression but always the products of a perfectly unified sensibility. As he wrote in the Preface to the final volume of *Modern Painters* (1860):

> All true opinions are living, and show their life by being capable of nourishment; therefore of change. But their change is that of a tree – not of a cloud.

In his exuberant confusion of scientific observation, aesthetic theory and personal morality, and his habitual mingling of subjects with no logic beyond the irresistible current of his own meditations, Ruskin is not only the 'mediaevalist' Kenneth Clark discovered, but a last flowering of the English Renaissance, a modern version of that Sir Thomas Browne beloved by the Romantic prose writers. Ruskin built on the complex, persuasive syntax of Carlyle, adding a seductive tone that Virginia Woolf had in mind when, as one committed to the relative austerities of twentieth-century prose, she wrote longingly of his grander passages where it is as if 'all the fountains of the English language had been set playing in the sunlight for our pleasure'. In his intellectual restlessness and his sense that man is inevitably a social being, Ruskin spoke to the Victorians; he is a Romantic in his delicate and responsive charting of the sequence of mental development and his belief in the 'innocent eye' that sees natural objects without the veil of familiarity, 'as a blind man would see them if suddenly gifted with sight'.

Attitudes that Matthew Arnold was to designate as 'Hebraic' and 'Hellenic' (the moral demands of a religious conscience, and the natural joy in the abundance of creation) fought it out in Ruskin's complex nature until the long silence of insanity came upon him twelve years before his death. He was an incurable solitary. His friendships, he wrote, were with works of art ('I am never long enough with men to attach myself to them; and whatever feelings of attachment I have are to material things'). Intellectual isolation led him frequently into arrogance and eccentricity; he had, as his biographer J. D. Rosenberg points out, masters but not colleagues and he lived in a private universe where each glance was a revelation but there were no eyes but his own.

Ruskin's works can be understood only with the constant gloss of his own life; all his writings are in some degree autobiography, and his intellectual stand is always referred back to his feelings. In his earliest volumes, writing was a necessary passion, 'a sort of instinct like that for eating and drinking', and a piquantly elaborate way of conveying a simple and fresh vision of reality. The prose of his middle period grew subdued, weighty and architectural, and towards the end of his life his utterances became the gloomy and terrible outpourings of *Fors Clavigera* and 'The Storm-Cloud of the Nineteenth Century', before the pellucid imagery and

tranquil emotions of those last reminiscences that Marcel
Proust, the inheritor of Ruskin's style, knew by heart.

The circumstances of Ruskin's life were abundantly sad,
though his genius (which he candidly admitted that he had)
depended on his early isolation, rigorous moral training and
intellectual forcing. He was the only child of a prosperous wine
importer, and the father and mother's Evangelical
exclusiveness and spiritual ambitions for their son kept him
rigidly from the contaminations of the world; the lonely infant,
playing with his bunch of keys, absorbedly following the
pattern in the carpet, and enjoying the restricted beauties of his
parents' garden and the chapel where they worshipped was
'narrowing himself to happiness' and establishing those habits
of intense observation that show in his critical writing, along
with a conviction that sensory pleasure must intensify the
moral life. Ruskin did not naturally share in the austerities of
his parents, and made anguished and largely ineffectual
attempts to free himself from the 'ceaseless authority' of a well-
meaning tyranny. His upbringing turned normal impulses
towards sexuality and affection to the pleasures of sight (the
luminosities of Turner and the carnality of the great
Venetians) and to the disciplined ecstasies of his prose and his
lectures. 'I should like to draw all St Mark's, and all this
Verona stone by stone; to eat it all up into my mind, touch by
touch'. He made folios of drawings of the most exquisite
refinement and precision, and later of murky intensity, that
just miss independent greatness.

The most emotional and sensual of writers, whose critical
power depends on his ability to seduce his readers into sharing
his vision, was notoriously wretched in his private life; first in
the arranged marriage with Euphemia Gray, the child for
whom he had written the fable *The King of the Golden River* in
1841, and later in the prolonged and distressing courtship of
another beloved child turned adult, Rose La Touche, whose
religious mania parodied his own painful doubts. His marriage
was annulled after six years and his former bride married his
brilliant protegé, the Pre-Raphaelite painter J. E. Millais.

Ruskin came to art criticism with no preparation save his
enthusiasm and his 'innocent eye': he remained entirely
ignorant of European aesthetic theory and relied instead on his
early training as a geologist, which provided him with an

invaluable stock of metaphor and a sense of the architectural forms approved by and latent within nature. He was goaded into writing for the public by a criticism of J. M. W. Turner, one of whose rare friends he became, and *Modern Painters* was begun in 1843 as a vivid evocation of those landscapes he and his father were collecting. The volumes that followed became a kind of *bildungsroman*, a frank diary of Ruskin's development of taste and conviction; the second volume, made after his first journey alone to Italy, begins the drama of his widening sympathies. In the famous 'unconversion' at Turin he walked out of the grim chapel of his family's faith and exchanged his 'pert little Protestant mind' for the humanist glories of Veronese (1528–88): 'things done delightfully and rightly were always done', he argued, 'by the help and in the spirit of God.' In *Modern Painters* Ruskin follows Wordsworth's method in *The Prelude* of amassing a wealth of sensory impressions and an uncensored avowal of mental states that justify his authoritative and joyful final position.

Ruskin's view of nature came to be more tormented than that of the early Romantics. Wordsworth had certainly faced the lassitude of spirit when nature seems to rebuke man's solitary egotism, and Coleridge portrayed a natural world from which joy had fled; for Ruskin, changes in nature did not reflect his own dejection but appeared to cause it. As a youth, he had seen God manifest in skies and mountain-peaks; in his maturity he saw instead poverty-stricken villages, shattered rocks and storm-clouds.

The Seven Lamps of Architecture (1848) was uncharacteristic of Ruskin's prose in its formal shapeliness and rapid composition, and it set the pattern of the later works by turning from art itself to man its creator and consumer, thus forming a necessary prologue to the masterpiece *The Stones of Venice*. Ruskin argued that architecture was the necessary index of a nation's values, and had probably developed this theory out of the *Contrasts* (1836) of the Catholic A. W. Pugin (1812–52) a work of the early Victorian spiritual renaissance with influential views on the role of 'the nobler powers of superstition' in elevating human social character. *The Seven Lamps* was an invaluable addition to English aesthetic philosophy, with its ideas of 'organic form', its belief that function and design should be interwoven and structure and materials honestly displayed; all concepts in revolt against the vulgar and mechanical embellishments that the industrial age made possible.

The Stones of Venice (1851–3) is the most moving and resonant of Ruskin's works; a labour of love begun on his wedding journey, and the memorial to a city that moved him more than any human being. Venice was the precious city of the Romantic imagination, from Wordsworth's 'Ode on the Extinction of the Venetian Republic', to Byron's *Childe Harold*, through Clough's *Dipsychus*, Browning's 'A Toccata of Galuppi's', and Turner's studies, to the valedictory *Death in Venice* by Thomas Mann (1875–1955). In its beauty, pride and decadence Venice symbolised the Promethean spirit in man. Ruskin claimed in later life that 'there is a kind of Divina Commedia – a dramatic change and power; – in all beautiful things', and this was his Christian epic, an unhistorical but emotionally persuasive drama of a great society's collapse as mirrored in its art; a lost Paradise.

In 1860 Ruskin's life changed course. His marriage was over, his championship of the Pre-Raphaelite artists begun, his reputation as a lecturer established, and in 1858 he had broken with the narrow Protestantism of his childhood. Yet his fame as an art critic left him unsatisfied, and the letters of his fortieth year are full of anguish: 'I see creatures so full of power and beauty, with none to understand or teach or save them . . .'; 'about me there is this terrific absurdity and wrong going on . . .'; 'I am tormented by what I cannot get said, nor done . . . .' His depression seemed a punishment for 'my having enjoyed too much of lovely things till they almost cease to be lovely to me'. He turned from art criticism to an attempt to revive moral sensations in his audience; a goal implicit in his earliest prose, but now the central issue of his life.

Spectators *ab extra*: deliberating outsiders

William Barnes (1801–86), the 'Dorset Poet', was an instinctive follower of Ruskin: his *Thoughts on Beauty and Art* (1861) was an unconscious echoing of the greater theorist by a man too isolated to have masters.

> Look for pleasure in the line of beauty, and other curves of charming grace in the windblown stems of grass, and bowing barley or wheat; in the water-shaken bullrush, in the leaves of plants, and in the petals of flowers; . . . and tell us whether nature does not show us graceful curves enough to win us from ugliness, even in a porringer . . . .

Barnes was the forerunner of Thomas Hardy in his loving imaginative dependence on the Dorsetshire countryside and in his collecting of 'old lore', his transmission of the speech of the people, and his densely imaged verse. Gerard Manley Hopkins learned from him and preferred him to the Scots dialect poet Robert Burns, setting some of his poems to music. Barnes himself had taken the seventeenth-century divine George Herbert (1593–1633) as a model: the entrancing nature study *George Herbert at Bemerton* (1861) by William Dyce (1806–64) indicates the reverence in which the homely mystics Herbert and Cowper were held by the Victorian Romantics.

Barnes was a skilled etymologist and linguist, a wood engraver and a morbidly modest schoolmaster turned clergyman. His use of the local dialect for his most striking poems was a classicist's whim rather than Clare's attempt to reclaim a corner of serious literature for the peasantry; the Dorset tongue was 'a bold and broad shape of the English language, as the Doric was of Greek'. His model was always Homer, who found 'the one proper epithet in describing', in imitation of nature itself, 'very sparing of showy contrasts'.

Barnes's poetry began with the neatly conventional Regency verse of *Poetical Pieces* (1820) and *Orra: A Lapland Tale* (1822), a crystalline, spare and oblique narrative. For twenty-two years he wrote as an antiquarian, but in 1844 brought out *Poems of Rural Life in the Dorset Dialect* with its experimental reconstruction of Old English rhythms. *Hwomely Rhymes* followed in 1858, and *Poems in the Dorset Dialect: Third Collection* in 1863. Sometimes he reverted to 'national English', but he concentrated on 'Doric': writing in dialect was 'not like work but like the playing of music, the refreshment of the mind'.

> 'Ithin the woodlands, flow'ry gleäded,
> By the woak tree's mossy moot,
> The sheenèn grass-bleädes, timber sheäded,
> Now do quiver under voot;
> An' birds do whissle auver head,
> An' water's bubblin' in its bed,

An' there vor me the apple tree
Do leän down low in Linden Lea.

Barnes had John Clare's gift for the magical phrase: 'the young that died in beauty', and 'our abode in Arby Wood'. He stimulated Hopkins's passion for word-coinages – 'The mother-holden child', 'healthjoy', 'limb-strength' – while Hardy developed Barnes's poignant reflections on the individual's brief share in the chain of generations.

Barnes's unemphatic talent, which Coventry Patmore described as 'a lack of vanity and ambition coupled with so much expert skill' captures those Romantic moments of piercing intensity when the natural world is completely apprehended: 'The Geäte a-Vallen To' goes beyond Hardy's humanism to the reductive twentieth-century art of William Carlos Williams (1883–1963), and the American poet's 'cool colloquy' of the mind of man with the objective world.

Edward Lear (1812–88) called himself 'by habit a wanderer, a humorist and a grumbler'. Like Charles Lamb and Thomas Hood, he was a Romantic working out of disappointment, and in his analytical nonsense poems he dwelt ruminatively on his shortcomings. His loving couples – the Owl and the Pussycat, the Yonghy-Bonghy-Bo and Lady Jingly – are hopelessly ill-matched, and his themes are of rejection, desertion and discomfiture, with the only possible refuges a crusty imperturbability ('How pleasant to know Mr Lear . . .') or a fanciful Nirvana ('under a lotus tree a eating of icecreams and pelican pie, with our feet in a hazure coloured stream with the birds and beasts of Paradise a sporting around us'). His universe is without logic or social cohesiveness, unlike those of Lewis Carroll and W. S. Gilbert, and is buffeted by strong currents of emotion, while its topography makes up a portrait of the artist.

Lear was 'brought up by women – and badly besides – and ill always'; an unwanted twentieth child, whose father speculated his way from modest affluence to a debtor's prison. The son was an epileptic and given from childhood to periods of depression. He supported himself from the age of fifteen, first by making 'morbid disease drawings' for teaching hospitals, and then ornithological plates. A commission to record the Earl of Derby's menagerie led him to the unofficial role of licensed jester to several great houses, and the writing of the first *Book of Nonsense* to amuse the Earl's grandchildren. In his professional life, Lear was a diligent landscape artist and a tutor to Queen Victoria, herself a creditable water-colourist. Lear claimed that his 'total unbroken application' to painting was 'the universal panacea for the ills of life', and travel and change relieved his melancholia and hypersensitive response to light and atmosphere.

Lear's poems, in their eccentric way some of the finest of the age, include *The Book of Nonsense* (1846), *Nonsense Songs, Stories, Botany and Alphabets* (1871), *More Nonsense* (1872) and *Laughable Lyrics* (1877). His letters, exquisite in themselves, are full of impatient, zany prose, exaggerated complaints and threats, cockney humour, spoonerisms and Joycean disturbances of language: 'become a sparry in the pilderpips and a pemmican on the housetops'. As an illustrator of his own comic verse he is the William Blake of nonsense, mournfully juxtaposing innocence and experience in an anticipation of the acidly wistful view of human limitations and failed relationships in the work of the gifted American James Thurber (1894–1961).

A character in a Grahame Greene novel observes laconically of Arthur Hugh Clough (1819–61): 'He was an adult poet in the nineteenth century. There weren't so many of them'. Clough's defenders take pleasure in their poet's poised ironies, delicate inflections, metrical inventiveness and intriguing vacillations between a mannered affectation of doubt and a genuine Romantic fear of 'some malpractice of heart'. He is refreshingly intellectual at a time when many poets appear to think through their imagery, and determinedly averse to calling his readers to action. A review of his *Ambarvalia* (1849) opened the general attack on Clough by urging that 'doubt . . . is not a poet's mood'. Uncertainty was not fashionable in the 1840s, though even the unimpeachable Goethe had cautioned that 'to act is easy, to think is hard'. In the provocative *Amours de Voyage* the hesitant hero ponders:

> *ACTION will furnish belief.* –but will that belief be
>   the right one?
> This is the point, you know.

Clough has a liberating sense of human absurdity and the courage to put this to work in serious poems rather than in the magical kingdom of nonsense. His work was not particularly popular in his own time; he wrote as much as his friend and rival Arnold, but no full edition appeared until 1951. That disapproving charge of 'doubt', the legacy of his earnest moral training at Rugby School, that forcing ground of conscience, and his struggles in the religious debates at Oxford, both defined and disabled him as a poet. 'Life loves no lookers-on at his great game', he wrote, mentally picturing himself in *Mari Magno* as prone

> To finger idly some old Gordian knot,
> Unskilled to sunder, and too weak to cleave,
> And with much toil attain to half believe.

His discriminating diffidence was balanced by the robust belief (anticipating both Freud and Yeats) that his craft and all the works of civilisation, 'exuberant, fervid and fecund', grew out of metaphorical excrement, or 'mixtures fetid foul and sour', a theory worked out triumphantly in the long-suppressed opening to 'O land of Empire . . .'. Clough was a truer successor to the classical poets than the chill and clean Hellenist Arnold; Clough belongs to the tradition of Horace (65 BC–8 BC), unflinchingly aware of the gamey, dangerous, public aspects of life, but convinced of the superior claims of civilised pleasures and cultivated emotions. Above all, Clough and Horace are enigmatic ironists whose positions it is never safe to assume. 'The Latest Decalogue', anthologised almost as often as the uncharacteristic or merely deceptive 'Say not the struggle nought availeth . . .', is the razor-sharp witticism of a man who was a spy rather than a citizen in the middle-class Victorian world.

Clough's public life was wholly unimpressive. A brilliant beginning was ruined by a crisis of faith at university, unsettled shuttling between England and the United States, resignation from two academic posts by the time he was thirty, and weary acceptance of a minor function in the Education Office so that he could marry. Yet he was deeply respected for his intrinsic quality: 'I cannot hear your essay this evening, Mr Symonds', said the Master of Balliol. 'I have just heard that Clough is dead'.

Of the poems published in his lifetime, *The Bothie of Tober-na-Vuolich* (1848) is the most buoyantly innovative, and the most eccentric tribute to Europe's year of revolutions. All Clough's poems bear un-English titles which have not helped their general popularity; *The Bothie* is, however, eloquently democratic. A reading-party of Oxford students on holiday in the Highlands climbs, bathes and philosophises, and the hero, Philip, falls in love with the daughter of a peasant-farmer; they emigrate to New Zealand in a mésalliance that looks forward to *The Ordeal of Richard Feverel* (1859), *Our Mutual Friend* (1865) and the preferred literary pairings of D. H. Lawrence (1885–1930). Clough anticipated Lawrence in his sturdy sense of sex as the mainspring of the human mechanism ('A London Idyll') and in his uncanny perception of the inner lives of his heroines. *The Bothie* is a celebration of Romantic joy freshly transposed into sexual terms; the possibility of retaining an innocence of feeling audaciously expressed in elaborately artificial hexameters.

Ambarvalia, published a month later, contains material of varying quality. 'Blank Misgivings of a Creature Moving About in Worlds Not Realised' argues the difficulty of applying Romantic concepts to contemporary experience, while 'Sic Itur' and 'Natura Naturans' are modern metaphysical poems. The first makes the new technology a metaphor of human existence, and the second, Clough's finest short poem, is a gorgeous erotic meditation on an unknown woman in a railway carriage; an analogue to the witty painting of Augustus Egg (1816–63), *The Travelling Companions* (1862) or Vronsky's falling in love with Anna Karenina in Tolstoy's novel (1875–7). Not until Hardy would the mystery of wayward sexual attraction be so unabashedly dramatised.

Amours de Voyage (1858) returned to the supple hexameters of *The Bothie* in a cooler, more heavily ironic narrative of an inconclusive courtship within the English community in Rome in 1850, with civil insurrection countered by the sceptical, pacifist sentiments of a drily observed hero who anticipates T. S. Eliot's Prufrock (1917). Clough's own doubt is most poignantly expressed in 'Easter Day', a rejection of Christianity kept back from publication, but the most unflinching gaze of its time at 'the empty vacant void' left by an absent God. The deliberate formality of the poem, far removed from the gaudy blasphemies of Swinburne, derives from and sadly challenges Milton's 'Ode on the Morning of Christ's Nativity' (1629).

Dipsychus, privately printed in 1865, is Byronically high-spirited, and revels in its metrical virtuosity until the fourth section becomes a racy cantata with the refrain:

> As I sat in the café, I said to myself,
> They may talk as they please about what they call pelf,
> They may sneer as they like about eating and drinking,
> But help it I cannot, I cannot help thinking
>   How pleasant it is to have money, heigh ho!
>   How pleasant it is to have money!

Dipsychus has the impudent fluency of the episodic, radical German dramas of Georg Büchner (1813–37) and looks forward to the plays of W. H. Auden in the 1930s. It is an endlessly diverting tug-of-war between a conscience-burdened man and his equally innate hedonism, and the prologue and epilogue in which Clough mocks his own fastidiousness make a necessary preface to his poetry.

Dante Gabriel Rossetti (1828–82) was as autonomous a poet as Clough, but a great deal more influential. He was, after Wordsworth, the most revolutionary poet of the century, though his achievement is more open to critical challenge; he turned the current of Victorian poetry from a Wordsworthian sense of the poet as 'a man speaking to men' to a belief that he was a much more privileged individual.

Rossetti's influence on the poets of the later nineteenth century was all the more remarkable since he wrote only by fits and starts in the intervals of his career as an unexpectedly fashionable painter, and he was entirely careless of the English poetic tradition. His example filled a need in Victorian poetry; the Romantic assumptions no longer matched an urban, industrialised and spiritually uncertain world, and prose fiction was succeeding to the high office Wordsworth had claimed for poetry. In 1849 a contributor to *The Prospective Review* predicted that the novel was 'the form in which much of the poetry of the coming age will be written', and Clough himself shrugged: 'Our novelists give us a real house to live in'. A poetry liberated from the need to guide and order actual experience became imaginatively ungoverned and supremely conscious of its form, following Rossetti's creation of a private dream world which was a blend of the sensual and supernatural.

Unlike the English Romantics, Rossetti was quite incurious about politics and social justice, despite being brought up in an exile's household. He regarded himself as a purely accidental participant in his century, rather like the ancient idol of his 'Burden of Nineveh', freakishly exposed to gaping London crowds. His literary interests were narrow and violent (Italian poetry up to and including Dante (1265–1321) and Romantic German ballads), and throughout his life he was impatient of reality, seeking to create by superstitious ritual, seances and the intervention of drugs those moments in which the physical world dissolved into a familiar mystical universe, 'a vain, strange land', full of sombre perils and vague promises.

Rossetti's family was as eccentric as the notoriously gifted Brontës; his father was obsessed with a private interpretation of Dante, his elder sister secluded herself as an Anglican nun, and another sister, Christina, lived in retirement as a poet whose gifts equalled or surpassed his own. William Michael, the ponderous Boswell of the family, was their editor, banker and biographer. Dante Gabriel picked up an irregular education, and in 1848, with the first draft of 'The Blessed Damozel' in manuscript, sought out the studio of the young Ford Madox Brown who was developing a new English art; deliberately insular, unacademic and heavily symbolic. Soon the unteachable Rossetti was gathering his own disciples in Brown's studio, including the dogmatic and fanatical Holman Hunt (1827–1910) and the precocious J. E. Millais. The circle called itself the Pre-Raphaelite Brotherhood, taking up the idea that art had degenerated since the creation of ideal types of physical and moral beauty by the Italian painter Raphael (1483–1520), and that the time had come to renew the ties of painting to nature. Where possible, they were to paint from non-professional models in the open air, and to take their inspiration from literature.

There was immediately what William Rossetti called 'a perfect crusade against the PRB' and 'a savage assault' on Gabriel in particular. His *Ecce Ancilla Domini*, a troubling portrait of Christina as a cowering Virgin, appeared to flaunt either Roman or blasphemist tendencies, in a period sensitive to threats to the English church. The attack by the academicians was expected, but Dickens's ill-advised invective against Millais's *Christ in the House of His Parents* ('a woman so horrible in her ugliness that . . . she would stand out from the rest of the company as a monster in the vilest cabaret') did great damage. Fortunately, at the urging of the poet Coventry Patmore, always willing to exert himself in the cause of a literary underdog, Ruskin decided that the group shared his philosophy of art, and in a famous letter to *The Times* of 13 May 1851, he became their champion.

'Pre-Raphaelitism' is hard to define. It encompasses both poetry and painting, and within a single genre, works as unalike as Rossetti's austerely spiritual *Girlhood of Mary Virgin* and the glaring portraits of his low-life mistress Fanny Cornforth swathed in brocade and jewels, which in turn co-exist with Hunt's crowd-pleasing moral lessons, *The Light of the World* and *The Awakening Conscience*. Yet all 'Pre-Raphaelite' painting is designed to waylay the spectator, lured insect-like by the bright colours, into coming uncomfortably close to the artist's perception of the world. Like modernism in the twentieth century, this sort of painting was designed to shock; whereas academic art had (in Clough's words) poised, retained, fixed and held the observer, Pre-Raphaelitism shattered the act of seeing and reassembled the fragments. Its artists are often criticised for not taking advantage of the climate in France that produced the Impressionists, but in a sense they bypass the revolutions of their own century and anticipate both Surrealism and the cult of the individual in Picasso (1881–1973) with the shameless advertisement of erotic and cultural obsessions. Even the pure abstractions of Piet Mondrian (1872–1944) and De Stijl (1917–28) were hinted at by Rossetti's own early preference for rectangular compositions and primary colours.

For all their fondness for mediaeval subject-matter, the Pre-Raphaelites were children of their century; in Ruskin's words, they surrendered no advantage which the knowledge of the invention of the present time could afford their art. Once Ruskin's support and the astute marketing skills of each member of the group had assured individual survival, they found patrons in the men and women made rich by industrial growth, who were flexible or uncertain enough in their taste to want a style so untried. Hunt, Millais and Brown produced the new icons of the age; social and religious subjects as full of symbolic meaning as those of Raphael had been. New techniques of reproduction, and in particular the heyday of wood and steel engravings in the 1840s, had made a wide repertoire of visual material available to a popular audience. The invention of a new range of colours, which was to add immeasurably to the thrill of the Great Exhibition in 1851, provided the singing blue-greens, magentas and violets which link the paintings in tone, as does the habit of laying down colour on a white ground for extra brilliancy. The mid-century's childlike joy in the possibilities of colour is slightly embarrassing to the modern spectator, but the vivid dissonances of Holman Hunt and the stained-glass glory of Millais's *Isabella* forced the watcher into a new relationship with the subject and the external world.

Rossetti and his group produced their own magazine for a brief four issues in 1850; *The Germ* was subtitled *Thoughts Towards Nature in Poetry, Literature and Art*, in the best Romantic manner. But the 'Round Table' dedicated to the anonymous creation of morally challenging art broke up by 1851, under the pressure of the intense egotism of its members.

Rossetti's creative development was guided by his complex and erratic emotional life, with its phases marked by a succession of women of great beauty and humble origins. Elizabeth Siddal, the favoured model of the Brotherhood from her discovery in 1850, remained his companion and uncannily apt pupil until their belated marriage in 1860 and her suicide in 1862; by then she had been replaced as a latter-day Beatrice to Rossetti's Dante by the magnificently enigmatic Jane Burden, who had inexplicably married the young William Morris in 1859. Morris, with Swinburne and the painter Edward Burne-Jones (1833–98) formed the nucleus of a second generation of Pre-Raphaelites that Rossetti gathered round him in the summer of 1857 during the painting of the soon-to-vanish Oxford Union frescoes on Arthurian subjects. In 1868, under the influence of Jane Morris, Rossetti returned to poetry, putting together much of his clotted, mystical sonnet sequence *The House of Life* while literally haunted, as he believed, by the ghost of his dead wife. The manuscript poems of 1847-54 which he had buried with her as a gesture of remorse or propitiation were disinterred and published in the volume of 1870; this Gothic episode leads to an uncommon degree of difficulty in ascribing date or context to most of Rossetti's poetry.

His guilty feelings were inflamed the next year by Robert Buchanan's gross attack in 'The Fleshly School of Poetry' in *The Contemporary Review*, which condemned Rossetti and Swinburne for their allegedly lascivious treatment of sexual themes. Rossetti spent the next two years in seclusion with Jane Morris at her husband's lonely manor house, turning out increasingly mannered portraits of her beauty, and returning to poetry in 1879 with elaborate ballads, *The Bride's Prelude*, an ornate psychological study of hapless guilt, and a yet more expanded version of *The House of Life*. He died in 1882, physically and mentally wrecked by fears and addictions, great in reputation and theoretically a rich man, and leaving an influence that would linger well beyond the century.

Rossetti's poetry is full of a painterly love of dense, fully-realised imagery. But the essential feature of his style is paradox, sometimes exploring constant Romantic dilemmas, and sometimes merely confused and despairing. *The House of Life* is freighted with oxymorons: 'Death-in-Love', 'Barren Spring', 'Vain Virtues', 'Newborn Death'. His celebration of sexual love is highly formalised; even the notorious 'Nuptial Sleep' has erotic imagery hardly distinguishable from Tennyson's universally acceptable 'Now sleeps the crimson petal . . .' and is closed with a sense of reborn innocence. Rossetti rarely described passion satisfied; he prefers an heroic chastity, as in 'The Staff and the Scrip', or a sanctified asexuality (the Coleridgean clarity of 'My Sister's Sleep'), and even the cautiously lubricious 'Jenny' is completely innocent in its situation, as a philosophically inclined client waits out the night in a sleeping harlot's room.

Often the Rossettian paradox is one of form; his ballads falsely sophisticate the convention employed by Romantic poets to ensure a simple and honest diction. The primitive and the artificial are counterpointed throughout Rossetti's poetry; heady, gorgeous imagery set against a tender response to fleeting patterns of water, wind and light, and a claustrophobic symbolism countered by a Wordsworthian impatience to rediscover experience unsullied by thought.

> The wind flapped loose, the wind was still,
> Shaken out dead from tree and hill;
> I had walked on at the wind's will --
> I sat now, for the wind was still.
>
> Between my knees my forehead was --
> My lips, drawn in, said not Alas!
> My hair was over in the grass,
> My naked ears heard the day pass.
>
> My eyes, wide open, had the run
> Of some ten weeds to fix upon;
> Among those few, out of the sun,
> The woodspurge flowered, three cups in one.
>
> From perfect grief there need not be
> Wisdom or even memory;
> One thing then learned remains to me --
> The woodspurge has a cup of three.

The best of Rossetti's poetry dwells on the Romantic impulse, that moment of insight at which the temporal and timeless worlds coincide, as they do in 'The Woodspurge' and 'Sudden Light'. His most ambitious poems, 'The Stream's Secret' and 'This is her picture as she was . . .' are autobiographical; a wavering between an impatiently rejected reality and a symbolic dream world, so that they combine a Lethean mysticism and a Tennysonian plangency ('Empty pastures wet with rain'). Rossetti is haunted by the dark side of Romanticism that came into English poetry through Coleridge; the fear of the extinction of life, and loss of the radiant creative vision. His gift died with him, like that of most surrealists, though it continued to lure his imitators.

'The school of experience': women writers of the 1840s

The Brontë family, Charlotte, Emily, Ann, and their tormented brother Branwell (an inarticulate De Quincey and failed painter) were at once inheritors, victims and critics of the Romantic tradition. The sisters' novels have sometimes been described as 'Pre-Raphaelite' in their disconcerting emotional honesty, clarity of imagery, and powerful suggestion of what Charlotte Brontë called 'the sympathies of Nature with man'.

What Elizabeth Gaskell, her imaginatively attuned biographer, terms in 1857 'the wild, strange facts' of their lives have made the family a legend: the proud and irascible clergyman father bringing up his four surviving children to be his intellectual companions; their invention of elaborate imaginary worlds as compensation for their isolation; privation and homesickness endured at school and out governessing; Charlotte and Emily's adventure as pupil-teachers in Belgium, and Charlotte's unrequited love for a master at the school there; Branwell's self-destruction through drinking and drugs; a brief taste of success with the publication of the first novels and poems of 'Currer, Ellis and Acton Bell'; the rapidly following deaths from tuberculosis of Emily and Ann; Charlotte's emotionally exhausted marriage to her father's curate, and her own death at the age of thirty-nine.

The literary life of the family began with the famous 'web of childhood' to which Charlotte Brontë paid tribute in her one genuinely fine poem.

> We wove a web in childhood,
> A web of sunny air;
> We dug a spring in infancy
> Of water pure and fair;
>
> We sowed in youth a mustard seed
> We cut an almond rod;
> We are now grown up to riper age --
> Are they withered in the sod?
>
> The mustard-seed in distant land
> Bends down a mighty tree,
> The dry unbudding almond wand
> Has touched eternity . . . .

The paired sagas of Angria and Gondal absorbed the children's energies so that their formal education and the later business of earning a living became tedious interruptions. Angria, shared by Charlotte and Branwell, and Gondal, managed by Emily and Anne, were radically different; in Angria, strength of feeling legitimised action, whereas in Gondal the only certain good was stoical endurance in the face of certain doom. Angria was dominated by its Byronic heroes for whom the heroines compete; the Gondal epic unfolds the career of one superbly amoral heroine, a 'glorious child', 'too blithe, too loving', who ruins her lovers, murders her infant, and suffers agonies of alienation during her long reign. Poems such as 'No coward soul is mine . . .' and 'Cold in the earth, the deep snow piled above thee . . .', traditionally presented (with Charlotte Brontë's editorial connivance) as Emily Brontë's own passionate outbursts, are speeches from the various women of Gondal. Charlotte Brontë, who had to move in the outside world, eventually felt her violent and reckless fantasies to be a danger to her religion and her sanity; Emily Brontë's universe was transmuted effortlessly into the world of *Wuthering Heights*.

Charlotte Brontë (1816–55) was the longest living and most prolific of the sisters. Her negligible poems and the tentativeness of *The Professor* (not published until 1857) are no preparation for the flawed but magnificent *Jane Eyre* (1847), with its grandiose claims for romantic love and the rapacious but tender ego of its heroine. It is a summation of contemporary themes: Elizabeth Barrett Browning's demands for female rights to 'nourishment for the mind', and the earnest reconciliation of the needs of the passionate individual and the demands of Christian conscience and duty in the novels of Charlotte Yonge (1823–1901) and Charles Kingsley. Like Charlotte Brontë, Dickens evokes a semi-autobiographical childhood in his own novel of 'the disciplined heart', *David Copperfield* (1850). Half of *Jane Eyre* grows out of the Gothic tradition (the accursed hero, the secluded house, and the supernatural threats to the heroine), but the other half dramatises the union of 'propensities' and 'principles'; that Romantic integrity of feeling that must be made to take account of its social context. *Jane Eyre* was admired by both sexes at its first appearance – a situation not always obtaining today – and the novel speaks for freedom in a general sense.

Shirley (1849) was designed as a corrective to *Jane Eyre*; the world in which Charlotte Brontë actually found herself, rather than the domain of fancy. It is absorbing but unsatisfactory, written at a time of fear and grief, and changing course uncontrollably after the death of Emily Brontë, who is effusively honoured in the heroine of the title. The salvageable sections of *Shirley* deal with the delicate but unserviceable intelligence of the infatuated Caroline Helstone. Though *Shirley* appears to address itself to topics current in the novels of the 1840s – social unrest and political theory – its violent episodes are only metaphors for personal relationships gone awry.

Villette (1853) is powerfully original, lacking the formal satisfactions of *Jane Eyre*, but rejoicing in its deliberate eccentricities. It is the most thoroughly autobiographical of the novels, set in a dreamlike version of Brussels, and making candid use of events not publicised during Charlotte Brontë's lifetime. Lucy Snowe is a defiantly prickly heroine, in search (at considerable risk to her reason) for authenticity of feeling. In the course of giving and receiving an education, she finds that very little in contemporary culture and permitted relationships can satisfy her needs, and her sceptical, suffering mind remains the one sure point in her phantasmagorical world. It is a novel as corrective in its impulse as *Shirley* had been, an intimate study of loneliness and unrequited love that embarrassed and repelled contemporaries like Matthew Arnold and Harriet Martineau. But the bleakness is balanced by an exalted conviction that 'Happiness is a glory shining far down on us out of heaven'; a Romantic belief that makes all lesser forms of joy contemptible.

Emily Brontë (1818–48) wrote only one novel, in the sense that Beethoven wrote only one opera, and her fiction is the more dramatic for its high polish. *Wuthering Heights* (1847) had been tested in the fantasies of Gondal until its characters and landscapes have the integrity of Thomas Hardy's novels and poems, or the Yoknapatawpha County of William Faulkner (1897–1962). Emily Brontë has no recognisable forebears (though earlier, consciously experimental writers like Mary Shelley and Bulwer Lytton had anticipated some of her effects); her precise and uncompromising craft was fostered by her native surroundings and abundant leisure.

Wuthering Heights is a bewildering novel, since so much in the outwardly crystalline narrative is called into question by the voices who contribute to it. The impercipient Lockwood can neither understand nor sympathise with the passions that he learns about from the manipulative, intermittently truthful Nelly Dean, and the central characters explain themselves fiercely without their creator making an attempt to discriminate between their clashing egos. Emily Brontë, no less than God, is disconcertingly absent from her world, in which a supernatural universe may or may not be imposed on the plane of mundane needs and violent loves, and nature is by turns malevolent, indifferent and benign. Heathcliff and Catherine enjoy a Romantically amoral will, and the next generation possesses a blessed ordinariness: each without a sign of approval from the author. Passages of the finest and most dramatic writing, including the famous conclusion to the novel, may be exercises in sustained anti-Romantic irony. The novel is a mixture of sophisticated artistry and the simplicity of the folk-tale; a foundling who suggests the Prince and Darkness and the loving siblings who are reunited. The bizarre, the supernatural and the sadistic elements of the novels are presented with a saving respect for physical actuality. *Wuthering Heights* remains a gigantic, beautiful conundrum which makes such immense claims for Romantic energies that it may well be a criticism of such yearnings.

Anne Brontë (1820–49) lived in the shadow of her more dynamic sisters, and suffered posthumously from Charlotte Brontë's protectively depreciatory care of her reputation. Her little-read poetry records a vigorous inner life and a more analytical temperament than either of her sisters possessed. She disdained imagery, and her understanding of family relationships, particularly in the grisly year of Branwell's collapse, is both rigorous and charitable.

Anne Brontë's novels, *Agnes Grey* (1847) and *The Tenant of Wildfell Hall* (1848) are marked by her habitual chastity of expression: *Agnes Grey*, the faintly fictionalised reminiscences of her own unhappy years as a governess, suggests an initial aversion to fiction as a paltering with the truth. But she has a keen eye for social detail, a relish for absurdity, and the family ability to contemplate cruelty without flinching; Agnes Grey, unlike Jane Eyre, is capable of a detached sympathy for people who do not share her imaginative bounty. *The Tenant of Wildfell Hall* shows Anne Brontë more at ease in the expansive form of the novel that contradicted her naturally economical utterance. A principled, religious and intelligent woman is fascinated by a philandering drunkard, in a relationship that recalls Samuel Richardson's *Clarissa* (1747–8); it is far from the tract that Charlotte Brontë found it, and halfway, in subject and treatment, to George Eliot's early story 'Janet's Repentance' in *Scenes From Clerical Life*. Of all the Brontë novels, *The Tenant of Wildfell Hall* lies closest to the Victorian mainstream and what the twentieth-century critic F. R. Leavis has called 'the Great Tradition'.

Elizabeth Gaskell (1810–65), the intelligent and scrupulous biographer of Charlotte Brontë, developed her art in middle life, like George Eliot and Joseph Conrad. Her deceptively leisured, understated fictions make her the archetypal 'minor Victorian novelist', and her reputation has been further diminished by her unembittered satisfaction in her double role as writer and as the active wife of a busy Unitarian clergyman in Manchester. Her novels probe the minute human consequences of the break-up of the feudal order and the growth of urban industrialism; her response to these social problems is intuitive, generously Christian, and respectful of individual needs. She refuses to generalise in terms of class, or to support specific legislation.

Mary Barton: A Tale of Manchester Life (1848) is a striking first novel, very much to the taste of the times in its attempt to understand the newly emergent and possibly dangerous working class. However, its best aspects lie not in the melodramatic plot, but in the fine observation of the petty stratagems by which the very poor and ill-used keep up their morale and extend the small charity in their command to even less fortunate neighbours. *Ruth* (1853) is a notable contribution to the mid-century's attempts to explain the phenomenon of prostitution, brought about by the economic impossibility of early marriage for the socially ambitious Victorian man, and the struggle for survival within an uprooted, newly urbanised and economically powerless female working class. The wholly admirable *Ruth* shows the seduction and despair of a dressmaker's apprentice, who is helped to find her way back to respectability by a genuinely Christian family. Once again, the incidental details, including the touchingly banal ruin of the inexperienced girl, are more affecting than the message of the whole. The material of *Ruth* was to be reworked in Hardy's *Tess of the D'Urbervilles* (1891) and George Moore's *Esther Waters* (1894); the latter's realism has affinities with the precise detail and feeling for social context in Elizabeth Gaskell.

Cranford (1853), derives from childhood memories of a world of stable social patterns, very different from 'ugly, smoky Manchester; dear, busy, earnest, noble-working Manchester' where Elizabeth Gaskell worked out her destiny. It invokes the world of Mary Russell Mitford and is an equally consoling fantasy; a village of women without the men whose zeal for change and intellectual rebelliousness break up the old traditions. But the gentleness of Cranford is already a holiday indulgence; it is threatened by the railway and by stock speculations, those staples of the world of Mr Dombey. *North and South* (1855) is a Victorian *Much Ado About Nothing*, that unites a majestic young lady of breeding with a captain of industry; the taming of the intelligent and passionate woman by a man of the future has more in common with Shaw's *Arms and the Man* (1894) than with Disraeli's *Sybil*. It is a novel of manners, but as in Jane Austen's fiction, these outward forms are expressive of different attitudes towards society itself.

Wives and Daughters (1866), the last of the novels and all but finished at Elizabeth Gaskell's death, reverts to a rural parish and is set, like the later *Middlemarch*, at the time of the 1832 Reform Bill. It is prescient of the greater novel; deliberately provincial in its setting, critical of its own nostalgic impulses, using the first hints of social chance to force new and experimental alliances between characters, and deeply interested in the promise of the scientist with his speculative and uncommitted mind. Mr Gibson, the physician married to a vapidly egotistical provincial beauty, is very close to Lydgate in *Middlemarch*; despite her principled aversion to George Eliot's irregular 'marriage', Elizabeth Gaskell had a great admiration for a gift which meshed so finely with her own.

Elizabeth Gaskell's novels explore the realm of necessity rather than that of freedom. Her heroines have to accept what fate their menfolk assign them; Mary Barton copes with a depressed and unemployed father who destroys her lovers, Margaret Hale is thrust into a world of servants' work and shabby lodgings by her father's religious doubts, Ruth is ruined by a womanising member of parliament, and Molly Gibson is saddled with an unprincipled stepmother. Elizabeth Gaskell shows their daily battles with the ignoble and their grace under these inescapable indignities much as Tolstoy ends his two great novels with the approval of those characters who submerge their ecstatic independent quests for enlightenment in their role as parents and heads of households; Kitty and Levin, Natasha and Pierre. George Eliot developed the Poysers of *Adam Bede* and the Garths of *Middlemarch* as intellectually satisfying versions of that family hearth which was traditionally the consolation of Victorian life. Dickens habitually stresses his sympathy with the human need to create an oasis of order, generosity and tenderness in a chaos of selfishness, and even for the discriminating Charlotte Brontë 'household joys and domestic endearments' are 'the best thing the world has!'

While Elizabeth Gaskell illustrates the tendency of·fiction in the middle decades of the century to move from indignant criticism of social ills to a leisurely and nostalgic analysis of social pressures on the individual, the poet Elizabeth Barrett (1806–61), from 1846 Elizabeth Barrett Browning, remained passionately committed to the idea of the artist as one who changed social attitudes by eager example.

The considerable romance of her life has outlasted her reputation as a poet; her incarceration as a mysterious invalid by her possessive father, her painstaking self-education in the classics, her correspondence and wide reading that kept colour in her banishment, her dramatic elopement with her colleague Robert Browning, and the rich satisfactions of her life in Italy. Her interest in character, shrewd observation and her wit should have made her a remarkable novelist, but her eccentric upbringing spoiled her for that. Virginia Woolf, who knew the value of an escape from 'respectable, mummified humbug' to an existence 'crude and impertinent perhaps, but living', is one of the most sympathetic commentators on a woman once considered for the laureateship but now confined to the 'servants' quarters' in the mansion of literature. 'Her bad taste, her tortured ingenuity, her floundering, scrambling and confused impetuosity' are admitted, but in compensation there remain 'ardour and abundance, her brilliant descriptive powers, her shrewd and caustic humour'.

Elizabeth Barrett Browning was forced by poor example and current taste into a false lyricism for which her voice was too strong. Of her copious output, the political poems of the Italian years are stone-dead, and only the verse-novel *Aurora*

Leigh survives, besides the grudgingly reprieved *Sonnets from the Portuguese* (1850) and a handful of isolated poems, including the social protest *The Cry of the Children*; and 'The Great God Pan', where her classical reading and her rank energy meet with unusual felicity.

She never tried, like the Brontës, to adopt a male persona in her poetry, which contains a bravely feminist repertoire of metaphors for 'the full-veined, heaving, double-breasted age', and heroines of the Demeter or Valkyrie stamp. Marian Erle's indignant narrative in *Aurora Leigh* of her rape and the birth of her illegitimate child is a wild, female exultation:

> Springing up erect,
> And lifting up the child at full arm's length,
> As if to bear him like an oriflamme
> Unconquerable to armies of reproach –

This has a visual equivalent in the troubling paintings of Ford Madox Brown in the 1850s. *The Pretty Baa Lambs* with its monolithic modern Madonna and her brawny attendant, and his imperious fallen woman sanctified by her maternity in *Take Your Son, Sir!* are far from the orthodox images of praise of motherhood and reminders of the wages of sin.

Sonnets from the Portuguese will always have appreciative if uncritical readers, though their strenuous but inexact language shows the poet at her worst. W. H. Auden dismissed them with a curt 'my taste abhors them, and my judgement tells me they are no good'. *Aurora Leigh* (1857) is also easy to mock, with its riot of influences (George Sand (1804–76), the melodramatist Eugène Sue (1804–57), Balzac, Victor Hugo and Charles Kingsley), but it is amazingly readable. Elizabeth Barrett Browning's feminism is of a heavily qualified sort; she is interested only in the emotional rights of gifted women, and bored by the plodding arguments for female suffrage and economic freedom. Aurora herself has an impeccably feminist ancestry; for George Sand herself, born Aurore Dupin in 1804, owes much to the *Corinne* (1807) of Madame de Staël (1766–1817), and her own Romantic excesses are coolly appraised in Meredith's complicated *Diana of the Crossways* (1885).

Despite its popularity (thirteen editions by 1873), *Aurora Leigh* was a false trail in literature. Clough and Coventry

Patmore shared Elizabeth Barrett Browning's desire to release poetry from its commitment to personal lyricism and a mediaeval past, and *The Bothie of Tober-na-Vuolich* (1848) and *The Angel in the House* (1854–63) also reinforced their deliberate modernity with an attempt to place sexual relations on a more authentic basis. But Clough and Patmore are genuinely original. Elizabeth Barrett Browning had trusted in Spasmodic fashion to the spirit making the form, and the blank verse she settled on was unsuited to her rapid and associative thought. In her attempt to make poetry as responsive to modern life as the novel, she failed to see that the divergence was already too complete.

3
The disinterested intelligence: 1850–70

COMMENTATORS on the nineteenth century have always regarded the 1850s and 1860s as a peculiarly favoured period; an interlude of prosperity, achievement and social harmony that is a vindication of responsibly applied Utilitarian theory. Despite the Indian Mutiny and the Crimean War that warned of the coming troubles and distractions of Empire, these decades were a time of happy relaxation after the doctrinaire 1830s and 1840s with their famine, epidemics and threat of revolution. Progress seemed assured, the more brutal aspects of a *laissez-faire* capitalism had been tamed, self-help was tactfully rewarded, and the citizens of Britain (for the first time largely urban) were growing accustomed to a degree of administrative control that would have seemed unthinkable two decades earlier.

Lord Palmerston (1784–1865), the architect of British foreign policy at this time, perfectly embodied the outlook of the newly powerful and articulate commercial and industrial middle class, more eager to see its economic achievements reflected in Britain's overseas prestige than to speed the pace of reform at home. Palmerston's high-handed and temperamental but extremely popular support of liberalism and nationalism in Europe was a form of political narcissism, as he and his supporters saw embryonic constitutional governments emerging along British lines, while the balance of power remained intact. Palmerston's exalted sense of a national mission – the creation of a virtual Pax Britannica – was to make him the victim in his lifetime of the ruthless pragmatism of the Prussian Bismark. But the years before

1865 remained, for all their dangerous glamour, the high point of British foreign policy.

Economic prosperity and political stability endowed fortunate men and women with 'the power to speculate, to wonder, and to enjoy', in the approving phrase of G. M. Young; a wise man, he added, would choose the 1850s to be young in. 'The age of improvement', 'the age of equipoise', 'Victoria's heyday' or 'the Victorian noon' as the period is variously called, was a remarkable interval of intellectual liberation within a context of generally shared assumptions; religious doubts, social indignation and the lure of the untethered imagination pointed the way to the divergences that came in the 1870s, but these disruptive forces were still under control.

If Lord Macaulay voiced a characteristic and almost universal satisfaction that 1851, the year of the Great Exhibition, would 'long be remembered as a singularly happy year of peace, plenty, good feeling, innocent pleasure, national glory of the best and purest sort', the pessimistic Thomas Hardy looked back from 1893 in his short story 'The Fiddler of the Reels' and saw that golden year marking an ominous shift in sensibility:

> an extraordinary chronological frontier or transit-line, at which there occurred what one might call a precipice in Time. As in a geological 'fault', we had presented to us a sudden bringing of ancient and modern into absolute contact . . . .

Hardy deliberately chose the simile of one of the 'Terrible Muses', as Tennyson called the sciences of geology and astronomy that were reducing the stature of man and calling religious orthodoxy into question. Charles Darwin's *The Origin of Species*, long foreshadowed, was published in 1859, at a period when men were not only re-evaluating their place in the universe but learning a more immediate historical self-consciousness; the term 'Victorian' is used for the first time in the 1850s, just as Disraeli had flourished 'the nineteenth century' in the 1820s. For the first time, it becomes comparatively easy to slip without much mental adjustment into the subjective context of literature; these people have much the same attitudes as ourselves.

'It is a privilege', Disraeli wrote to a friend in 1862, 'to live in this age of rapid and brilliant events. What an error to consider it a utilitarian age. It is one of infinite romance.' Romance had filtered down, very agreeably, to a banal level of taste and custom; popular poetry and fiction, a taste for machine-made exotica and pseudo-mediaeval ornament, and the picturesque exaggeration of outward sexual differences. A true Romanticism was being reborn at a more significant level with a new generation of independent thinkers who had been reared in an atmosphere of industry and piety and who were now committing themselves to a personal search for the right basis for faith and action. Ruskin changed course dramatically, abandoning art criticism for a vehement attack on capitalism; Browning and Meredith developed intricate fictions discovering newer and subtler bases for ethical judgement; Matthew Arnold's poetry dwelt intently on the poet's separation from the populace he must lead to 'sweetness and light'. Tennyson's poetry, far from enhancing received ideas, became more and more a warning against 'the lust of gain, in the spirit of Cain', and that 'Demos' which ends in 'working his own doom'. George Eliot, the most famous example of the emancipated intellect, replaced 'the miserable etiquette of sectarianism' with a discriminating belief in 'truth of feeling' as 'the only universal bond of union', and her novels became the true successors to Wordsworth's poetry.

The core of the Victorian period is often spoken of as complacent, a charge which would have surprised its writers. Very few of them can be charged with a lack of subtlety when they are attentively read. Social change was already challenging the code of self-restraint that had come in with the earliest nineteenth-century reformers of religion and manners, and poets and novelists recorded the new perplexities. The deceptively aquiescent novels of Anthony Trollope prove to be energetically ironic studies in the erosion of conservative social values, and Dickens and Charles Kingsley dramatise a want of social cohesiveness; even the popular 'sensation' novels of Wilkie Collins and his imitators suggest complex middle-class guilts and fears. The remarkable flowering of Victorian mediaevalism was not so much a decorative escapism as a search for stability, since those who felt trepidation at the power promised to the labouring classes or at the disappearance of God through the challenge of the sciences, could look back to an emotionally satisfying mythical feudal order, while the idea of chivalry legitimised the engrossing concept of 'the gentleman'. This key word of the nineteenth century, richly glossed in all the novels of the period, underwent many changes of meaning until a term originally applied only to people of 'gentle' birth came to be used more broadly of anyone who had acquired a liberal education, a reasonably polished demeanour and a Christian conscience: or whose son could be expected to possess those things through the influence of the public schools.

Despite the intellectual vitality of these decades, there is the hint of a divison between writers and the reading public that becomes a rift with the *Poems and Ballads* of Algernon Swinburne in 1866. Whereas the early Romantics had sought to establish bonds of common feeling and a shared culture, the poets emerging in the 1850s and after urged their non-conformity and their right to indulge in private fantasy. It was the inevitable reaction to the effects of a general but hardly liberal increase in education, and the constant reinforcing of the middle class with recruits from below. For the first time, those with money to spend on the embellishments of life were not necessarily sophisticated. The 'big men with heavy purses' were too often like Dickens's Mr Podsnap in *Our Mutual Friend* (1864–5).

> Mr Podsnap's notions of the Arts in their integrity might have been stated thus. Literature; large print, respectfully descriptive of getting up at eight, shaving close at a quarter past, breakfasting at nine, going to the City at ten, coming home at half past five, and dining at seven. Painting and Sculpture; models and portraits representing Professors of getting up at eight . . . .

These unreflective lives bred a reaction of distaste in many writers and artists, and led directly to the Aesthetic Movement of the 1870s and 1880s, with its charming but dilapidated Pre-Raphaelitism stripped of moral energies, and the Decadence of the 1890s.

These decades of a brief, harmonious balance began with a symbol of Romantic imagination wedded to technological power. The 'blazing arch of lucid glass' that was the Crystal Palace with its treasures of scientific invention and the riches of commerce was a stately pleasure dome for the masses, and a union of fancy and practicality, high and popular art, that was not to be seen again in the nineteenth century.

'Scenes of an awful drama': the condition-of-England question

Henry Mayhew (1812–87) produced one incontestably great work in the course of a mysteriously unsuccessful life: *London Labour and the London Poor* was completed in 1862 after thirteen years of effort, interrupted by disputes with unpaid printers and disappearances abroad to escape creditors. The exhaustive survey of the Victorian urban underclass, told mostly in their own words (Mayhew was addicted to conversation), seems another monument to mid-Victorian industry, and it comes as a shock to discover that Mayhew ('whom God make wiser') was a byword for idleness and improvidence. He had worked as a journalist after being dismissed from his father's law firm, and scraped a living from penny journals and knockabout farces, nearly betraying himself into solid success when he co-edited the first volume of *Punch* with Mark Lemon in 1840; he was soon demoted to 'Suggestor-in-Chief' and his time taken up with his disgraceful bankruptcy proceedings. *London Labour* began as a series of articles for the *Morning Chronicle*, cancelled when an advertiser objected to the disclosure of conditions in his tailor's shop, and the vignettes were issued instead as a periodical selling at twopence the weekly instalment, with the first collection appearing in 1851. Mayhew ended his self-effacing career as a ghost-writer, and his obituarists found his life unaccountable; he was unable to take the values of his own class seriously, and courted failure as a protest, giving society the slip as effectively as the vagabond 'Waring' of Browning's poem.

London Labour and the London Poor ('a picture of London life so wonderful, so awful, so piteous and pathetic . . . lying by your door and mine', wrote Thackeray with unwonted enthusiasm for the underprivileged) gives a paradoxically accurate version of mid-century society; contemporary, urban and proletarian, whereas the world of the novelist tends to be historical, rural and provincial, and wholly middle-class in attitude. Mayhew's documents present a curious, almost satirical view of respectable life seen from an underside that has parallel codes and conventions; even the scavengers of the most disgusting offal have their rigid caste system, and the costers, those aristocrats among the poor, are motivated by that same 'love of self' that drives the industrialist. Not only do Mayhew's poor live on the refuse of the middle classes; they use cast-offs of its language and morals, 'Redeemer' suggesting the pawn-shop rather than religion. They live off the misfortunes of others, from the river-finders who dredge corpses from the Thames to the 'running-patterers' who provide an illiterate public with doggerel versions of crimes and gallows-scenes: Dickens was able to use Mayhew's documents almost without exaggeration for his nightmare world of *Our Mutual Friend*.

Mayhew allows himself hardly any editorial comment, unlike the later French Hippolyte Taine (1828–93), whose *Notes on England* (1872) were illustrated eerily by Gustave Doré (1832–83); Mayhew's portrait of a vast and unacknowledged society emerges by slow accumulation. It is far from artless in its details, however; Mayhew shapes each monologue for maximum effect, employing a spare language which suggests strong emotions and heightened experience in an almost Wordsworthian manner. Stabbing phrases evoke whole sad histories:

If I had money enough to buy a stock of oranges, I think I could be honest.

No mother couldn't love a child more than mine did me, but her feelins was such she couldn't bear to see me.

Each encounter contains the same unspoken drama; the flattered egotism with which the speaker lays bare his stratagems for survival in the most squalid circumstances, and a growing despair as his newfound articulacy reveals the hopelessness of his plight. *London Labour and the London Poor* is the *Inferno* of the nineteenth century.

Mayhew has strong affinities with the visual arts; the genre painters Wilkie and Mulready with their Wordsworthian sympathy for the small tragedies of the rural poor, and the more assertive Victorian depictors of depressed lives, Abraham Solomon (1824–62) in his *Second Class: The Parting* (1854) and *Waiting for the Verdict* (1857). Both reached a wide audience through engravings, while *Applicants for Admission to a Casual Ward* (1874) by Luke Fildes (1844–1927) is a compositionally ravishing and emotionally harrowing study in the manner of Mayhew himself.

If Mayhew impresses the reader by his rigorous self-effacement, Charles Kingsley (1819–75), no less a sympathiser with the poor, was rash in all his dealings and uncritically fluent in his prose. He exemplifies to the point of caricature the best and worst in the intellectual of the mid-century: an organiser and an optimist, a blend of the mystic and the sanitary reformer, savagely angry at the shameful conditions in which the poor lived, but blind to the limiting effects of social class since to him all souls were equal. He welded Darwinism and faith into a theory of spiritual evolution and sang the praises of wedded love and family life, jovially celebrating his nation's propensity 'to discover and to traffic, to colonise and to civilise, until no wind can sweep the earth which does not bear the echoes of an English voice'. His confident moral fictions repelled other, more sensitive minds; George Eliot, no less typical of the mid-century, granted that 'Kingsley sees, feels and paints vividly', but she added that 'he theorises illogically and moralises absurdly'.

Kingsley provided the form and the audience for more sophisticated writers, rather as Bulwer Lytton had done in the 1830s. George Eliot's fastidious *Romola* (1862–3) was to use the scheme of Kingsley's *Hypatia* (1852), where real and fictional historical characters at a cultural watershed are presented with choices that reflect current problems. Rudyard Kipling was to capture Kingsley's verve for the practical challenges of Empire, but with a greater sense of moral ambiguity, so that his *Traffics and Discoveries* (1904) comments adversely on Kingsley's facile self-congratulation; like Kingsley, Kipling was at his best in the fable for children written with adults in mind. D. H. Lawrence developed the social and sexual themes of *Yeast* (1848) in his most famous novels: Kingsley's immunity to criticism had fostered his freely-developing, eccentric art in which poetry and social commentary were interwoven.

Kingsley came from a clergyman's family, and his life was shaped by his faith. An early, uncharacteristic episode of doubt was resolved as soon as he fell in love, and his wife helped him enthusiastically to reclaim a neglected parish to Christian orderliness, while he wrote her *The Saint's Tragedy* (1848), a poem based on the somewhat perverse theme of Elizabeth of Hungary's exacting penances. His relative candour in sexual matters has little to recommend it; he was forced by the reticence of the time to a taste for insulted and imperilled beauty that is unpleasantly bizarre, and his attitude to women was wholly Miltonic; they remain the demure pupils of the blonde giants of heroes, while labouring beside them to do God's will on earth.

In the 1840s Kingsley the 'Working Parson' was the co-founder of the Christian Socialist movement which sought to replace the revolutionary programme of Chartism with a plan for educating the working man so that he might deserve those democratic freedoms which were 'the idea of the Bible and the cause of God'. Kingsley was a publicist of great forcefulness and charm, a lecturer as spell-binding as Ruskin. His desire for universal moral improvement went along with a practical enthusiasm for drainage reform and the control of epidemics, and this eminently sensible mania provided crucial episodes in *Alton Locke* (1850) and *Two Years Ago* (1857). His immediate success as a novelist paid for a curate and freed him from his parish for a busy career in literature and controversy.

Yeast (1848) is emotionally autobiographical, identifying the enemies of society as capitalism (which denies man's spiritual nature) and Catholicism (which thwarts his sexuality and his natural charity). *Alton Locke* turned from the agricultural poverty of *Yeast* to the sweatshops of London and a hero whose poetic genius alienates him from his own class. Kingsley, like Carlyle, forces the horrible realities of poverty stripped of the suave jargon of political economy upon the reader, and Dickens's *Bleak House* (1853) was to build on the frankness of Kingsley's tirade against society.

By the 1850s Kingsley had become a very eminent Victorian. He became an apologist for Empire and an amateur scientist and anthropologist, writing *Glaucus: Or, The Wonders of the Shore* (1854) for children, and *The Heroes: Or, Greek Fairy Tales for Children* in the next year. This attractive volume, gracefully and simply written with touches of unemphatic poetry, put classical legend into a Christian context, and so helped to maintain the ancient languages as cornerstones of the public school curriculum.

In those old Greeks, and in us also, all strength and virtue come from God. But if men grow proud and self-willed, and misuse God's fair gifts, He lets them go their own ways, and fall pitifully, that the glory may be His alone.

Hypatia (1852) used the recondite setting of the beginning of the Dark Ages to argue out issues that Kingsley felt still burned in his own day: a democratic creed replacing an effete aristocracy, and energetic and instinctive Teutons doing battle with a monkish church. *Westward Ho!* (1855) was bloodthirsty even by Kingsley's standards; it was written out of indignation over the mishandling of the Crimean War and the permission by which the Roman church re-established its hierarchy in England. Kingsley's novel of the sixteenth-century colonial wars between England and Spain shows an unreflecting bigotry and the violent and prejudiced novel remained a classic for children well into the twentieth century.

Two Years Ago (1857) is a return to the contemporary scene; a weltering and vastly enjoyable novel which defies summary, but centres around a cholera epidemic and reads as though Tennyson had attempted *An Enemy of the People* (1882) by Henrik Ibsen (1828–1906). There is some entertaining satire at the expense of Spasmodic poetry and the usual approval of a bullying hero who is already muscular and is soon made Christian.

By 1859 Kingsley had been offered the post of chaplain to his exact contemporary the Queen, and Prince Albert suggested that he be given the professorship of Modern History at Cambridge, where Kingsley was popular with the students if not with the dons. Throughout the 1860s he was to involve himself in religious controversy on the side of a bluffly commonsensical view of a God who intervenes directly in his creation. He had no patience with the theological subtleties of English Roman Catholicism or of modern German scholarship. Marian Evans's translation (1846) of *Das Leben Jesu* (1835–36) by D. F. Strauss (1808–74) had made an English audience aware of the theory of the German idealistic philosopher Georg Hegel (1770–1831) that religion was not a factual revelation but 'the perception of truth . . . invested with imagery'. Many Broad Churchman were able to incorporate this purely metaphorical truth of scriptural events into their understanding of religion, since for them Holy Writ was not the sole foundation of faith; God also revealed himself to the individual heart. But to Kingsley, Strauss was 'a vile aristocrat, robbing the poor man of his Saviour – of the ground of all democracy, all freedom, all association'. An even greater wrath was reserved for the convert to Catholicism, J. H. Newman, whom Kingsley accused of lying in order to gain more conversions. Newman resented the slander; Kingsley offered an even more offensive retraction, and an exhausting public correspondence continued until friends intervened and Newman concluded his defence in the famous, emotionally intricate *Apologia Pro Vita Sua* (begun in 1864). The feud ended when Newman withdrew his attacks from the *Apologia* itself, and Kingsley, in return, sincerely admired Newman's devotional poem *The Dream of Gerontius* (1866). In the end, Newman said a mass for the Protestant's soul.

   The Water Babies (1863) is a fanciful key to the absorbing hobby-horses of this period in Kingsley's life; a tract for 'a generation who are not believing, with anything like their whole heart, in the Living God'. Kingsley was one of the few Victorians whose faith was not shaken by the Terrible Muses; the vast time-scale of evolutionary theory enhanced his comfortable certainty of God's greatness. Intellectual events moved fast in his century; the placid universe described by Paley (1743–1805), the English theologian and forerunner of Utilitarian theory in his *A View of the Evidences of Christianity* (1794), presided over by a purposeful God, had been challenged by the geologist Sir Charles Lyell's (1795–1875) theory in 1830 that the age of the earth must be reckoned in millions of years. In the anonymously published *Vestiges of Creation* (1844) God was no longer postulated as a first cause, and Darwin's *The Origin of Species* (1859) replaced Lyell's theory of life evolving according to design with the idea of evolution according to the laws of chance alone. Darwin's *Descent of Man* in 1871 implacably applied scientific methods to the study of human beings, and the refuges for the literal believer were closed. William Dyce painted the magically lucid *Pegwell Bay* (1858), with its minute figures on the seashore dwarfed by the immensities of Geology and Astronomy in the cliffs and the comet, as a ritualised and majestic tribute to the eeriness of a world perceived by a scientific intellect but still clinging to Romantic values. Kingsley, more brusquely, saw

God as 'living, immanent, ever-working', and using the complex medium of evolution in the individual soul as well as in the physical world; the notion of Hell, Kingsley decided, was ecologically wasteful.

Kingsley contributed to literature by the vast amount of pleasure he gave at the time, and by identifying issues which finer intellects pondered more closely. His resemblance to Charles Dickens remains a superficial one; though both were indefatigable authors with a huge public following, and both argued the need for a society based not on greed but on mutuality, Kingsley brushed away material facts in order to disclose the developing souls of his characters. After 1850, Dickens developed a commanding trilogy – *Bleak House, Little Dorrit* and *Our Mutual Friend* – that demonstrates the power of a corrupt social system to warp and destroy human relationships and the individual personality.

The 1850s saw Dickens increasingly concerned with social problems; professionally, as the editor of *Household Words* and *All the Year Round*, as an enthusiastic supporter of a variety of charities, and as a novelist whose fictions contained bitter satires against industrialism and government. His furious energies masked a dread of growing old: in 1858 he left the languid wife who had borne him ten children, and began a discreet liaison with a young actress. He became more introspective, studying the nature and obligations of his extraordinary talent, probing his own personality, and fascinated by those 'roads not taken': the people he and his characters could have been under different circumstances. He reached out almost desperately from the solitary act of writing to an immediate contact with his public in a series of exhausting dramatic readings from his works, which certainly hastened his final collapse, and he died on 8 June 1870, after a full day's work on his uncompleted mystery, *Edwin Drood*.

Dickens, like Scott and Thackeray, did not theorise in print about the novel. The frankness with which later writers such as Henry James the American novelist and George Meredith discussed aesthetics would have struck him as both improper and unnecessary. But his developing sense of the nature of his art is a fierce undertow in his novels, and his deepest hatred is reserved for characters like Skimpole and Sir Leicester

FARE THEE WELL.

FARE thee well! and if for ever—
  Still for ever, fare *thee* well—
Even though unforgiving, never
  'Gainst thee shall my heart rebel.
Would that breast were bared before thee
  Where thy head so oft hath lain,
While that placid sleep came o'er thee
  Which thou ne'er canst know again:
Would that breast by thee glanc'd over,
  Every inmost thought could show!
Then, thou would'st at last discover
  'Twas not well to spurn it so—
Though the world for this commend thee—
  Though it smile upon the blow,
Even its praises must offend thee,
  Founded on another's woe—
Though my many faults defac'd me,
  Could no other arm be found
Then the one which once embraced me
  To inflict a cureless wound?
Yet—oh, yet—thyself deceive not—
  Love may sink by low decay,
But by sudden wrench, believe not,
  Hearts can thus be torn away;
Still thine own its life retaineth—
  Still must mine—though bleeding—beat,
And the undying thought which paineth
  Is—that we no more may meet.—
These are words of deeper sorrow
  Than the wail above the dead,

Both shall live—but every morrow
  Wake us from a widowed bed.—
And when thou would'st solace gather—
  When our child's first accents flow—
Wilt thou teach her to say "Father!"
  Though his care she must forego?
When her little hands shall press thee—
  When her lip to thine is press'd—
Think of him whose prayer shall bless thee—
  Think of him thy love had bless'd,
Should her lineaments resemble
  Those thou never more may'st see—
Then thy heart will softly tremble
  With a pulse yet true to me.
All my faults—perchance thou knowest—
  All my madness—none can know;
All my hopes—where'er thou goest—
  Wither—yet with *thee* they go—
Every feeling hath been shaken,
  Pride—which not a world could bow—
Bows to thee—by thee forsaken
  Ev'n my soul forsakes me now.
But 'tis done—all words are idle—
  Words from me are vainer still;
But the thoughts we cannot bridle
  Force their way without the will.
Fare thee well!—thus disunited—
  Torn from every nearer tie—
Seared in heart—and lone—and blighted—
  More than this I scarce can die.

PUBLISHED BY J. JOHNSTON, CHEAPSIDE.

1. *Fare thee Well* (1816) by George Cruikshank. Byron leaving England.

2. Chatterton (1856) by Henry Wallis. George Meredith was the model. The suicide of the marvellous boy became a symbol of the tragic and baleful aspect of the Romantic temperament.

3. *Lorenzo and Isabella* (1849) by J. E. Millais. An illustration to Keats's *Isabella*.

4.   *The Bard* (1817) by John Martin.

5. Title page to the monthly instalments of *Vanity Fair* 1847.

6. The first manuscript page of the cancelled final chapter of *Persuasion*.

7. *The Small Hours in the Sixties at 16 Cheyne Walk* (1916) by Max Beerbohm. Swinburne reading 'Anectoria' to Gabriel and William Rossetti.

8. *The Awakening Conscience* (1853) by Holman Hunt.

9. *Family Prayers* (1864) by Samuel Butler.

10. *Mrs. Siddons as Lady Macbeth* (?1812) by Henry Fuseli.

11. *Work* (1865) by Ford Madox Brown.

REFINEMENTS OF MODERN SPEECH.

SCENE—*A Drawing-room in " Passionate Brompton."*

*Fair Æsthetic (suddenly, and in deepest tones, to Smith, who has just been introduced to take
her in to Dinner).* " ARE YOU INTENSE?"

12.   'Are you *Intense*?' from *Punch*.

HERE BEGINNETH THE TALES OF CANTERBURY AND FIRST THE PROLOGUE THEREOF

The tendre croppes, and the yonge sonne
Hath in the Ram his halfe cours yronne,
And smale foweles maken melodye,
That slepen al the nyght with open eye,
So priketh hem nature in hir corages;
Thanne longen folk to goon on pilgrimages,
And palmeres for to seken straunge strondes,
To ferne halwes, kowthe in sondry londes;
And specially, from every shires ende
Of Engelond, to Caunterbury they wende,
The hooly blisful martir for to seke,
That hem hath holpen whan that they were
seeke.

Bifil that in that seson on a day,
In Southwerk at the Tabard as
I lay,
Redy to wenden on my pilgrym-
age
To Caunterbury with ful devout
corage,
At nyght were come into that hostelrye
Wel nyne and twenty in a compaignye,
Of sondry folk, by aventure yfalle
In felaweshipe, and pilgrimes were they alle,
That toward Caunterbury wolden ryde.

THAT Aprille with his shoures soote
Thedroghte of March hath perced to the roote,
And bathed every veyne in swich licour,
Of which vertu engendred is the flour;
Whan Zephirus eek with his swete breeth
Inspired hath in every holt and heeth

13.   The first page of the Kelmscott Chaucer.

The great bespeak for Miss Snevellicci

14. 'The great bespeak for Miss Snevellicci.' Drawing by Phiz for *Nicholas Nickleby*.

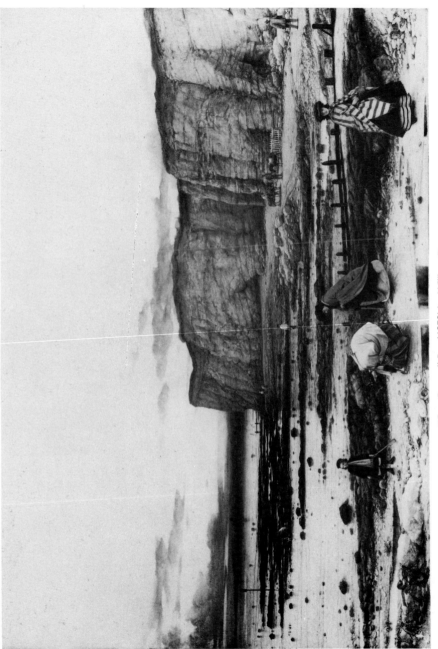

15. *Peqwell Bay* (1858) by William Dyce.

16.   Children Sleeping in a London Street.

17. George Eliot (1860) by Samuel Lawrence.

18. Charles Dickens (1842) by Alfred Comte D'Orsay.

19.   The Opening Ball in the New Assembly Rooms, Manchester, 1859.

20. The Crystal Palace in the 1860s outside London. Originally built for the Great Exhibition in 1851.

Dedlock in *Bleak House* and Henry Gowan in *Little Dorrit* who treat art as a mere incidental embellishment of life. David Copperfield, himself a novelist and a hero very close to Dickens's heart, speaks openly about the role of fiction:

> . . . I do not enter on the aspirations, the delights, anxieties and triumphs of my art. That I truly devoted myself to it with my strongest earnestness, and bestowed upon it every energy of my soul I have already said. If the books I have written be of any worth, they will supply the rest. I shall otherwise have written to no purpose . . . .

Dickens saw the literary arts as an aspect of that panacea of *work* prescribed by Goethe, Carlyle and Ruskin, and he shared Scott's view that the novelist was 'a productive labourer', whose works are an effectual part of the public wealth. The vivacity and violence of the early novels were pruned into a disciplined, yet still rich and copious study of how the individual achieves self-mastery and a place within the social order, which is a necessary but corrupting environment; he may have to relinquish some of his most precious qualities in making terms with society.

David Copperfield (1850) calls upon the reader to respond in a full, unembarrassed and alert way to a strong and often troubling emotional range, conveyed so eagerly that the novel is always slipping into the present tense. *David Copperfield* is notoriously uneven in quality, but its flaws are intimately bound up with its finest achievements. There is a solemn inevitability in the stages by which David acquires his 'disciplined heart', and the candid weighing of the gains and losses of maturity and the constant rejoicing in the powers of the imagination closely resemble the themes of *The Prelude*, finally published in the same year. It is at once the most artless and the most sophisticated of narratives, the fairytale clarity balanced by the subtlety of Steerforth's tragedy, and the romance of David and Dora which is as wisely understood as that of Rosamund and Lydgate in George Eliot's *Middlemarch*, or that of Lisa and Andrei in Tolstoy's *War and Peace*.

Bleak House (1852–3), a vast, sombre and poetic novel in the style equally of William Blake and of Carlyle, was Dickens's self-confessedly Wordsworthian attempt to dwell 'on the romantic side of familiar things'. Too often misunderstood as a Victorian satire on curable social evils, *Bleak House* is a much darker study of the power of inescapable aspects of civilisation – the past, progress, the ideas of law and family – to subvert and warp the individual personality and all human relationships. It is a mystical version of a human world sinking back despairingly into a primeval chaos; a gloomy and deceitful universe where religion is without compassion, philanthropy exists without charity, law without justice, and love without honour. Its characters are stumbling, hurt and puzzled, and very few of them manage to overcome their 'discouragements' in order to labour in the service of their fellows.

Hard Times (1854) is a somewhat unsatisfactory retreat from the complexities of the novels surrounding it; Dickens had shown how even the most sympathetic characters were implicated in the evils of the world of *Bleak House*, but here he sets up a group of utilitarian villains to free readers from self-criticism, and provides the circus as a haven for the imagination and affections. *Little Dorrit* (1855–7) rejects these easy answers and the rhetorical brilliancy of *Bleak House*; it is an assured, lucid and ample study of what John Lucas has called 'undefeated decency', and Dickens's considered decision that the ordinary person can survive the malignancy of society. Dickens abandons that pride in caste, subtle intelligence and wide experience implicit in David Copperfield as his new hero, Arthur Clennam (suffering from that Romantic disenchantment so thoroughly analysed in nineteenth-century poetry) is drawn back to fulness of feeling by Amy Dorrit, a heroine at once totally unremarkable and full of mysterious power. The novel is an unconscious gathering up of Romantic symbols with its resonant references to the innocent female spirit, its Mediterranean and alpine vistas, the prisons of society and self, and its themes of retribution and atonement. Disinterested love works its transformation on a world of selfishness, in the manner of the late comedies of Shakespeare.

A Tale of Two Cities (1859) is a novel of famous passages and febrile plot, as rhetorically excessive as *Little Dorrit* had been chaste in its expression. Dickens turned back to Carlyle in his treatment of the French Revolution, but the scenes of turmoil and carnage are mere representations of his inner life at this period, and not honestly related to contemporary England or to human relationships.

Great Expectations (1860–1) is, by contrast, the most formally perfect and emotionally sombre of Dickens's novels, retaining the mould of the folk tale but resolutely denying the optimistic sentiments. Pip is no gentleman in distress but a labourer raised into gentility by a mysterious bequest, at great cost to his self-respect and natural affections; the opposite of the resilient and confident David Copperfield. Only those without worldy hope can afford to be loving, and the characters of the novel develop repellent stratagems for keeping a portion of their lives unsoiled by a society they must manipulate as a matter of business.

Our Mutual Friend (1864–5) returns to the fascination with exaggeration that had begun in *Bleak House*. It is prodigal in its invention, containing enough material for a dozen ordinary novels, and strangely prescient of developments in quite different writers like Henry James and Meredith. The world of Mayhew is given imaginative life; it is a London of scavengers and dustheaps, offal and sham veneer that is soon heightened into something as grotesque as the satirical comedies of Ben Jonson (1572–1637) but on a vaster scale, where people see each other only as objects to be made use of in a scramble for status. *Edwin Drood* (1870), which owes much to the 'sensation novel' of the previous decade, has great charm and expertise but survives largely as a mystery whose secret was carried to the grave. It returns to the theme of the twin-souled man begun in *A Tale of Two Cities*, which was to be so inviting to the romancers of the last quarter of the century, culminating in *Dr Jekyll and Mr Hyde* (1886) by R. L. Stevenson.

Like Mayhew and Kingsley, Dickens dramatised the balder social injustices of his time with vivid indignation, but the novels are not limited to goals of immediate reform. He railed against stupidity and enjoyed giving a villain a drubbing in print, but he saw the roots of evil in the unloving and unimaginative hearts of men and women; in failures of sympathy which were beyond the reach of legislation, but which permitted the suffering that took its toll in pestilence and revolution. Alone among the writers of a century crammed with achievement, Dickens can stand his fictions beside those of Shakespeare, as an innate, exquisitely observant and morally acute artist, a page of whose writing (as one terse critic said) gives the reader more than a page of anyone else's.

'The hopeless tangle of our age': the poet in his public role

The success of *The Princess* (1847) had enabled Tennyson to marry, and *In Memoriam* promised him financial security; the laureateship which came to him on the death of Wordsworth in 1850 confirmed the direction his career had taken by giving him the congenial role of mentor and master of ceremonies to his age.

Current taste, warned off by the empty mausoleum of *The Idylls of the King* (finally arranged in 1888) has tended to prefer the younger Tennyson's dallying with Romanticism, and he has suffered from a twentieth-century conviction that poetry written to order to celebrate national events must be insincere. Yet Tennyson tacitly reconstructed the office of laureate, as confidently as the Romantic painter Delacroix set about the epic decoration of the great public buildings of Paris, and his commissioned poems are only rarely accomplished ceremonial pieces like the pleasingly ornate 'Welcome to Alexandra'; they are more usually perversely sober warnings to the age, like the subdued, spectral and ill-received 'On the Jubilee of Queen Victoria', or praise of defeated or beleaguered heroism (the charge of the Light Brigade, the siege of Lucknow, or the loss of the polar explorer Sir John Franklin). The greatest of the declamatory poems is the elaborate *Ode on the Death of the Duke of Wellington* (1852), with its intricate and intelligent interweaving of physical detail and symbolism, private apprehension and public exhortation, grasp of individual character, and a Carlylean sense of national identity, as a poet secure in his own heroism salutes another titan.

Tennyson spent his years of public life defining his idea of the heroic, often in the teeth of public opinion, as the most powerful way of confronting his world with the chasm between its values and its practice: his Carlylean rage is vividly, if roughly voiced in 'Locksley Hall Sixty Years After':

> Pluck the mighty from their seat, but set no meek ones in their place,
> Pillory Wisdom in your markets, pelt your offal at her face,
> Tumble Nature heel o'er head, and yelling with the yelling street,
> Set the feet above the brain and swear the brain is in the feet.
> Bring the old dark ages back without the faith, without the hope,
> Break the State, the Church, the Throne, and roll their ruins down the
> slope.

Authors -- essayist, atheist, novelist, realist, rhymester, play your part,
Paint the mortal shame of nature with the living hues of art.

He remained politically naive, and like most of his generation, deeply distrustful of democracy; the lurid sermon on the French Revolution in *Aylmer's Field* and all of 'Locksley Hall, Sixty Years After' are prompted not by Carlyle's gleeful expectation of a cleansing catastrophe, but a fear of radicalism in which Tennyson included that socialism that made him 'vomit mentally'. This deliberate lack of sympathy with political realities made Tennyson unusually aware of the delicate emotional roots of the social organism: 'desolation' is the worst fate that can befall the human soul, and like the novelists of the mid-century, he traces the network of obligations and affections that bind men and women together.

Tennyson's unhappy but sheltered boyhood, his early poverty and his intellectual and finally aristocratic companions gave him an unusually detached attitude to his age; there was nothing of Grub Street about him. If Dickens and Thackeray had given their readers a real house to live in, Tennyson provided it with an airy and spacious landscape. He had no direct contact with the raw energies of his middle-class readers, though he is exactly aware of the effect that change had on the current of feeling; the results of religious doubt, rampant financial speculation and the temptations of Empire and military adventure. He was not an intellectual poet: 'Flower in the crannied wall' suggests deep and satisfied affinities with Keats's doctrine of negative capability and an unquestioned acceptance of his richly intuitive faculty.

> Flower in the crannied wall,
> I pluck you out of the crannies,
> I hold you here, root and all, in my hand,
> Little flower – but *if* I could understand
> What you are, root and all, and all in all,
> I should know what God and man is.

Maud (1855) is a deliberately disorienting poem, in which the gentle disquiets of *The Princess* have become a universal malaise. It is superficially similar to Spasmodic self-absoption, or to Browning's dramatic monologues, but unlike either in Tennyson's underlying calm presentation of a permanent moral order with which the hero has lost touch. The chaos of the speaker's mind results from a world fouled with reckless speculation and inhumanity, and the long, brilliantly artificial poem looks forward to *The Waste Land* by T. S. Eliot (1922) as much as it harks back to Carlyle's *Sartor*, with its drama of the subtle mind making the discovery that 'I am one with my kind'.

Enoch Arden, *Aylmer's Field* and *Sea Dreams* appeared in the volume of 1864, and comment in different ways on the precious nature of the individual and the destructive effects of the 'cash-nexus' on fragile human bonds. Often dismissed as sentimental, these narratives have a subtle vigour that recalls Crabbe's matched stories of love perverted by greed, and his unabashed interest in the physical texture of daily living. Giacomo Puccini (1858–1924) once considered *Enoch Arden* as a subject for an opera in his *verismo* style; the robustly tender treatment of small tragedies with the assumption that 'sorrow's springs are the same', became a hallmark of late nineteenth-century art, anticipated by Tennyson.

The Idylls of the King, which occupied Tennyson over forty years (though most of it appeared in the 1850s and 1860s), is more impressive in outline than in execution. Though Tennyson had done much to establish the Victorian fascination with Arthurian legend by his early poems, the epic defeated him. Like a design by Edward Burne-Jones for tapestry, the linked poems have a null beauty with their grandly inexpressive figures, pondered composition and a redundant treatment of foliage and architecture dwelt on because human passion is so lacking: *Aylmer's Field* had dramatised much more cogently the theory that the whole social fabric depended on the bond between men and women. Tennyson's shadowy Arthur derives from Carlyle's heroes, and his feudal order dies when his companions sink back into introspective misgivings or sensual indulgence, yet the stirring message of *Heroes and Hero-Worship* is betrayed by the undertow of the imagery which suggests that the decline of the Round Table is one with the 'creeping year' itself, Nature (as in *Tithonus*) always tending to decay.

The minor poems offer many rewards to the venturesome reader: dialect poems which expand the grittiness of Crabbe, and grotesqueries like 'Rizpah' and 'Happy' which overcome the horrors of their subject matter (as Browning's do not always do) to celebrate decent feeling in a world where natural affections have become extraordinary. 'In the Children's Hospital', a poem much praised by the unsentimental George Orwell, is a telling example of Tennyson's distance from 'easy tears', as it evaluates and rejects various attitudes to the problem of suffering.

As a poet of private emotions, lyrically expressed, Tennyson was able to resolve the paradoxes he discerned; as a critic of society, he was aware that his readers lived in a world too complex and too troubled to be helped by an art which could only warn or console. His model as laureate was the greatest of the Roman poets, Virgil (70 BC-19 BC), with whom he identifies himself in one of his commissioned poems; a writer both of national epic verse evoking the roots of his culture, and praise of nature that is essentially didactic. Even the greatest of poets, Tennyson argues through Virgil, must be limited in his effect: one could be a 'landscape-lover, lord of language' without solving the intractable problem of the 'doubtful doom of human kind', which could only be acknowledged with 'majestic sadness'.

Matthew Arnold (1822-88) was as sheltered and intellectual a poet as Tennyson, 'knowing the shady side of life only out of books', as his friend, the unhappy controversialist J. A. Froude (1818-94) put it. Arnold and Tennyson were both dedicated to finding assured beliefs in a climate of change and doubt, and each possessed a strong lyric gift conscientiously reshaped into a public voice. Tennyson took on the duties of the laureateship; Arnold abandoned poetry for persuasive prose. Arnold was sceptical and fastidious, judging his own amateur and insular culture by European standards, and finding temptations but no solace in the commonplace domestic pleasures that Tennyson had built into an emotional defence against the chaos of democracy, rootlessness and religious doubt.

Arnold was, in the poet Swinburne's phrase, 'David, the son of Goliath', the intellectual successor to his redoubtable father Thomas, who had been appointed headmaster of Rugby School when Matthew was only six. The potential political and professional élite under his care soon became a new breed of conscientious and idealistic gentlemen; as a supporter of Dr Arnold's candidacy had promised, the headmaster changed the course of English education. A study of modern languages made his pupils aware of Europe, and the classics became not a badge of caste but a lively introduction to literary criticism and social theory; Goethe's and Carlyle's gospel of work became a cornerstone of education, and an even greater stress was placed on the habit of self-criticism that fitted the scholar for leadership. Every Sixth Former became a Carlylean hero in the microcosm of the school.

Matthew Arnold shared his father's passion for education and his conviction that the individual must attain self-mastery and a place in the 'general life'. Dr Arnold, a daily witness to 'the spring and activity of youth . . . unsanctified by anything pure and elevated in its desires', was echoed by the witty son's similar distaste for the unreflective life.

Arnold's schooldays were far from brilliant; like Wordsworth, whose neighbours the family had been on their summer holidays, he made better use of his vacations. He visited Europe 'like a young Milton on his travels', according to his fitful Muse, George Sand, and toyed with continental revolutionary theory as well as new German classical aesthetic theory. The bantering manner that distinguished him from his father was perfected in University debates, and Charlotte Brontë was struck with 'regretful surprise' at the seeming foppery of his whimsical wit that masked a painful detachment from the age. His outward life ran smoothly, with none of the public crises of conscience that ruined the careers of his friends Clough and Froude, though he wrote privately to the former that

> these are damned times – everything is against one – the height to which knowledge is come, the spread of luxury, our physical enervation, the absence of great *natures*, the unavoidable contact with millions of small ones, newspapers, cities, light profligate friends, moral desperadoes like Carlyle, our own selves, and the sickening conscience of our difficulties . . . .

Lord Lansdowne, the Whig politician whose secretary Arnold had become on his return from Europe, helped the newly married man to a secure future as an Inspector for Schools, following the rapid growth of interest in education since the first disbursement of public funds in 1833. Arnold's work took him both to Europe and into the respectable but very dull homes of dissenters and Evangelists whose lives he determined to enrich. For thirty-five years he committed himself to the general training of 'all who are born men to all which is human', and his poetry belongs to the 1850s and 1860s, while the two remaining decades were given over to essays in social and literary criticism and religious and education theory. Critics are usually divided in their emphasis on his achievement.

'Man must begin', wrote Arnold, 'where Nature ends', and he set himself regretfully but firmly against the Wordsworthian outlook. Nature in Arnold's poetry is cruelly indifferent to man's innate sense of justice and compassion; the 'impulse' which had once sprung from a 'vernal wood' to teach 'of moral evil and of good' comes in Arnold's estimation from man's own 'deepest, best existence'. He had a thirsty longing for that Romantic 'joy' so richly conveyed by Wordsworth and Coleridge, implying an intuitive creativity and union with nature, but he rejects it as a probable delusion; the 'generous fire' of Romantic ardour is spurned as 'mere hurrying fever' and a 'tedious, vain expense' of emotion. Throughout Arnold's poetry, Romantic and Tennysonian settings and metaphors are stripped of their consoling enchantment; he remains Romantic only in his strict adherence to emotional truth. If Tennyson had modelled himself on Virgil, Arnold the poet sat, like the Greek tragic dramatist Sophocles (c.496–c.406 BC) in 'sad lucidity of soul', obliged to be an 'adverse voice' preaching self-discipline and self-knowledge without the allurements of imagery and musicality; of all the Victorian poets, Arnold has the weakest visual sense. In all this, he did not reject the achievement of the Romantic poets: merely their relevance to his own time.

> Too fast we live, too much are tried
> Too harass'd, to attain
> Wordsworth's sweet calm, or Goethe's wide
> And luminous view to gain.

The poet of the present age, 'self-school'd, self-scann'd, self-honour'd, self-secure' was one who 'saw life steadily and saw it whole' from his lonely vantage point 'above the howling senses' ebb and flow'. In practice, Arnold's stoicism is an uneasy matter; 'Requiescat' (1853) is more restless and unsatisfied than its models in Landor's verse, and *Sohrab and Rustum* (1853) and *Balder Dead* (1855) are oblique treatments of a subject that no doubt moved Arnold profoundly; the son's relationship to a brilliant father.

Inevitably there is in Arnold's poetry a sense of passions reined in too self-consciously. His ideal vision of the poet as a purged, considerate mind rejecting all specious charm in favour of classical sternness was fortunately counterbalanced by a yearning for human attachments, and he sought honesty rather than consistency. He had in addition Wordsworth's habit of returning at intervals to subjects and emotions exhaustively treated at an earlier stage, and 'Rugby Chapel' (1867), 'Thyrsis' (1866) and 'Obermann Once More' (written in 1849) are among such retrospective flights. At his best, Arnold balances irreconcilable moral and aesthetic attitudes with the detachment of the French Novelist Gustave Flaubert in 'The Forsaken Merman' (1849) and *Tristram and Iseult* (1852).

The famous group of poems dealing with a lost love 'Marguerite' (1852) are uncomfortably uncontrolled. Arnold could not, like Tennyson, show romantic love as an escape from egotism, since for Arnold love interrupted the individual's quest for self-mastery.

> This is the curse of life! that not
> A nobler, calmer train
> Of wiser thoughts and feelings blot
> Our passions from our brain;
>
> But each day brings its petty dust
> Our soon-choked souls to fill,
> And we forget because we must
> And not because we will.

'The Strayed Reveller' comments chillingly on emotional self-indulgence, and like Emily Brontë, for whom he was to write a chastely elemental elegy, Arnold indulges emotion only in order to judge it rigorously.

'Dover Beach' (1867) is the most famous and assured of Arnold's poems, and the most memorable single statement of the intellectual and spiritual malaise of these decades; a poignant avowal of man's perplexity in his newly enlarged universe.

> The sea is calm tonight.
> The tide is full, the moon lies fair
> Upon the straits; – on the French coast the light
> Gleams and is gone; the cliffs of England stand,
> Glimmering and vast, out in the tranquil bay.
> Come to the window, sweet is the night air!
> Only, from the long line of spray
> Where the sea meets the moon-blanch'd land,
> Listen! you hear the grating roar
> Of pebbles which the waves draw back, and fling,
> At their return, up the high strand,
> Begin, and cease, and then again begin,
> With tremulous cadence slow, and bring
> The eternal note of sadness in.
> Sophocles long ago
> Heard it on the Aegean, and it brought
> Into his mind the turbid ebb and flow
> Of human misery; we
> Find also in the sound a thought,
> Hearing it by this distant northern sea.

But the most pleasing poems are the muted, sometimes wryly amused elegics, which evaluate character and achievement with a view to the improvement of the living. 'The Scholar Gipsy' (1853) with its delicate echoes of Keats's Odes is a cautious rapprochement with the beginnings of English Romanticism, with its central figure of the outcast merged in nature; *Thyrsis* is a late reconciliation with the spirit of Wordsworth as it reviews familiar scenes through a changed sensibility.

Arnold's essays do not prolong the puzzle of his poetry with its uncertainty of tone and divided aims: they have a straightforward elegance in their witty phrase-making and merciless pillorying of opponents. He began his didactic career in *Essays in Criticism* (1855) by defining the critical faculty as 'a disinterested endeavour to learn and propagate the best that is known or thought in the world', and set out on a long course of giving his countrymen 'a conscience in literary matters'. *Culture and Anarchy* (1867–8) is eminently readable today in spite of its topicality, with its underlying permanent theme of the need to reconcile forces within the individual and society; like a benign Carlyle, Arnold suggests grand powers at work beneath the contemporary urge for 'Doing as One Likes' and the 'bondage of Bentham'. Whereas Carlyle looked forward to the apocalypse, Arnold saw society revitalised through an individual cultivation of an inward 'sweetness and light' that was superior to 'the mechanical and material civilisation in esteem with us', and which would bring men into harmony with their past. The new order would come about through the regeneration of the middle class, at present given over to an unlovely religiosity and careless of intellectual refinement, but more capable of improvement than the 'barbarian' aristocracy or the 'vast residuum' of the working class, too underdeveloped for anything beyond Arnold's distaste and a hope for improvement before they were inevitably enfranchised. Arnold's theory that the English sensibility had overstressed 'Hebraism' or strictness of conscience at the expense of an 'Hellenic' spontaneity of judgement based on the cultivation of the senses and sympathies, is very similar to the Romantic argument of Dickens's later novels.

Arnold's writings on religion were an attempt to salvage an ethical guide from a creed attacked by science and rationalism, at a time when the crisis of faith was at its height. Christianity remained for him 'the greatest and happiest stroke ever yet made for human perfection', and was a metaphor for the individual aroused from 'blind selfish impulse' to the life of obedience to an eternal moral order.

Essays in Criticism, Second Series, seen through the press posthumously, is, next to Coleridge's *Biographia Literaria*, the most important nineteenth-century contribution to literary criticism. If religion had lost its power, then poetry remained a repository of human ideals. Arnold's survey of English poetry was both magisterial and intuitive, and he looks forward to his twentieth-century successor, F. R. Leavis, who summed up Arnold the critic as 'an extraordinarily distinguished mind in complete possession of its purpose and pursuing it with easy mastery.'

In 1869, summing up his poetic career, Arnold agreed that he had less poetical sentiment than Tennyson and less intellectual vigour than Browning, but an excellent fusion of the two qualities that would ensure his place in 'the main line of modern development'. Arnold remains an excellent guide to the sensibility of an age from which he was so unhappily estranged, and beyond praise as a critic; Browning, in the long run, has been the more influential poet. Many poets owe their being to Browning's example: Kipling's vivid descriptions of process, Hardy's wry love lyrics and grotesqueries, Robert Frost's (1874-1963) use of the singular event, and Ezra Pound's passion for the outstanding individual, and his criticism of his world from a private, scholarly universe unfixed in time. The modern poet Edward Lucie-Smith (1933-) sees Browning moving in twentieth-century literature like yeast in dough; 'a kind of quarry, from which modern poetry continues to be hewn'. An acquaintance with Browning's later poetry in addition to his anthology pieces helps to renew a sense of his experimental urgency.

Men and Women (1855), the fruit of his happy Italian years, was an epoch in Victorian poetry, though critics initially complained of its 'perversity, carelessness and bad taste', and only a perceptive minority approved, including George Eliot and the young William Morris. By *Dramatis Personae* (1864) the public was ready for the new form of the dramatic monologue, and Browning entered on his years of public adulation following his widowerhood and return to England. The fiction and poetry of this period almost merge in *Men and Women*; like Dickens, Browning uses the grotesque to give his moral lessons a pulsing energy, while his deepest sympathies lie with commonplace experience freshly felt.

Browning's fictional portraits all have a strong moral bias; like George Eliot, he is fascinated by the process by which the individual heart is corrupted by egotism, and his famous casuistical monologues compress this degradation of character into a few hundred lines. Browning is a Romantic in his fear that a perverted reason will thwart the impulses of the heart, and in his idealistic striving for a good dimly perceived. Many of his speakers suggest the fixity of damnation; their revelations are gratuitous, accomplishing nothing in the external world, while the situation of the unseen listener and the relentlessly articulate defendant goes back to the *Inferno* of Dante and looks forward to the fluent but paralysed sufferers of the plays of Samuel Beckett (b. 1906).

Browning was fascinated by the problem of style. The Romantics had not bothered, in their empirical way, to forge a distinctive form of expression, and put the new wine of their sensibility into the old bottles of blank verse. Browning continued to use this passe-partout form, though he took a perverse pleasure in skewing its regularity unmercifully with colloquialisms and interjections. In *The Ring and the Book* (1868–9) the straitjacket of the metre shows off his ability to create thoroughly differentiated characters in spite of this handicap. His translations, hardly read today, show how fiercely Browning was prepared to manipulate language in order to mime the violence and intricacy of his favourite subjects; his version of the *Agamemnon* (1877), is as densely original as Hopkins's early poem *The Wreck of the Deutschland* (1875).

> Thus in the mind of him he rages, falling,
> And blowing forth a brisk blood-spatter, strikes me
> With the dark drop of slaughterous dew – rejoicing
> No less than, at the god-given dewy comfort,
> The sown-stuff in its birth-throes from the calyx.

Even Browning's considerable musicality is far from simple; his love lyrics, with their weaving intricacies, act out the theme of the eternal inequality of passion ('where one eludes, must the other pursue') which is a part of his philosophy of the imperfect: life can only be lived in an endeavour to encompass an ideal beyond human powers to attain.

The late poems of Browning, with their riddling titles, sophisticated analyses of human motive and obsession with secrecy, make no concessions to readers; hidden in amongst them are the insinuating 'House' (on the theme of the privacy of the artist) and the incomparably poignant 'Development', published in *Asolando* on the day of Browning's death. Ostensibly a meditation on a cultivated man's deepening understanding of the Greek epic poet Homer, it is an eloquent defence of the role of fiction in keeping the moral sense alert, and at the same time, Browning's own testament to the trial of religious faith challenged by scientific scepticism.

The illumination of the commonplace

Nathaniel Hawthorne (1804–1864), the American novelist much admired by his English contemporaries, left an unforgettably attractive tribute to the forty-seven novels of Anthony Trollope (1815–82). His densely peopled and richly textured fictional world was, Hawthorne said, 'just as real as if some giant had hewn a great lump out of the earth, and put it under a glass case, with all its inhabitants going about their daily business, and not suspecting that they were being made a show of'. However, the careful ordinariness of Trollope's version of mid-century life – he is the most deliberately unremarkable of writers – led very rapidly to the undervaluing of a man who rivalled the French Balzac in his indefatigably thorough imagination. His reputation was not enhanced by the *Autobiography* published a year after his death; in an age of aestheticism, he concentrated defiantly on the mechanics of his craft.

The writers of the late nineteenth century were ungrateful to Trollope. Henry James, who developed his own habit of authorial interjection out of Trollope's example, remarked that the novelist was 'safe', and that reading his fiction was like sinking into a gentle slumber. Arch-realists such as George Gissing found Trollope's actualities 'pedestrian', and admirers of the experimentation of George Meredith's novels were unwilling to believe Trollope's insistence that 'once upon a time, with slight modifications, is the best way of telling a story'. The critic Leslie Stephen decided that Trollope had nothing to do with art at all, though his daughter Virginia Woolf, who drew upon Trollope's unemphatic finesse in dissecting human relationships extending through time, found endless 'refreshment and delight' in the solidity of his imaginary world: 'in whatever direction we reach out for assurance, we find it'.

Trollope had remarkable integrity as an artist. He accepted dwindling offers from his publishers without changing his style in accordance with public taste, so that *The Duke's Children* (1880) remains a satisfying conclusion in keeping with the tone of the Palliser series of novels. It is only recently that this writer, never out of favour with a discerning middlebrow public, has been suspected of more than a genius for competence, but he is in fact the direct heir of Jane Austen and Thackeray, deeply attached to his invented characters and anxious to prove that their inner lives are often at variance with the showing they make in the world. He is a liberal conservative, the upholder of traditional values of a rural and aristocratic society that is under permanent attack from outsiders who have no real beliefs: *The Way We Live Now* (1875) shows the old codes of conduct failing to answer in the scramble for status and economic survival. Trollope's novels are working definitions towards the term 'gentleman', and the great enemy in his fiction is untruthfulness, that certain dissolver of social bonds recognised as such by Jane Austen.

Trollope's frank intrusions into his novels are a part of his zeal for truth, as well as a means of persuading his readers to relax their vigilance so that the implications of the story take them by surprise. He found the mystery-mongering of the 'sensation' novels of the mid-century offensive, and set himself resolutely against plot for plot's sake: *Phineas Redux* (1873) throws its emphasis on to the hero's reaction to being suspected of murdering a colleague, rather than inviting speculation as to the identity of the criminal, or to the outcome of the trial.

> The reader need hardly be told that, as regards this great offence, Phineas Finn was as white as snow. The maintenance of any doubt on that matter, – were it even desirable to maintain a doubt, – would be altogether beyond the power of the present writer.

His style is similarly transparent – 'in truth' is a favourite phrase – and he has a habit of using clichés with a startling aptness. In his immediately recognisable style, each paragraph is a supple balancing of attitudes, with a concluding sentence summing up the moral outcome in the astringent manner of Jane Austen.

Trollope's early life was wretched, and his later success as a popular novelist and senior official of the Post Office came as a happy surprise to him. He was sent into the world from his impecunious family as a very junior clerk, and many of his fictional characters echo the callow youth he must have been; a type he made his own before H. G. Wells (1866–1946) studied Kipps and Mr Polly. An Irish romance, *The Macdermots of Ballycloran* (1847), came out after a lucky posting to Ireland where he had gained a proper idea of his abilities.

Like Thackeray, Trollope shows the effect of the passage of time on human relationships. The interwoven 'Barsetshire' and 'Palliser' novels show a cast of characters evolving over twenty-four years, and his fictions convince by their slow accretion of detail and that relentless exposure of the effects of moral choice at which George Eliot was to excel. Despite his reliance on the traditional plot of comedy ended with a marriage, his novels suggest the underlying dissatisfactions of the mid-century. His central characters are outwardly optimistic and well-adjusted, but secretly living on the shadow-side of Romanticism: *The Small House at Allington* (1864) and *Phineas Redux* describe spoiled lives, as does the masterly, nearly tragic *The Last Chronicle of Barset* (1867). Trollope understood the pressure of Romantic yearnings for a fuller life as well as Arnold, and Glencora Palliser, mourning her lost love Burgo Fitzgerald, suffers as much as Margaret separated from her Merman. Trollope's men and women, like those of Tennyson, can exist only within the social fabric, and the outsider or misfit is driven to madness; yet, like Jane Austen, Trollope knows the price the individual pays for such security. His women must marry and give up a precious independence of spirit, and several of his heroines are driven frantic at the prospect; men are subject to the parallel discipline of party allegiance and professional censure. Trollope is an uncompromisng analyst of good and ill in marriage, and takes the world of work with absolute seriousness.

Trollope analysed a society in which cracks were starting to appear. The old certainties of Church and State were being challenged not by Demos and the Terrible Muses, but by various forms of social counterfeit. Interlopers like Melmotte and Lopez with their swindling schemes, Mr Slope and Mr Emilius with their fashionable parodies of religion, and Lizzie Eustace and Lady Carbury with their sham literatures paralyse the men and women of integrity who can no longer call upon an established sense of right and wrong to repel the outsider who is unfairly protected by the assumption that all outwardly respectable people must be honourable. Trollope refuses to minimise these threats to a conservative order, any more than Wordsworth had flinched from the implications of the new age in *Michael*.

George Eliot, born Mary Ann Evans (1819–1880) was the natural descendant of the English Romantics, and her novels are imbued with their scrupulous habits of description and essential conservatism. She shares Wordsworth's and

Coleridge's emotional primitivism, using childhood as a symbol of pure feeling, even while sympathetically exploring adult complexity. Like these poets, she believed that life must be lived in the afterglow and expectation of moments of transcendent joy: 'I cannot help believing in glorious things in a blind sort of way', confesses the intuitive heroine of *Middlemarch*. Although George Eliot was a formidable intellectual, she was concerned that 'general doctrine' could 'eat out our morality' if unchecked by 'the deep-seated habit of direct fellow-feeling with individual fellow men'. Her novels took up the Romantic theory that human beings must overcome their egotism by the perpetual exercise of a vivid moral sympathy. Shelley had anticipated the central idea of her fiction in his *Defence of Poetry*, written in 1821:

> The great secret of morals is love, or a going out of our own nature . . . . A man, to be greatly good, must imagine intensely and comprehensively, he must put himself in the place of another and of many others; the pains and pleasures of his species must become his own. The great instrument of moral good is the imagination . . . .

Her art, like that of the great Romantics, reproduces the common universe, lifting 'the film of familiarity which obscures from us the wonder of our being', as Shelley had said. The narrative is supplemented by her controlling authorial voice, interjecting and interpreting, so that the novelist becomes a Wordsworthian intelligence endowed with 'greater knowledge of human nature and a more comprehensive soul'. Such intervention is nothing less than a 'reaching forward of the whole consciouness towards the fullest truth, the least partial good', as *Middlemarch* has it.

Mary Ann Evans was the daughter of a Warwickshire land agent, whose conservatism and moral intransigence were both a burden and an inheritance. The intelligent and emotional child was freed from her narrowly evangelical education by a fortunate introduction to a liberal-minded manufacturing family who helped to develop her affectionate nature and sceptical intellect. These new friends were in various stages of retreat from sectarian Christianity and familiar with the new German scholarship which was secularising religion, as well as with the philosophy of Auguste Comte (1798–1857) that replaced metaphysics with a new ethical system based on the

emergent sciences of psychology and sociology. Mary Ann
Evans soon went through her own 'unconversion' but never
abandoned the ethical side of Christianity, or its emotional
coloration.

In 1864 her translation of D. F. Strauss's *Das Leben Jesu*
came out to great acclaim, and a legacy allowed her to live
briefly in Switzerland, so that she became one of those who
argued for the advantages of combining an English sensibility
with European culture. 'Marian Evans' returned to London in
1850 and was retained as a reviewer and then as assistant
editor for the newly refurbished version of the *Westminster
Review*, a distinguished journal of advanced liberal opinion.
The bohemian, intellectually abrasive atmosphere suited her,
and her influential friends soon included the ugly and talented
George Lewes, a peppery drama critic and populariser of
'positivist' or Comtean philosophy, as well as the author of a
creditable *Life of Goethe* (1855). His main occupation was to be
the fostering of 'George Eliot's' latent abilities as a novelist.
Lewes's extra-legal marriage to Marian Evans lasted from
1854 until his death; his humane refusal to repudiate his wife
when she bore a child to another man made later divorce
impossible. The extraordinary couple gradually acquired an
awesome respectability, and George Eliot became an
unimpeachable arbiter of moral standards.

An earlier friend, the evolutionist and natural philosopher
Herbert Spencer (1820–1903) had attempted to get Marian
Evans to capitalise on her 'quick observation, great powers of
analysis, unusual and rapid intuition into other's states of
mind, deep and broad sympathies, wit and humour, and wide
culture', by writing fiction. Lewes was more persuasive; *Scenes
From Clerical Life* was begun in 1856 and came out in 1858 to a
promising reception. It is an uneven work, with its roots in the
social analyses of Jane Austen and Crabbe, and the mature
novels are hinted at in the faithful depiction of humble life and
blundering intelligence, and the theme of moral aid between
fellow-sufferers.

Adam Bede, the first full-length novel, was begun in 1857
under the stimulus of Dutch domestic paintings seen on
holiday in Germany; a genre which proved to be the ideal of
English Romantic taste in the visual arts, feebly satisfied at
home by Wilkie and Mulready. 'I have written a novel which

people say has stirred them very deeply – and *not* a *few* people, but almost all reading England', she wrote proudly in 1859; like Trollope and Dickens, she enjoyed a responsive and scrupulous relationship with a vast public. The faults of *Adam Bede* mature into the virtues of her later fiction; the passive but ardent central figure, a melodramatic action performed by exactly understood characters, and an elaborately patterned plot.

The Mill on the Floss (1860) stays, like its predecessor, within the orbit of George Eliot's childhood experience, and the passionate and thwarted Maggie Tulliver is a partial self-portrait. Though written *con amore*, it is a sombre novel, resembling Dickens's *Great Expectations* in its theme of innocence abused, its poetic evocations of landscape, and the acidly economical sketches of petty rural tyrants. George Eliot is already ambitious enough to be hampered by the demands of conventional plotting and the limitations of autobiography; the adult Maggie is less absorbing than the child, and in her last two novels George Eliot was to abandon the idea of an absolute resolution, leaving her characters on the brink of fresh developments in their lives.

Novel-writing left George Eliot exhausted, and a recuperative journey to Italy led to the great abortive project of her creative life; an historical reconstruction of events in the career of the fifteenth-century religious reformer Savanarola. But research was interrupted by a sudden inspiration; 'a story of old-fashioned village life, which has unfolded itself from the merest millet-seed of thought'. *Silas Marner* (1860) is the most perfect of her novels, a Wordsworthian story of an individual's rebirth as part of the human community, and the triumphing of the heart's affections over a narrow understanding of religion and duty, along with the darker message of the ineffaceable results of wrong action. Silas the weaver is exiled from a religious sect on a false charge of theft, and lives as a miser until his hoarded gold is stolen and miraculously replaced by a living child whom he comes to cherish. The subtle mind of the author moves without condescension among her ignorant characters whose motives are not altered by period, class or education. The theme of change, so defeating to Victorian poetry, becomes something wonderful and optimistic in this resonant fable.

Romola, written between 1861 and 1863, marked the passing of the shadow-line between youth and age during a period of inner turbulence and public missteps. 'I finished it an old woman', George Eliot wrote mournfully, adding that 'great, great facts have struggled to find a voice through me, and have only been able to speak brokenly'. The painstaking research, so carefully concealed in the later novels, overpowers fragile issues of personality, and (like Scott in *Ivanhoe* and *Quentin Durward*) George Eliot betrayed her special gifts in trying to write of a world to which she had no personal link. Yet *Romola* makes possible the great achievements of her maturity, by freeing her from the restraints of autobiographical fiction. *Middlemarch* and *Daniel Deronda* were to analyse the provincial world she knew in the context of grand ideas and European history, and Romola herself, like the later heroines, endures the consequences of marriage to a man who cannot appreciate her moral fineness. The novel brings into focus the core of the last three novels; that the intellect is pernicious without the discipline of sympathy.

Felix Holt the Radical was written just before the passing of the Second Reform Bill (1867) and looks back to the time of the First (1832). The title is something of a misnomer, since Felix's radicalism lies in his emotional honesty and an impatience with money and caste that predicts the attitudes of D. H. Lawrence. It is an ironic novel, at once cautious and abrasive, that reminds the reader of Scott's claim that 'There is no private life which has not been determined by a wider public life', and of Dickens's belief that the past nourishes the present.

Middlemarch (1871–2) is the summation of English fiction to that date, with its roots in Scott's analyses of cultural evolution, Jane Austen's incisive studies of the social contract, and Thackeray's sense of character modified by the passage of time. But it looks beyond the English tradition to Flaubert's studies of the romanticising of the self in a provincial setting, Tolstoy's measuring of the individual against great national events, and the ample but austere novels of cultural transition and individual egotism by Thomas Mann. In Virginia Woolf's dashing judgement, *Middlemarch* was 'one of the few English novels written for grown-up people'. Lewes had the happy thought of bringing it out in serial publication over a year, so that the stories of Lydgate the physician and Dorothea the heiress were intimately meshed as twin studies in defeated ambitions, subject to the delicate discipline of interwoven themes, linked characters and a controlled tempo. The historical analogies become subtler, with the Reform Bill suggesting the grand effort by which human beings overcome individual selfishness and achieve social harmony as facets of 'that myriad-headed, myriad-handed labour by which the social body is fed, clothed and housed'.

Daniel Deronda (1876) was set ten years earlier, so that the events of the American Civil War in the background set the theme of 'a new life of terror or of joy'. The public has long divided the novel into the highly approved story of Gwendolen Harleth's reluctant and terrible marriage to the sadistic Grandcourt (a narrative which Henry James reinvestigated as *Portrait of a Lady* in 1881), and the more problem-ridden story of Deronda's search for his Jewish inheritance. George Eliot had not foreseen the magnitude of resentment; Hans Meyrick, Deronda's troublesome friend, ironically dismisses that part of the novel as 'the tragedy of a fellow who signed himself over to be good, and was uncomfortable ever after'. It is a novel of extremes and experiments, and the difficulties cluster around Deronda himself, so close to his creator in his 'imaginative lenience' and his 'meditative interest in learning how human miseries are wrought'. The twin plots cannot be divided, and reconciling them remains a fascinating critical challenge.

In 1878 Lewes died, and George Eliot was desolate; her companion in grief was a young kinsman whom she married in the spring of 1880. The marriage was as outrageous and inevitable as one of her fictional endings, and the strange coda to an emotional life so perfectly analysed in her novels was ended by her sudden death late in the same year.

'We lack, yet cannot fix upon the lack': the poetry of introversion and fantasy

The poet A. C. Swinburne wrote in his old age that 'it must be a somewhat sad thing to be born a minor poet . . . in an age, to say the least, not wanting in great men'. His reflection on lesser talents was prompted by his criticism of a former associate, William Morris (1834–96). Morris was more than a poet; he was a Victorian Renaissance man who had begun with an undergraduate yearning to found a semi-monastic order among his friends at Oxford in the 1850s, which evaporated as soon as he met Rossetti, whom he was soon emulating as painter and poet. *The Defence of Guenevere* (1858) was a quirky portrait of a mediaeval world that is violently cruel as well as dreamily idealised, and his one painting (of Jane Burden, later his wife, as an Arthurian queen) is overfinicky and tentative, but independent of Rossetti in its reflective treatment of sensuality from a woman's point of view.

Morris trained as an architect and became adept in the decorating of private homes and churches, reacting against the florid coarseness of current taste in his habitual use of clear colours, 'elegant' trails of foliage based on Persian pattern, and a rigorous avoidance of anything machine-made. His workshops produced stained glass and tapestries from his friend Burne-Jones's designs, and his printed books, including the famous 'Kelmscott Chaucer', had their paper, ink and type copied from mediaeval models so that they set standards of 'decorative honesty' that still prevail. He was a literary man of many guises, a perfectionist and a successful tradesman, a capitalist and a revolutionary socialist, a civilised and loyal comrade, the friend of George Bernard Shaw and inspirer of W. B. Yeats, but enigmatically detached from human relationships. His most powerful feeling was, like Ruskin's, extra-human: 'an intense and overweening love of the very skin and surface of the earth on which man dwells, such as a lover has in the fair flesh of the woman he loves'.

Morris's eventual commitment to socialism is the inescapable fact of his life. He learned a passionate 'hatred of modern civilisation' from Ruskin; as a young man, he had attempted to create private oases of beautiful dwellings for his family and friends, but he soon rejected such partial reforms. He decided that the Great Exhibition accurately reflected the corrupt values of Victorian society, and only social revolution could redeem this base vulgarity; 'the ornamental part of life is already rotten to the core and must be utterly swept away', he wrote, envisaging a commonwealth based on the comradely sharing of 'useful work' as opposed to the servile endurance of 'useless toil'. The pleasure of the eyes was 'as necessary to man as his daily bread', and the constant handling of beautiful objects would set before men and women 'the true ideal of a full and reasonable life'. This Ruskinian vision of a changed world, lovingly elaborated in *News From Nowhere* (1891) grew out of Morris's hearty identification with the Middle Ages as he imagined them; not the heroic feudalism of Scott, Carlyle, Tennyson and Ruskin himself, but a world 'trim and clean, orderly and bright', where no man was good enough to be another man's master, and where, as in the utopias of William Cobbett, the life of the mind mattered less than good fellowship and the work of the hands. Morris suspected that the higher forms of imaginative literature, such as the novels that he personally enjoyed, were by-products of the neuroses of capitalism, and like Plato he banished such fictions from his ideal republic.

Morris was a prolific writer; his lectures, including 'Hopes and Fears For Art' (1882) and his socialist pamphlets have the air of performances doggedly undertaken for the sake of the matter, and his political views are far more engagingly presented in the socialist romances *News from Nowhere* and *A Dream of John Ball* (1886). His poetry, beginning with the richly promising *Defence of Guenevere* (1858) trailed off into the vapid, pseudo-Chaucerian *The Earthly Paradise* (1868–70), written before the resolution of his personal and aesthetic dilemmas in socialism. The opening invocation to 'Forget six counties overhung with smoke' is called into question (for readers capable of lasting out the soporific couplets) by the mediaeval characters who are themselves in flight to another dream-world, this time to an heroic Viking past, in response to one of the plagues of their idyllic period. Morris creates an uneasy, flaccid half-world of statues coming to life and humans stricken into stone by enchantment; art without motive or direction. His later prose fantasies have none of this queasy glamour; they are straightforward escapes from the daily battle with socialist argument.

Morris is at his best in the precocious *Defence of Guenevere*, which was inspired by his enthusiasm for Browning's *Men and Women*. However, his mediaeval world is more amoral than any of Browning's settings; Guenevere does not offer a 'defence' at all, in Browning's casuistical manner, but simply asserts superbly what it is to be herself.

Yea also at my full heart's strong command,
See through my long throat how the words go up
In ripples to my mouth; how in my hand

The shadow lies like wine within a cup
Of marvellously colour'd gold; . . . .

His mediaeval world is brought to life with an uncanny thoroughness; Morris knows, as Tennyson does not, what snow looks like when it melts on armour, and that the bells of Camelot are 'back-toll'd'. There was no point in imagining a knight, he said, if you couldn't see him toasting a herring on the point of his sword; a picture a junior member of his circle, Rudyard Kipling, was delighted to provide in 1906. But Morris's early imagination is amoral, recording with equally calm precision the details of garden, feast and meadow, and also the heat-haze above a woman burned at the stake, mail-rings showering from murderous men, the contortions of a hanged victim, and 'a slain man's stiffened feet'. He may well have been appalled by such a degree of aesthetic detachment, which may have hastened his flight into socialism.

The Icelandic poems show an older Morris more at ease with his gift, and in comfortable reaction against his age. W. H. Auden and his contemporaries found the bleakness of 'Iceland First Seen' more congenial than the 'harps and arbours' of most Victorian mediaevalism. Morris had made his way to a real-life version of the infamous 'Victorian Wasteland' that had been the mirror of human despair in Tennyson's *Idylls* and the 'Morte D'Arthur', and Browning's 'Childe Roland', and discovered there not horror but a liberation of the spirit. His translations of Icelandic sagas, an extension of that pre-Romantic interest in Northern mythology expressed most typically in *The Descent of Odin* (1768), by the experimental poet Thomas Gray (1716–71) are allegories in thorny prose of the growth and decline of civilisation, in the manner of the *Ring* cycle (1853–74) by the German composer of opera Richard Wagner (1813–83) and Ruskin's and Carlyle's historical fables. *Sigurd the Volsung* (1876) with its loping, virile rhythms, finds a utopia in the past, in a compact and dignified world of labour where heroes and their consorts built and spun, and the poet, whose role was so doubtful and insecure under capitalism, was the honoured preserver of culture and tradition.

R. W. Dixon (1833–1900) was an early associate of Morris and Burne-Jones, and his poetry hovers between Pre-Raphaelite pastiche and a genuine eeriness and mysticism; Beddoes with religion. Dixon combined a genuinely Romantic temperament with a crippling diffidence, and needed a supportive circle of stronger talents around him, in which he contrived to hold his own. He had helped to found the *Oxford and Cambridge Magazine* which had flourished for a year in 1856 as the spiritual successor to Rossetti's *The Germ* (1850), and after 1878 Dixon became part of a second circle of talents, including his former pupil the Jesuit priest and poet Gerard Manley Hopkins and the theoretician and later laureate, Robert Bridges. Dixon had recognised Hopkins's extraordinary gifts at once, while Hopkins praised Dixon's own 'rich and exquisite work', and understood the older man's problems of reconciling a Romantic egotism and the demands of Christian humility.

Dixon grew up in the family of a Methodist clergyman serving parishes in the industrial cities of Manchester and Birmingham, and so had first-hand knowledge of 'slums of shocking squalor and misery, and . . . incredible scenes of debauchery and savagery'. Like his school-friend Burne-Jones, he was astounded by the beauty of Oxford, and with William Morris they developed the idea of a latter-day chivalric order that would do unspecified good among the poor; in the end, only Dixon took holy orders and went to work in the East End of London. After years of obscurity and hard work he was made a minor canon and librarian of Carlisle Cathedral.

The religion which is purely decorative in most Pre-Raphaelite poetry is integral to Dixon's work; his verse, at once precise and ghostly, suggests that of Tennyson Turner who had also lived in retirement in the shadow of greater talents, and wrote of a natural world alternately illuminated by faith and threatening to dissolve into dispair. Dixon's conscientious attempts to broaden his poetic range were mistakes, and *Christ's Company* (1861), *Odes and Eclogues* (1884) and *Lyrical Poems* (1887) show how he progressively refined the lavish imagery of Rossetti into the delicacy of *fin de siècle* verse, where poetry aspired to the condition of book illustration:

> In one great line her body thin
> Rose robed right upwards to her chin;
> Her hair rebelled in golden bands,
>   And filled her hands.

Dixon stripped the Romantic imagination down to its essentials, and the virtues and limitations of his poetry were exaggerated in the art of Christina Rossetti, the most substantial talent among the minor poets.

Christina Rossetti (1830–94) mismanaged a gift at least as fine as that of her flamboyant brother Dante Gabriel. Possibly because of his example, her life was restrained and unworldly, and she took full advantage of her age's tendency to refuse women of her class an independent life. She cultivated an extreme delicacy of conscience, refusing two suitors who could not claim her degree of piety, and her poetry emphasises the denial of human love for the greater glory of God. Enough excellent poems remain ('Goblin Market', 'A Birthday' 'After Death' and 'Remember') to indicate the strength of the gift for fantasy, passion, sensory exactitude and lyric keenness that she tried conscientiously to suppress. 'In An Artist's Studio' is a gently inexorable criticism of Pre-Raphaelite egotism, in its ironic move towards the climax –

> Not as she is, but was when hope shone bright;
> Not as she is, but as she fills his dream

– which suggests the disinclination Christina Rossetti had to find herself a place in the lush, masculine imaginative world of her brother's circle.

Christina Rossetti's life was a melancholy one; the free-thinking Virginia Woolf regretted the sacrifice of one who 'mounts irresistibly to the first place among English women poets', adding tartly that 'if I were bringing a case against God, she is one of the first witnesses I should call'. Christina Rossetti's torment was imposed on her by her own nature, unhappily divided between what Charlotte Brontë had called 'propensities' and 'principles'. She did not have the sceptical independence of the American poet Emily Dickinson (1830–96) whom she superficially resembled, and she did not retain that fresh response to the natural world that nourished the tradition of retirement in the English poetic line of Cowper and Clare. Like Beddoes, she flirted obsessively with the idea of Romantic dissolution, and her deep-rooted guilt at this escapism and her double nature is expressed most trenchantly in 'Amor Mundi', with its lilting rhythms and bitter message: 'The downhill path is easy, but there's no turning back'.

Her habitual attitude was that of an Eve cast out of Paradise, yearning for that innocent enjoyment of natural beauty that consciousness of sin forbade. She could occasionally allow herself to revel in sumptuous imagery and dramatic fancy, in the spirit of an Esther decked out in the service of God, and only rarely did she manage the triumph of the almost entirely secular 'A Birthday':

> My heart is like a singing bird
>   Whose nest is in a watered shoot:
> My heart is like an apple-tree
>   Whose boughs are bent with thick-set fruit:
> My heart is like a rainbow shell
>   That paddles in a halcyon sea;
> My heart is gladder than all those
>   Because my love is come to me.

The heroines of her poetry illustrate her divided nature; the sinful nun, the princess yearning for the common life, the deflowered girl and the doomed bride. The drama of her verse centres around her longing for human affection and a Romantic fear that such a commitment would threaten her private vision of unattainable glory; she wrote approvingly of the dead Cardinal Newman:

> thy will
> Chose love not in the shallows, but the deep:
> Thy tides were spring tides, set against the neap
> Of calmer souls; thy flood rebuked their rill.

The strain of rejection shows in excesses of guilt like 'Repining' and two unusual poems of 1855, the nightmarish 'My Dream' with its obscene crocodile of execrable appetites, and 'Cobwebs', her own vision of the Victorian Wasteland, ruined by her sterile asceticism: 'a land with neither night nor day . . .'

Although Christina Rossetti poured out most of her talent

wastefully on formal exercises of devotion, her distinctive voice, balancing the innocence of sensation and the sophistication of language, continued to emerge. The pellucid imagery of the mournful Christmas carol 'In the bleak midwinter . . .', with its close echoes of Keats's lament on the human condition 'In a drear-nighted December', continues into the pristine aptness of her poems for children, which have the assurance of the early poems of Hopkins, who resolved the tension between his sensuous and spiritual nature more happily.

'Goblin Market' (1859) is the crowning achievement of Victorian fantasy; an intuitive combination of simplicity and sophistication, innocence, and a sensuality that promises delights far beyond sexual indulgence. Illustrators have been inflamed by the Coleridgean ambiguities of this most pictorial of poems; Rossetti dwelt on its secretive eroticism, the goblins of Lawrence Houseman (1865–1959) were shrouded and murderous. The paintings of Arthur Rackham (1867–1939) evolve writhingly from the tormented forms of nature itself. Laura buys the luscious but accursed fruit with one lock of hair and wastes and pines after gorging on it; Lizzie, the wise virgin, withstands the onslaught of enraged goblins to bring the antidote to her sister. The slight story, with its intimations of nameless evil and infinite good, becomes a distaff version of *The Rime of the Ancient Mariner*, celebrating the sweet joys of natural affection as well as the perilous need of the individual to go in quest of supreme experience.

Coventry Patmore (1823–96) had a similarly mystical temperament, but found no difficulty at all in reconciling human and divine love. He had Tennyson's Romantic ability to discern a transcendent joy in daily realities and universal emotions, and he is, after Hopkins, the most serious religious poet of his time. Hopkins himself praised Patmore's 'really profound' insight, and 'an exquisite, far-fetchedness of imagery worthy of the best things of the Caroline age'. Patmore was a Victorian Metaphysical poet, as daring as John Donne in his use of commonplace metaphors for the deepest erotic and spiritual mysteries:

> His only Love, and she is wed!
> His fondness comes about the heart,
> As milk comes, when the babe is dead.

Patmore's Coleridgean mysticism was enhanced by his serious study of the speculative theologian Emanuel Swedenborg (1688–1772) whose *Heaven and Hell* and *Conjugal Love* shaped the themes of his poetry. Patmore's father had gone abroad after the loss of his fortune in 1845, and the son scraped a living studying law and writing for magazines, until he became assistant librarian at the British Museum. The laureate of wedded love married happily three times; his first wife bore him six children and was the inspiration for *The Angel in the House* (1854–63), a novel in verse which is also a meditation on the spiritual lessons of courtship. Two years after her death he became a convert to Roman Catholicism, and the elegy and mystical essay *The Unknown Eros* (1877) explores his new faith. His second wife brought him a fortune which enabled him to live in leisured, literary retirement.

Patmore's 1844 volume contains narratives which suggest the powerlessness of human beings unaided by God, and the *pièce de résistance* is the Swiftian 'A London Fête' with its mordant description of a crowd watching a public hanging. But Patmore achieved his more characteristic style with *The Angel in the House*, ingenuous in outline and sophisticated in execution, which did for marriage what Tennyson had done for the shared human experience of bereavement: all readers could find their own private key to

> The warmth of her confided arm
> Her bosom's gentle neighbourhood
> Her pleasure in her power to charm.

By the end of the century, any intelligent reader was likely to approach this most accessible poem with extreme caution; Felix Vaughan, running his eye over the matrimonial prospects in the daughter-filled household of a Dean of the Church of England is uncomfortably like Jane Austen's Mr Collins, wincingly confusing worldly and spiritual advantages. For Patmore there can be no such comic confusion, because the mundane and the holy are so perfectly interwoven in the human sensibility. He had a saving, delicious sense of scale

and proportion, and Tennyson's ability to find enlightenment
in the ordinary:

> I, while the shopgirl fitted on
> The sand-shoes, look'd, where down the bay,
> The sea glow'd with a shrouded sun.
> 'I'm ready, Felix; will you pay?'
> That was my first expense for this
> Sweet Stranger, now my three days' wife.
> How light the touches are that kiss
> The music from the chords of life!

If the course of true love runs exceptionally smooth for Felix
and his Honoria, it is because Patmore needs a muted
narrative to emphasise the profundity of the change in the
lover from egotism to a new awareness of his spiritual and
emotional capabilities; the 'preludes' to each 'idyll' outline
these developments. Inevitably, *The Angel in the House* fails to
please the modern reader's sense of sexual equality. It has the
uneasy excellence of the song cycle of Robert Schumann (1810–
56), *Frauenliebe und Leben* (1840), where the artistry is
indisputable but the emotional content and assumptions of
female dependence and purity are shown up as the unexplored
attitudes of a particular time, rather than as genuine Romantic
investigation of feeling. Patmore's best-known poem
'Unthrift', equating a woman's chastity with the Eucharist, is
incomparably deft and profoundly unlikeable.

   Like Rossetti, Patmore can enter a mystical state by
dwelling intimately on the simple events of a lover's life. The
best parts of *The Angel in the House* take on the brooding,
Romantic refinement of Rossetti's drawings of Elizabeth
Siddal sleeping, sketching or laying the table, and *The
Unknown Eros* is filled with that idea of heavenly reunion
familiar from 'The Blessed Damozel'. In that poem, Patmore
set out to show, as Wordsworth had in *The Prelude,* the process
by which the soul matures through its initial contact with
nature and then through human love, social ties and study.
The meditation begins with the loss of a wife who dies 'with
sudden unintelligible phrase / And frighten'd eye', and goes on
through essays on grief ('The Toys', 'Departure', and
'Eurydice') to daring attacks on the public world of politics
and science, where Patmore shows a fierce prejudice against

reform and the 'twin deserts' of telescope and microscope that may be most kindly viewed as his Romantic refusal to have his imagination coerced. The Victorian Wasteland has spread, in *The Unknown Eros*, to the heavens themselves.

> View'd close, the moon's fair ball
> Is of ill objects worst,
> A corpse in Nature's highway, naked, fire-scarr'd, accurst:
> And now they tell
> That the sun is plainly seen to boil and burst
> Too horribly for hell.

The first Book deals with the general human experience of bereavement and penitence; the second is more waywardly mystical. However, 'The Child's Purchase' is one of the most underrated religious poems of the century; a Romantic litany to the Virgin who becomes the interpreter of human individuality, 'our only saviour from an abstract Christ'.

William Allingham (1824–89) was a far from negligible minor Victorian poet whose technical expertise, emotional sensitivity, creation of evocative symbols ('the wind among the reeds') and reliance on the Irish ballad tradition strongly influenced the more greatly talented W. B. Yeats. Although the Irish poet was a member of the Protestant minority, a government officer, and a sophisticated literary man at home in the circles of Tennyson and Rossetti, he identified passionately with the peasantry of his native land: 'I would give the waste lands of Ireland into toilful Irish hands', he proclaimed. He believed (as John Clare had before him) that agrarian and political reform went hand in hand with a change in poetic style; a blend of personal and folk myth, and the simple language of the ballad. Even while he was composing 'The Maids of Elfenmere' for Rossetti's illustration, he was producing ballads with cheap woodcuts for halfpenny sale at Ireland's fairs: 'I have for some part of my verses, a little audience such as few poets can boast of'.

Allingham's imagination was essentially visual; he displayed his private world of fancy with the disconcerting precision of Christina Rossetti in 'Goblin Market', and he is the master of the well-placed adjective and the striking image:

> . . . all the wood, alive atop with wings
> Lifting and sinking through the leafy nooks,
> Seethes with the clamour of a thousand rooks.

Despite his convictions, Allingham is more concerned with observable reality than with politics. Even when he writes of emotionally charged subjects. such as the poverty and evictions in *Laurence Bloomfield in Ireland* (his 5000-line novel in verse about a progressive landlord), his subject is his own complex attitude to his native land, analysed with finesse. In *George Levison, or, The Schoolfellows*, which has the ready appeal to sentiment of the genre paintings of the 1850s, and which its publisher, Dickens, found 'mournfully true', Allingham achieved the flexible verse form and neat observation of Coventry Patmore; a woman's hat-ribbon 'whirring in the wind' captures the vanishing moment in which all the charm and mystery of physical existence is bound up.

Allingham is best remembered for his delicately sinister fantasy with its strong roots in Celtic folklore ('Up the airy mountain . . .') and his fine-drawn grotesquerie in the spirit of Beddoes ('The Crucible', with its wittily gruesome jests on the effects of 'Chemist Death'). But despite his genuine political commitment and his freakish imagination, he is at his most characteristic and Romantic when drawing his message 'learn to live' from the trivial but intensely perceived occurrences of daily existence.

In 1889 the dramatist, wit and critic Oscar Wilde attributed much of the literary spirit of the *fin de siècle* to the poet and novelist George Meredith (1828–1909), an intellectual and theorist of sexual relationships whose mysticism was more idiosyncratic than Patmore's.

> Ah! Meredith! Who can define him? His style is chaos illuminated by flashes of lightning. As a writer he has mastered everything except the language; as a novelist he can do everything except tell a story; as an artist he is everything except articulate.

Wilde, whose paradoxical prose had been adapted from Meredith's own, did not imply that these mannerisms were a disadvantage; Meredith himself felt that wit was something that 'had an outline in vagueness, and was flung out to be apprehended, not dissected'. He was that precious and necessary thing, a legitimate ancestor within the English tradition for the decadents and poetic novelists of the late nineteenth century who would otherwise have been mere translators of French culture.

Meredith survives as much in his influences as by his actual achievement: 'My name is celebrated, but nobody reads my books', he admitted ruefully. He gave practical encouragement to Hardy and Gissing, and freed writers such as Henry James and Virginia Woolf from a dependence on pleasing a broad audience; they were able to adapt his experiments in the suggestion of the fluctuating inner lives of characters rather than concentrating on the meticulous provision of a material world in fiction. Oscar Wilde purveyed a simplified form of Meredith's arcane wit, and his comedies, like Meredith's, hover on the brink of tragedy as artifice is defeated by genuine feeling at the last minute. The Irish novelist James Joyce had Meredith's feeling for the glamour of linguistic invention and his insatiable appetite for literary allusion, and D. H. Lawrence used *The Ordeal of Richard Feverel* (1859), itself an ironic development of two studies in Romantic educational theory (Rousseau's *Emile* and Carlyle's *Sartor Resartus*) as a model for *The Rainbow* (1915) and its sequel *Women in Love* (1920), with their interplay between man and nature, and instinct and intelligence. E. M. Forster (1879–1970) developed the vivacious yet principled Meredith heroine who had emerged from the practical-minded charmers of his father-in-law the satirical novelist Peacock, and the conflict between egotism and sympathetic intuition.

Meredith's poetry is too rich for modern taste; it has an intense musicality and lyrical emotionalism that is less embarrassing when it occurs in the frankly experimental prose of the novels. The ornate personifications and extravagant metaphors of the Rossettian *Modern Love* (1862) obscure the psychological realism of a tale of mutual infidelity and the narrator's own poignant untrustworthiness, rather as the melodrama of Augustus Egg's accomplished *Past and Present* series of paintings distracts the onlooker from the compassionately ambiguous emotions of husband and wife thrust into the public roles of avenger and sinner.

Meredith's full-hearted treatments of nature in 'Love in the

Valley', 'The Lark Ascending' and 'The Woods of Westermain' have been as unfairly neglected as Millais's later landscapes; in both artists, there is a slightly embarrassing wealth of talent, an unabashed sentimentality, and a pervasive thread of melancholy and warning. Poet and painter find man moving in nature without affecting it, as he does later in Hardy's novels and poems: the *Times* critic had written perceptively of Millais's *Ophelia* (1852) that 'there must be something strangely perverse in an imagination which souses Ophelia in a weedy ditch . . . while it studies every petal of the darnel and anemone floating on the eddy . . .' Meredith's musicality, like Swinburne's, comes from Shelley, whose skylark he implicitly evokes in 'The Lark Ascending', that passionate Romantic yearning for 'spaciousness' and imaginative freedom. His violent heroine in 'The Nuptials of Attila' recalls Shelley's Beatrice Cenci in a bloody celebration of instinct and liberation that lies at the farthest possible remove from Arnold's glacial evocation of Northern heroism in *Balder Dead*.

Nature warns the inner self of the dangers of not responding avidly to instinctual feeling, and the 'Comic Spirit' is invoked for the same purpose in the much more complex novels, where Meredith demands a Romantic directness of sensation in heavily artificial language. Emotion may be trusted and indulged only after 'blood and brain and spirit' have been brought into balance; 'you may love, and warmly love, so long as you are honest'. Meredith's wry comedy involves the near impossibility of achieving honesty; it is a quality subverted in the child by the unsuspecting egotism of parents and teachers, and a dangerous quality in adulthood at the best of times, as Clara Middleton discovers in *The Egoist* (1879).

Meredith is a curious blend of the subtly intuitive analyst, anticipating some of Sigmund Freud's researches into the unconscious mind, and an impatient moralist who shared Charles Kingsley's theory that man is evolving irresistibly to a higher state, and ridicule and physical abuse only hurry that process. Meredith never resolved his contradictory impulses; he treated his runaway wife with unfeeling cruelty, and then presented her case remorsefully in *Modern Love* and *Richard Feverel*. His taste was extremely conservative in his life as a publisher's reader, but he was cynically abusive of his own public who 'read not for the sake of judging human nature, but to escape from it'. *Diana of the Crossways* (1885) is an oblique self-portrait; his woman writer, ardent but paralysingly fastidious, and intelligent without self-knowledge, is a less sympathetically presented version of George Eliot's Dorothea Brooke in *Middlemarch*, and Meredith is not interested in achieving the imposing solidity of character that Trollope and George Eliot portrayed. He concentrates instead on the fascinating fluidity of a capricious personality, always capable of redirection with a fresh motive, and borne along on unacknowledged currents of desire and resentment.

Meredith's intense and individual art broke the power of plot in the nineteenth-century novel; his disciple E. M. Forster described the action of a Meredith novel as 'resembling a series of kiosks most artfully placed among wooded slopes, which his people reach by their own impetus, and from which they emerge with altered aspect'. Meredith was deliberately indifferent to the apparently unavoidable demand of fiction – that it tell a story with some degree of consistency – and was so engrossed in the subtleties of pure feeling that even words, he suspected, gave such ideal sensations 'the stamp of the world'. In his reverence for emotion uncontaminated by intellect he was an arch-Romantic, and his experiments in conveying this intuitive appreciation of the world took time to bear fruit in English fiction. Of his own novels, many are fascinating, but only *The Egoist* is an unqualified masterpiece, as reflective in its comedy as Mozart's *The Marriage of Figaro* (1786) which it intermittently resembles.

Algernon Charles Swinburne (1837–1909) was the most distinguished of the minor poets in his time, and a self-conscious successor to what he called the 'large, liberal, sincere' tradition of Byron and Shelley's Romanticism, for whom 'the large motions and the remote beauties of space were tangible as flowers', and whose works explored 'the high places of emotion and expression'. His own reputation, great in his century following the enthusiastic reception of *Poems and Ballads* in 1866, when students marched through Oxford chanting 'Dolores', underwent a catastrophic eclipse after his death.

The main passion of a life notorious for hectic political

enthusiasms and erotic experiment was literature itself. Like Shelley, Swinburne was a poet-critic of excellent judgement and wide-ranging knowledge, occasionally marred by violent personal antipathies (towards Browning and Arnold in particular). He had been an omnivorous reader from his unhappy schooldays, and his capacity for literary hero-worship in several languages was unlimited. He adopted the grandiose egotism and liberal politics of Victor Hugo, Charles Baudelaire's challenge of conventional morality by a perverse sense of beauty, Landor's classicism, Rossetti's religion of sexual love, and the mingling of the ribald and the pious in the *Testaments* of the mediaeval outlaw François Villon (b. 1431). Like the American Romantic Edgar Alan Poe he produced the most idealised expressions of Romantic love out of descants on corruption and torment; his master in this was the marquis de Sade (1740–1814) who had reduced human ethics to a study of the stratagems of sexual tyranny; in Swinburne's devoted understanding, this lost its original satirically anti-Romantic bias and became a path to self-forgetfulness in the manner of Keats's 'Ode to a Nightingale' and the exultantly savage paradoxes of 'Ode on Melancholy'.

Swinburne saw himself as a latter-day Byron, weighed down by the impediments of 'youth, genius, and an ancient name'. The sickly child of well-born parents, he left both Eton and Oxford under a cloud, and met Rossetti and Morris in time for the famous 'Jovial Campaign' at Oxford in the summer of 1856, where he learned metaphysics from Rossetti and poetry from Morris. Swinburne took great trouble with the form of his verse, compensating the swooning flow of metre and assonance with a sinewy Anglo-Saxon diction that is satisfactorily balanced in 'The Triumph of Time'. His verse dramas, on which he lavished much effort, show his debt to Morris most completely, along with a Romantic admiration of seventeenth-century playwrights. *Atlanta in Calydon* (1865) is the most exquisite product of Victorian hellenism, the ruthless stylisation of the action balanced by the piercing lyricism of the commentary in a combination of sweetness and austerity that the Dutch-born Laurence Alma-Tadema achieved in his genre paintings on classical subjects.

> When the hounds of spring are on winter's traces,
>   The mother of months in meadow or plain
> Fills the shadows and windy places
>   With lisp of leaves and ripple of rain;
> And the brown bright nightingale amorous
> Is half assuaged for Itylus,
> For the Thracian ships and the foreign faces,
> The tongueless vigil and all the pain.

Swinburne's poetry deals obsessively with those destructive aspects of love that emerge in Romantic poetry from Coleridge's subtle *Christabel* to Rossetti's 'The Orchard Pit' and 'Sister Helen'. His own 'darker Venus', 'Our Lady of Pain', is not simply a feverish personification of those prostitutes from whom Swinburne sought his strange gratifications in the underworlds of Paris and London, but a symbol of intense feeling; the 'antagonist alike of trivial sins and virtues'.

The years 1860 to 1879 were poetically productive, but Swinburne's health was ruined by his excesses, and in a notorious capitulation he put himself in the hands of Theodore Watts-Dunton (1832–1914), one of those figures who had a self-appointed mission of saving the more exuberantly gifted Pre-Raphaelites from themselves. Watts-Dunton was a literary man in his own right, though his works, once famous for their apparent mystical revelations, are now largely forgotten. His novel *Aylwin* (1901) enjoyed fleeting esteem as a 'message to the soul' that rebuked modern materialism by returning, through a 'Renascence of Wonder' to a Coleridgean Romanticism with overtones of Meredith. He nursed Swinburne into thirty years of additional life: 'an existence of the greatest calm, passivity and resignation, without a struggle and apparently without a wish for liberty of action', according to Swinburne's biographer Edmund Gosse (1849–1928). The poet devoted himself mildly to blank verse drama, unsuccessful attempts to imitate the 'innocence' of William Blake (rediscovered through Rossetti), and his more influential critical essays.

Swinburne was as indifferent as Rossetti to the public concerns of his age, so far as England itself was concerned; *Songs Before Sunrise* confuse political issues in Europe and extravagant personal emotion. 'A Forsaken Garden' remains a powerful expression of the melancholy consequences of spiritual feeling set adrift without an object in God; it is more moving than the violently pagan attacks on Christianity in the 'Hymn to Proserpine' or the brutal 'Before a Crucifix'.

Swinburne's flamboyance and the wearisome length of his lyrics conceal the exquisite craftsmanship and variety of tone in his work as a whole. He was an expert forger of the styles of several centuries; from the just simplicity of the cavalier lyric –

> We are not sure of sorrow,
>   And joy was never sure;
> Today will die tomorrow;
>   Time stoops to no man's lure; –

and the uncannily primitive ballads he favoured, to the neat pungencies of early English diction ('Clasped and clothed in the cloven clay'). His translations of Villon have a crisp bawdiness, and are in a sense his best work. The enchantingly ribald satirical burlesques in anglicised French (*La Soeur de la Reine* and *La Fille du Policeman*), once unknown outside a circle of appreciative male friends, show a sense of humour usually repressed in his poems, save for his self-parody 'Nephelidia' and some neat epigrams. *Lesbia Brandon*, a semi-autobiographical novel not published until 1952, is rescued from its place in the populous realm of Victorian pornography by some prose *tours de force* (including the death of the heroine) in the manner of Walter Pater.

Swinburne will always be disliked by many readers; he demands to be judged by a canon of taste that he invented himself, which depends on the appreciation of excess, and an ignoring of reason in the quest for sound. He takes emotions latent in early Romanticism to alarming or indefensible lengths, but at the same time he has a reckless strength of feeling and a sense of belonging to a universal culture, American as well as European, that comes as a relief from the narrow limits of minor Victorian verse.

'A moral, if only you look for it': popular fiction

The 'sensation novel' and the associated tale of terror were two of the most durable and successful kinds of fiction produced at the mid-century, and their crowd-pleasing properties (in 1860 Wilkie Collins's *The Woman in White* did much better than *The Mill on the Floss*) had a marked influence on serious novels. Dickens's *Great Expectations* (1860) and George Eliot's *Daniel Deronda* (1876) borrow the 'sensation' novel's intricate plots of concealed parentage, illegitimacy, sudden loss of fortune, mysterious legacies and disputed wills, forced marriages and tyrannical husbands, imprisonment in lonely houses, premonitory dreams, insanity and murder. The theme of *The Woman in White* and the incomparably finer *Great Expectations* is the same; the invoking of the law at whatever psychological cost to protect the advantages of civilised life.

The 'sensation' novel grew out of the 'Newgate' fictions of Bulwer Lytton and others, with their disconcerting sympathy for the criminal intelligence, and the genre came to include works of very unequal merit, from the sentimental melodrama of Mrs Henry Wood's *East Lynne* (1861), which is so very good in its incidental characterisation, and Mary Braddon's much dramatised murderous bigamist in *Lady Audley's Secret* of the same year (the sensation novel increased the range of female emotion and characterisation), to Wilkie Collins's addled *No Name* (1862) and his psychologically acute *The Moonstone* (1868). All drive home a common fear of the loss of self-respect and social status, and they provide, more powerfully than more ambitious fiction, a sense of the roots of those Victorian taboos that more intellectually adventurous novelists chafed against.

Middle-aged readers of *The Woman in White* had grown up in a world where revolution was a constantly apprehended threat, kept from occurring by a harsh and inefficient criminal code; the eighteenth century lingered on into the nineteenth, disappearing under the influence of improved communications, the growth of cities, a reformist religious sentiment, and the growing willingness of an expanded properties class to submit to a previously unimaginable degree of centralised authority (fostered, some suggest, by that classic document of nineteenth-century civil law, the railway timetable). But the fear of reeling back into the beast was deeply ingrained; Tennyson, like most of his contemporaries, viewed society as only superficially civilised. The middle class was made uneasy by its awareness of a vast and potentially dangerous proletariat whose demands for suffrage had to be met; Arnold spoke with a weary wit that does not mask his disquiet of

> that vast portion . . . of the working class which, raw and half-developed, has long lain half-hidden amidst its poverty and squalor, and is now issuing from its hiding place to assert an Englishman's heaven-born privilege of doing as it likes . . . .

The cruel vigour with which the division between respectability and 'squalor' was maintained was in itself a force for the general improvement of society, by allowing a reward to those who sought to be admitted to the middle class. Snobbery and hypocrisy admitted that there were higher standards of social behaviour in force, and prudishness was an understandable reaction to that unregenerate and filthy world outside the comfortable home filled with disciplined domestic servants, an expanding family and a clutter of machine-made possession; streets were noisy and disgusting with horse-drawn traffic, overcrowding and as yet inefficient sanitation made gross assaults on the senses, and drunkenness and prostitution were still flagrant facts of life. The overcossetting of women in protected circumstances was an inevitable overreaction to the gross insults offered as a matter of course to any unescorted woman in the previous century; in the long run, the development of street lighting (beginning in 1807) and a reliable police force (from 1829) did more for the general emancipation of the sex than the offer of professional education to a select few.

The sensation novels are as useful in points of law as they are absurd in plot, giving an excellent sense of the grounds for the complex taboos with which the propertied classes surrounded their daughters in order to safeguard fortunes; the Married Women's Property Act (1862) was more a charter for exasperated fathers than a refuge for abused wives. In addition, the sensation novels suggest the degree of protection and support a tax-paying citizen felt free to demand from the state in return for certain limitations on Doing as He Liked. Ultimately, the novels of Collins and his imitators show, like *Middlemarch,* the sociological effects of material change; the annihilation of time and distance by the railway, and a growing reliance on the wise materialism of the expert, usually a local physician or a London detective. The latter is the symbol of the new centralised rule of law and the gravely codified administration of justice, which culminates in the almost godlike powers of the folk-hero Sherlock Holmes in the short stories and novels of Sir Arthur Conan Doyle (1859–1930); the former is a fictional symbol of the Promethean intellect, conquering pain through anesthetics and epidemics through courage and experiment, and deeply aware of a Romantic union of mind and physical matter.

Wilkie Collins (1824–89) was the son of a repressively pious landscape artist, from whom he developed the ability to gauge his market, a vividly pictorial imagination, and an insight into the mind of the hypocrite. A Collins novel was automatically designed for illustration, atmospherically lit and rising at intervals to the melodramatic tableau required by serial publication; the first appearance of the Woman in White herself has a theatricality that hovers on the verge of poetic symbolism:

> There, in the middle of the broad, bright high-road – there, as if it had that moment sprung out of the earth or dropped from the heaven – stood the figure of a solitary Woman, dressed from head to foot in white garments, her face bent in grave inquiry on mine, her hand pointing to the dark cloud over London, as I faced her.

Ann Catherick materialises like the speaker in Wordsworth's 'Stepping Westward', and she has many echoes of *Lyrical Ballads* about her. Collins's fiction lures the reader not only by its promise of pages to be turned greedily, but by a puzzling sense of considerable imaginative abilities deflected to trivial ends. The plot of *The Moonstone* (1898), in which a young man of unimpeachable moral standing is led to steal a jewel of great price from the bedroom of the girl he hopes to marry, is essentially the same as in the sardonic novella *The Marquise of O—— (1810) by Heinrich von Kleist (1777–1811), but Collins could hardly have known that. The eerie landscape of *The Moonstone* is repeated with a thorough knowledge of its symbolic potential in Swinburne's desolate seashores, and in Theodore Fontane's (1819–98) intricate German analysis of unsatisfied adulterous feeling in *Effi Briest* (1894). Collins's habit of having half a dozen narrators share the tale, one crime reflected in many monologues, may have been suggested by the criminal court, but it also anticipates the method of Browning's *The Ring and the Book*.

Collins, who had been sent to work for a tea merchant, began writing in 1850 for Dickens's magazines, and his efficient journalism gives a wittily precise sense of the mid-century: 'Give us Room!' outlines the social perplexities of the crinoline, beloved of *Punch* cartoonists, and 'The Unknown Public' evokes that submerged end of the market he wrote for; penny journals with their fatuous serials and advice to correspondents aiming for a nervous gentility. 'Laid up in Lodgings', the best of the ephemera, is an excellent familiar essay, as good as Dickens's brilliant and moving *The Uncommercial Traveller* (1860), where well-known sights and sounds are acted upon by 'involuntary egotism' to produce a fantastic, De Quinceyish vision.

Collins enjoyed a mutually enriching partnership with Dickens: the families intermarried and travelled together, and acted in Collins's melodramas. *Edwin Drood* is Dickens's attempt to imitate Collins directly; his influence had appeared before that in masterly 'curtain-effects' and tighter plotting, and the late development of assertive but chaste heroines like Estella, Bella Wilfer and Helena Landless, who owe much to Collin's wildly popular Marian Halcombe in *The Woman in White*. Like Dickens, Collins cherished a secret life; he was an opium addict, and never married his principal mistress. The anarchic products of his own mind were transmuted into palatable middle-class fictions through a reversal of the conventions of the contemporary stage, where the most improbable scenes between stock characters were played out in surroundings of impeccable realism; in Collins, only the circumstances are bizarre, and the characters are as solid as those of Trollope, thoroughly imagined even when they are most outrageous.

The fictions of crime and the supernatural of Sheridan Le Fanu (1814–73) bore no relation to those of Wilkie Collins, with their middle-class emphasis on logical deduction and the consolations of the law. Le Fanu habitually worked from inside the mind of a central character, invariably a representative of religion or justice, who is destroyed by guilt and fear; his phantoms are not capable of rational explanation. They have an unblinking immediacy that uses the evidence of the senses to destroy a faith in the material world; a feat Emily Brontë had achieved in *Wuthering Heights*, and which Le Fanu can match.

> Mrs Prosser, quite alone, was sitting in the twilight at the back parlour window, which was open, looking out into the orchard, and plainly saw a hand stealthily placed upon the stone window-sill outside, as if by someone at her right side, attempting to climb up. There was nothing but the hand, which was rather short but handsomely formed, and white and plump, laid on the edge of the window-sill.

Le Fanu left behind fourteen novels, few if any read today, though *The House By the Churchyard* (1863) and *Uncle Silas* (1864) are known by title; his frequently praised volume *Ghost Stories and Tales of Mystery* (1851) has long been out of print, and he is best known for the masterly *In A Glass Darkly* (1872), which includes 'Green Tea', an obscure but horrible story of a hounding to death with a perception of the unconscious mind that seems to pre-date Freud. 'Carmilla' in the same volume is a link between Coleridge's *Christabel* and the thriller *Dracula* (1867) by Bram Stoker (1847–1912) whose melodrama had been learned from his employer the actor-manager Henry Irving (1838–1905); all three take a Romantically morbid view of female sexuality. Henry James's *The Turn of the Screw* (1898) deftly manipulated Le Fanu's technique of leaving no gap between the victim's consciousness and that of the reader, to produce maximum disquiet.

After the death of his wife in 1858 Le Fanu lived as a hermit in his Dublin house, where his studies of Swedenborg convinced him, as the unhappy heroine of *Uncle Silas* puts it, that 'the world is a parable – the habitation of symbols – the phantoms of spiritual things immortal shown in material shape'. Le Fanu is a deeply Irish writer, his themes embedded in his country's fiction; Maria Edgeworth's tragically whimsical analyses of the frailties of the gentry, and the heady mingling of history, folklore and Byronism in *Melmoth the Wanderer* (1820) by Charles Maturin (1780–1824). But at the same time, Le Fanu takes up Beddoes's Europeanised Romantic disgust at a disintegrating contemporary culture that has failed his idealism.

By contrast, the novels and plays of Charles Reade (1814–84) show the world to be a hugely agreeable place. All his exuberant fiction announces the generous spirit and innocent candour of a writer who preferred popularity to excellence; his contemporaries mourned the way he lavished his talent on melodrama, and George Orwell paraded him as a 'typical Victorian' who 'never makes a fundamental criticism' of his acquisitive society. Reade inherited Charles Kingsley's fondness for reformist fiction, but took no trouble to dress it up with poetry or philosophy, though his themes suggest an intuitive sophistication not done justice to by the words on the page.

Reade became a Fellow of his Oxford college, largely through academic inertia, and found his colleagues and the celibate life extremely irksome. A visit to Paris opened up a much more congenial career when he translated one of the popular melodramas of Eugène Scribe (1791–1861) for the English stage, and discovered a lifelong passion for the theatre. His playwriting was little more than outright plagiarism, summed up in the memorandum: 'Conscience a drama by Dumas is in 6 acts. 3 admirable. 3 bosh. Cut away the 3 bosh and invent or steal 3 quite different'. This was a common practice; Wilkie Collins, another natural dramatist forced by the literary market-place into fiction, explained in 1863 that:

> The few men of practical ability who now write for the English Theatre . . . know that they are throwing away their talent if they take the trouble to invent, for the average remuneration of 150 pounds. The well-paid Frenchman supplies them with a story and characters ready-made.

For all his enthusiasm, Reade was not a very successful dramatist and his theatrical ventures cost him some of the profits of his novels. One of the few original mid-century dramatists, the civil servant Tom Taylor (1817–80) helped reshape his *Masks and Faces* (1852) for the stage; the theme of the strong woman rescuing a weakly imaginative man is Reade's own, and Taylor supplied his own hallmark of the realistic routines of daily life that would eventually oust the old melodrama and spectacle.

Reade produced a wide range of fiction. His semi-autobiographical romances introduce a new, literally uncorseted working-class heroine who can lift her hands above her head, such as his *Christie Johnstone* (1853) who otherwise has no existence until *fin de siècle* sentimentalism (such as *Trilby* (1894) by Du Maurier) or the realism of George Moore and Gissing. Reade took the wrongs of women very much to heart, believing them the superior sex, and the muddle-headed but earnest *A Woman-Hater* (1877) with its praise for the 'cautious, teachable, observant' female intellect is a precursor of Henry James's ironic but strangely compassionate *The Bostonians* eight years later; the fastidious James regarded Reade, somewhat curiously, as 'a real master'.

The monosyllabic or proverbial titles of Reade's novels of social problems promise the righteous indignation and satisfying resolutions of stage melodrama: *It's Never Too Late to Mend* (1856) exposed the inhumanity of the prison system and contained well-researched material on the Australian goldfields that were luring emigrants, while *Hard Cash* (1863) looked into the scandal of lunatic asylums that harboured unwanted relatives, and *Foul Play* (1868) uncovered the racket by which ships were overloaded and sunk for the insurance money. Reade was prolific and organised, and could animate facts as tellingly as Harriet Martineau, Disraeli, or Dickens himself. His realism, however qualified by melodramatic romance, may have influenced Zola's much more famous intensified sense of actuality; Emile Zola (1840–1902) was translating English novels for Hachette et Frères while they were pirating Reade's novels in Paris, as Reade himself had snatched Zola's brooding study of addiction, *L'Assommoir* (1877) for an unlikely stage adaptation as *Drink* (1879).

Reade's most passionately personal novel is *The Cloister and the Hearth* (1861). It grew out of his vehement dislike of Carlyle's philosophy; ten years before *Middlemarch*, Reade elaborated a contrary belief in the value of the unremembered life. 'Not a day passes over the earth, but men and women of no note do great deeds, speak great words, and suffer noble sorrows.' His novel is a long romance about the forgotten parents of the sixteenth-century humanist and scholar Erasmus (1469–1536), during the first stirrings of the Protestant Reformation, and none of his loving preparation is wasted in his capacious narrative. His study, more graceful and humane than Kingsley's *Hypatia* nine years earlier, and making more concessions to popular taste than George Eliot's

Romola a year later, dramatises a similar individual crisis of conscience at a moment of profound cultural change, and lays Romantic stress on the holiness of the heart's affections, in an endearingly unemphatic and ordinary way.

'The pulse of thought': the private man in public life

In 1860 John Ruskin's attitude to his world changed in emphasis. He had always felt the stresses of his isolated emotional existence, unresolved tensions with his parents and with women, the spectre of inherited insanity and the additional instability forced on him by his partial rejection of Evangelical puritanism; now he became uneasy with his status as the arbiter of taste to a class unconscious of its privileged dependence on the miseries of an industrial economy. He turned from a personal response to art and nature to a furious indictment of a civilisation not worthy to enjoy beauty, and unlikely to produce it.

At the same time, his exquisitely sensitive eye and his emotional response to nature were changing character ominously as he underwent an intensified version of that Romantic eclipse of joy understood by Wordsworth and Coleridge:

> We Poets in our youth begin in gladness:
> But thereof come in the end despondency and madness.

The mental collapse that came in 1878 lifted only occasionally before the final silence of 1886, long before death in 1900. It was prefaced by nearly two decades of heroic attempts to subdue or rationalise his misgivings and the poignant adaptation of his prose style to make a virtue of his growing incoherence and subjectivity, as the struggle with all aspects of life became the hidden subject of his dialogue with the public.

A sense of the futility of all the labours and arts of life oppressed Ruskin even as his labours to change society gathered strength. Nature and society alike seemed defiled and menacing to him: 'The Storm-Cloud of the Nineteenth Century' (1884), a lecture delivered shortly before his final collapse, is an agonised rejection of the Wordsworthian sense of spontaneous joy implicit in the early volumes of *Modern*

Painters, where 'every argument, and every sentiment . . . was founded on the personal experience of the beauty and blessing of nature'.

The magnificent decline began with *Unto This Last* (1860) which was abruptly curtailed by its editor Thackeray after only four issues, so intense was the public uproar at the new tack their favourite critic was taking. The obscure title refers to Christ's parable of the labourers in the vineyard (*Matthew* 20: 1–16), with its eternally troubling contrast of human ideas of equity and God's divine generosity: Ruskin was proposing a new definition of 'value' to counter the political and economic philosopher J. S. Mill's contention that political economy was an amoral science. In doing so, he added a new dimension to Romantic feeling; in the past, Romantic poets and novelists had withdrawn in despair or contempt from the new industrialism. Wordsworth had found 'getting and spending' a tiresome irrelevance in 'The world is too much with us . . .', and Keats had ridiculed the mercantile spirit in *Isabella*. Ruskin saw the new bonds of Victorian industrialism as an area in which the Romantic exercise of imaginative sympathy could root out a dangerous egotism.

Ruskin excelled at this time in the lecture, which imposed its own saving discipline on his discursive imagination and allowed him that immediate relationship with his readers that Dickens sought in his famous readings. The Slade Professorship of Fine Arts at Oxford was a handsome recognition of his influence and abilities, but Ruskin reacted guiltily to such intellectual luxury by producing *Fors Clavigera* (1871–84), the personally revealing open letters on general social themes, addressed to 'the working men of England'. Prose-poems such as 'The Mystery of Life and its Arts' (1868) and *The Queen of the Air* (1869) anticipate the meditative poems of T. S. Eliot in the *Four Quartets* (1935–42) in their attempt to see the natural world suffused with extra-human meaning.

The brilliant success of his career as lecturer was ended by the action for libel brought against him by the American gadfly artist J. M. Whistler late in 1878. Ruskin had used *Fors* to attack Whistler's impressionistic *Nocturne in Black and Gold: The Falling Rocket*, which had been one of the minor exhibits in the resplendent new Grosvenor Gallery, the flagship of the Aesthetic Movement. Ruskin berated Whistler's 'cockney impudence' in asking 'two hundred guineas for flinging a pot of paint in the public's face', and Whistler, with his habitual enmity and daring, called the unstable but still intimidating critic to account. The two-day trial, which involved the major artists of the day on both sides, was as epigrammatic and tragic an affair as that of Oscar Wilde a decade later, and Whistler, who won token damages of one farthing, was forced to sell up and go abroad, while Ruskin resigned his professorship in defeat. His attack seemed to many the symptom of a sad decline in one who had once been the defender of new movements, but Ruskin was showing a deeper consistency with his principles; the young critic who had rejoiced in Turner's painted luminosities forever dissolving into that great light that is a symbol both of the act of seeing and the creative process itself, was not as an old one taken in by Whistler's flashy imprecisions of darkness lit with stagey artificial glitter. Ironically, Whistler's greatest achievements were to be those etchings of that Venice to which he removed himself after the bankruptcy that followed the trial: he reinterpreted, with a fastidious clarity, those scenes which Ruskin had drawn so hungrily earlier in his career.

Ruskin had little sympathy for modern art, and was depressed and disgusted by contemporary literature. *Fiction, Fair and Foul* (1880–1) is an eccentric but insightful tract of his decline, a condemnation of 'the modern infidel imagination' that was 'amusing itself with the destruction of the body, and busying itself with the aberration of the mind', when Dickens, the sensation novelists and the French realists purveyed a literature 'of the prison-house'

> because the thwarted habits of body and mind, which are the punishment of reckless crowding in cities, become, in the issue of that punishment, frightful objects of excessive interests to themselves . . . .

'The Storm-Cloud of the Nineteenth Century' was his fullest exposition of a blighted imagination existing in a degraded nature. Ruskin, the most powerful Romantic successor, amplified a vision of the Victorian Wasteland into a universal holocaust, with its 'plague-wind' and 'plague-cloud' yielding 'Blanch'd Sun – blighted grass – blinded man.' At its most banal level, 'The Storm-Cloud' describes the literal effects of a coal-based industrial economy, but there is a fierce poetic intensity that composes the blighting wind of 'dead men's souls' rather than the effluvia of factory chimneys. Ruskin is by now a Victorian King Lear, aware of the madness that distorts his vision, but imperiously forcing his once beloved surroundings to conform to his inner turmoil, and exaggerating the malignity of those enemies who must be great indeed to overpower his strength.

After the anguish of 'The Storm-Cloud' and the final letters of *Fors*, and the admission in *St Mark's Rest* and *Mornings in Florence* that the oldest sources of delight had failed him, Ruskin passed (like Shakespeare after his tragedies) to a period of calm, deliberate myth-making and a reconciliation with the past. *Praeterita* (1885–9) is a visionary reminiscence, a lightening before death of the intellect; 'the "natural" me, only . . . peeled carefully', as the sophisticated autobiographer explained. Marcel Proust, who had discovered Ruskin through another late book, *The Bible of Amiens* (1880), learned from this technique of the recall of the past through sense impressions, and transcended the subtleties of *Praeterita* (which he came to know by heart) in *Remembrance of Things Past*. In the unembittered intimacies of *Praeterita* Ruskin escapes from his despairing battle with his world and his insanity, into a safe country of memory where the child once more sees and feels with an uncorrupted Romantic intensity.

John Henry Newman (1801–90) was the most celebrated of Victorian converts to Roman Catholicism, and the author of forty volumes of sermons, essays, letters, an autobiography (*Apologia Pro Vita Sua*), poems (including *The Dream of Gerontius*) and a novel (*Loss and Gain*). He resembles Ruskin in his perfection of a thoroughly personal self-revelatory style in controversial prose, in a century that wanted public argument to be conducted in the emotionally persuasive tones of the sermon, that universally appreciated art form.

Newman's innately religious temperament found full expression initially in his guidance (with John Keble, R. H. Froude and Edward Pusey (1800–82)) of the Oxford Movement which had begun with Keble's Assize Sermon in 1833. The series 'Tracts for the Times' involved the Established Church in the spiritual revival that had preceded and kept pace with Romantic developments in literature, and the careers of brilliant men were made or broken by the intellectual battles as the English Church reorganised itself into an Evangelical or Low Church wing, a Broad faction which accommodated itself to political liberalism and the scientific criticism of scripture, and a 'High' Church (also called 'Tractarian', 'Ritualist' or 'Puseyite') that sought to revitalise itself through the revival of doctrine and ceremonial customs associated with the Roman roots of Anglicanism. The wearing of vestments, intoning of services, hearing of confessions, establishment of Angelican sisterhoods and the beautification of churches became agitating public issues, and the High Church was not friendly to liberalising forces.

English Romanticism was closely linked to religious feeling, and had a great deal in common with Evangelism and Dissent; a passionate interest in the individual conscience, a discriminating aloofness from 'the world's slow stain', a sense of great spiritual power discerned in nature, and an evocation of those 'spots of time' that are the equivalent to the conversion experience. The Oxford Movement had its intellectual origins in the conservative and individualist philosophy of Coleridge, and it exaggerated a Romantic tendency to clarify present problems by contrasting them with an idealised past. Tractarianism was responsible, along with a re-emergent and increasingly tolerated Roman Catholicism, for the neo-Gothic architecture of the period that left ineffaceable traces all over Britain in its nostalgia for a settled and feudal past in an age of steam and democracy.

Newman became the leading example of the perceived danger of the Oxford Movement; his conversion in 1845 warned that the English Church was in danger of losing autonomy and drifting towards Rome. Then suddenly (though other, notable conversions followed during the renaissance of the Roman faith in England), the Romantic spirit in religion was countered, as it had been in literature, by a general utilitarian impatience. The railway boom of 1847 and the excitements of revolution abroad and Chartist agitation at home made those who had been cultivating their spiritual nature aware of the advantages of pragmatism, and there was even a feeling, as one disaffected Puseyite put it, that Christianity itself had become 'an open question'. Ritualism continued to be a strong force within the English Church and in many cultivated lives: Charlotte Yonge's *The Heir of Redclyffe* (1853) influenced William Morris and his circle at Oxford, and young officers in the Crimea, in its strict but imaginative piety. But Trollope was able to treat Ritualism in the Barchester novels that begin 1855 merely as a matter of social nuance; it is a part of Mr Arabin's cultivation of superiority.

Religion was still the great issue in public debate, particularly in the intellectual centre of Oxford itself, but the battles of the 1860s and after were with scientific unbelievers and those within the church itself, like the eminent Greek scholar and Master of Balliol, Dr Benjamin Jowett (1817–93), who seemed to encourage threats to the faith.

After his conversion, Newman entered upon a prolonged, unfamiliar and chastening period of obscurity during which he devoted himself to the theory and practice of teaching (his *Discourses on the Scope and Nature of a University Education* in 1852 was intended as a rebuke to Arnold's humanist views), and grew into his role as the keeper of the religious conscience of the nation in a time of materialism. He saw the Church as the mirror of the world of nature with its ordered energies, 'so vigorous, so reproductive amid all its changes', and he conveyed this vision through the metaphors of the Romantic poets; surging seas, starry skies, and the 'unexplored and unsubdued world' of Holy Scripture. His universe where everything bodies forth the Creator's praise and the individual is precious for that spirituality that 'lives in the tips of his fingers, and in the spring of his instep' anticipates the equally Romantic and intensely personal poetry of another convert, Gerard Manley Hopkins.

Newman's urbane, unassuming delicacy in his written style was an elaborately artificial manner, despite his disapproval of 'the mere literary ethos' itself. *Loss and Gain* (1848) contains a great deal of discreetly suppressed hilarity, like Clough's contemporary piece of Oxford high spirits, *The Bothie of Tober-na-Vuolich; Lectures on Certain Difficulties Felt by Anglicans* (1850) and *Lectures on the Present Position of Catholics* (1851) make their points by suave but ludicrous transpositions between the temporal and spiritual planes. Newman wrote for the greater glory of his argument and ultimately in the service of his God, with a constant eye to effect. His simplest sentences are full of emotional suggestion; the famous climax to his autobiography is as deliberately moving an example of the distance between his idealism and the coarse materialism of his age as Arnold's 'Rugby Chapel':

> I have never seen Oxford since, excepting its spires, as they are seen from the railway.

Newman's apparently modest concentration on his own feelings allowed him to undermine his readers' convictions from his own seemingly defensive position. Geniality and candour masked his imperturbable beliefs and a dazzling intellectual agility, but he was no mere calculating propagandist: he needed the solace of writing and the intimate contact with a receptive audience as much as Ruskin himself, and his listeners became 'spiritual wives and children', while the motto of the cardinalate eventually granted him in 1879 was to be 'Heart speaks to heart'. George Eliot, recognising a fellow Romantic who might not share her faith but followed her vision, paid tribute to the *Apologia* as 'the revelation of a life – how different in form from one's own, yet with how close a fellowship to its needs and burthens.'

The naturalist Charles Darwin (1809–82) had many points in common with Newman, however opposed their eventual positions on religion: each man spent his mature years in retirement, drawing an elaborate map of existence from one crucial episode in his life. Newman meditated on his conversion and its meaning; Darwin upon the findings of his five years (1831–6) as the official naturalist on the *Beagle's* journey to South America.

Darwin's realisation that individuals with the most favourable variations within a species tended to transmit those characteristics to their more numerous offspring (evolution by means of natural selection) was sparked by his reading of Thomas Malthus's (1766–1834) rationalist theory of poverty and population growth (promulgated in the year of *Lyrical Ballds*, and a cornerstone of utilitarian principles). But *The Origin of Species* (1859) and *Descent of Man* (1871) had their beginnings less in Malthusian analysis than in the Romantic attitude to the visible world. Like Wordsworth, Darwin theorised creatively from a multitude of sense impressions recollected in the tranquillity of a mysterious retirement from public life, and he had the Romantic artist's ability to see the world as if for the first time: 'I think I am superior to the common run of men in noticing things which easily escape attention, and in observing them carefully'. He had the Romantics' feeling for balanced forces of creation and destruction, and for the operation of time on relationships: on the *Beagle* he had read Milton's *Paradise Lost* (1667) and it had given him the key to a time span to which the single experience of man cannot be the measure. *The Voyage of the Beagle* (1845) is a real-life *Rime of the Ancient Mariner*; the journal of a feeling man witnessing an unknown natural world of barely understood powers that enforce great suffering to some obscure end.

Darwin's prose is plain and self-effacing, though far from scientifically clinical. *The Voyage of the Beagle* is touched with gentle humanity and astringent wit, and occasionally heightened to rhapsody by the magnificence of the subject-matter. The famous conclusion to *The Origin of Species*, with its purely conventional reference to a First Cause, sounds the note of dignified melancholy that becomes the hallmark of agnostic argument later in the century.

> There is a grandeur in this view of life, with its several powers, having been originally breathed by the Creator into a few forms or into one; and that, whilst this planet has gone cycling on according to the fixed law of gravity, from so simple a beginning, endless forms most beautiful and most wonderful have been, and are being, evolved.

'Unsanctified intellects': the realm of nonsense

Charles Lutwidge Dodgson (1832–98), better known as 'Lewis Carroll', explored another universe; a world of imaginative freedom and delight where ordinary morality could be suspended. Such strategic retreats from reality were frequent throughout the nineteenth century, and eloquently justified by Charles Lamb, who called such temporary escapes 'a mastery over fortune' and an incentive to continue shouldering the burdens of moral existence: 'I wear my shackles more contentedly for having respired the breath of an imaginary freedom'.

Whereas Edward Lear had written self-revelatory nonsense verse filled with longing and nostalgia, 'Lewis Carroll' jealously guarded his real identity and explored a world of ruthlessly logical materialism; the utilitarian view, traditionally un-friendly to fancy and childhood, was exaggerated into a toy for the imagination. The real Dodgson was a scrupulously conventional professor of mathematics whose sole eccentricity was an apparently blameless passion for little girls, whom he entertained to tea, photographed, and for whom he invented puzzles, stories and absurd letters. The 'original righteousness' of childhood uncontaminated by adult sexuality appealed to his Romatic idealism that was still 'unbeguiled' by the sophistication of Oxford; once one of his many young friends passed into womanhood, she symbolically died to him.

> Still she haunts me, phantomwise.
> Alice moving under skies
> Never seen by waking eyes . . . .

The logical play of *Alice in Wonderland* (1865) and *Through the Looking Glass* (1871) led the professionally conservative Dodgson to make startling unconscious predictions of later discoveries; in particular, the consequences of the theory of relativity and the optical tricks of the cinema. *Alice* had a marked effect on literature; *Ulysses* (1922) and *Finnegans Wake* (1939) show Joyce imitating Carroll's layers of linguistic invention, random allegory and satirical parody, and *Ulysses*, like *Alice*, is the labyrinthine drama of a wanderer who pits a strongly intuitive ego against social ritual through a series of encounters. But *Alice* is closer to the world of John Ruskin; the possessor of the innocent eye of childhood struggles to preserve that integrity despite the ridicule of characters who have already capitulated. The triumphant illogicality of the end of *Through the Looking Glass*, where all players become queens and sharing enhances possession, is the divine unreason of *Unto This Last*. But at the same time Alice herself is an unsentimentally observed child, trying to make sense of a social world of rules, alien culture and adult passions, like Henry James's young heroine in *What Maisie Knew* (1897). Carroll remained happily innocent of the extent of his achievement, and was so conscientious in his role of children's friend that he turned (after the success of *Alice*) to the mawkishly educational and deservedly forgotten *Sylvie and Bruno* (1894).

The text of *Alice* is brilliantly supplemented by the drawings of Sir John Tenniel (1820–1914), the political cartoonist. These enhance the richly loaded prose with an independent network of allusions to the contemporary arts and politics; the illustrations are as immediately recognisable even when out of context as the quotation 'jam tomorrow and jam yesterday – but never jam today', and 'it takes all the running you can do, to keep in the same place'.

C. S. Calverley (1831–84) was an incisive comic writer who never lived up to the promise of his alarming gifts. In the elegant parodies of *Verses and Translations* (1862) and in his deadly use of Byronic bathos, he reinvents Clough's pose of the detached visitor to Victorian society. Calverley's own intermittent intellectual efforts were somewhat derisively confined to translating contemporary poets into Latin; he was a Peacockian character who won a garland of school and university honours but withdrew after an accident into absolute retirement. To his Cambridge friends he represented 'the incarnation of private judgement', while his enemies, piqued by his insouciant, improvisational wit, found him an 'unsanctified intellect.' He infused a wicked, dancing wit into the leaden metrics and philistine pomposity of Martin Tupper (1810–89), whose *Proverbial Philosophy* (1838) was much in favour with the court at Windsor:

> Read not Milton, for he is dry: nor Shakespeare, for he wrote of common life:
> Nor Scott, for his romances, though fascinating, are yet intelligible:
> Nor Thackeray, for he is a Hogarth, a photographer who flattereth not:
> Nor Kingsley, for he shall teach thee that thou shouldest not dream, but do.

A congenital disbeliever in authority, though too urbane for outright rebellion, Calverley pioneered the concept of 'Found Humour' in his drolly disobliging 'Notes Taken at College Meetings', and in his parodies of examination papers he mocked the 1860s obsession with competitive examinations, by which means the army and civil service were being reformed after the signal disasters of the Crimea and the Indian Mutiny.

As a decorously anarchic absurdist, the intellectual equivalent of the numerous Victorian practical jokers, he found poetry as ridiculous as most sorts of intellectual endeavour, and no different from the unprofitable art of the street organ-grinder. His suave parodies of the serious verse of the period will last in anthologies quite as long as the poems they undercut.

The eventual librettist for the 'Savoy Operas', W. S. Gilbert (1836–1911) was an unsuccessful barrister with an unsentimental love of the theatre. Actor-managers such as Squire Bancroft (1841–1926) and Henry Irving were bringing a respectability to acting that Scott and Dickens had won for novelists, and Millais for painters; Gilbert, knighted in 1907, was the forerunner of Oscar Wilde and Bernard Shaw who exploited his neat plots and fertile, paradoxical wit. The nineteenth-century theatre had been a wasteland, its vivacity lurking in the lawless 'penny gaffs' and music-halls, and great actors transcending the indifferent or mutilated material of the legimate stage by the sheer force of their personalities: Gilbert, almost single-handedly, reclaimed the profession of dramatist to respectability. His adroit and thoroughly respectable operettas were to form a complete middle-class social history of the nineteenth century from 1875, set to the captivating music of Sir Arthur Sullivan (1842–1900).

Gilbert's independent literary fame rests on his plays without music, and the much more interesting collections of *Bab Ballads* (1869 and 1873), fugitive pieces written for *Fun*, the most successful of *Punch*'s rival papers. The overgrown, deplorable little dwarves of his accompanying illustrations acted out fantasies of incredible savagery and rudeness, expressed in jauntily recitable verse, some of which anticipates the unstrung metrics of the laconically witty American Ogden Nash (1902–1971).

> She was a good housewife too, and wouldn't have wasted a
>   penny if she had owned the Koh-i-noor;
> She was just as strict as he was lax in her observance
>   of Sunday,
> And being a good economist, and charitable besides, she
>   took all the bones and cold potatoes and broken pie-
>   crusts and candle-ends, (when she had quite done with
>   them), and made them into an excellent soup for
>   the deserving poor.

The elephantine humour of G. K. Chesterton (1874–1936) is learned from Gilbert, though Gilbert is more dapper in his wit, and has no political or religious axe to grind, and his comic mayhem paradoxically preached the virtue of a relaxed tolerance. 'Bab' lives on most happily in the elegant and irreverent art of Max Beerbohm (1872–1956), whose deservedly famous cartoons show royalty and literary worthies reduced to the social undress of childish tantrums.

The Victorian humourists ought never to be forgotten. They remind the readers of the present day that a great deal that is spoken and written about as 'typically Victorian' was first located by the jesters of an age not always apt to take itself too seriously.

4
'Thunders in the distance':
1870–1900

THE last quarter of the nineteenth century saw a reorganisation of literary life almost as complete as that which had occurred in the 1830s. The great figures of a mid-century rich in achievement and blessed with shared attitudes had reached their term, and the period which followed was, though fascinating, full of division and disharmony. This time, the advances in legislation and technology offered no solutions to aesthetic dilemmas; the late Victorian world seemed infinitely complex, fragmented into mutually hostile nations with their separate empires to protect, suspicious classes and political factions, sciences and arts beyond the grasp of the common man, with human beings alone in a post-Darwinian universe. The power and prestige of Palmerston's Britain was becoming a fiction in a world where a European depression and the end of the American Civil War had made the United States an avidly successful industrial competitor, and where imperialist Prussia was taking the initiative in foreign policy. The increasingly desperate question of Ireland – more and more of an armed camp – engrossed and exhausted the energies of the English parliament where 'politics was Ireland', and the last chance to bring about constitutional Home Rule came and went with the 1893 defeat of Gladstone's second bill in the Lords. The political reform that had seemed only a step away from achieving complete social justice in the 1830s had swelled into an infinite agenda of democratic rights to be fought for, and writers like Joseph Conrad were beginning to ask what political institutions were for, and what toll they took of the human spirit. The malaise in the late century was general: Tennyson, in his *Jubilee Ode* to the Queen (1887) looked coldly on

> Fifty years of ever-broadening Commerce!
> Fifty years of ever-brightening Science!
> Fifty years of ever-widening Empire!

as he had once looked on the specious allurements of his Palace of Art: he asked his countryman instead:

> Are there thunders moaning in the distance?
> Are there spectres moving in the darkness?

A lesser figure, the civil servant Arthur Munby (1828–1910), wrote in his private diary:

> So ends 1870: hateful and villainous year, bloody with wars still raging, treacherous with newly broken treaties; in which the hopes of human progress, cherished twenty years at college, have at length finally died out. . . . And we even see our England drifting away from her colonies as well as decayed in Europe; . . . barren of hope and large wisdom at home . . . . I am gaining an income by administering obsolete laws, and a system which has in reality passed away.

The home-grown culture of the mid-century was no longer all-sufficient, and England hankered after French literary artifice and German armaments, becoming an importer of influence from across the Channel, as she had exported it through Scott, Constable and Byron in the post-Napoleonic period.

By the 1870s universal education was increasing the number of those who wanted to read, until the old, mutually respectful bond between writer and public was snapped. The key to the new age, in which the middle class was politically and culturally disenfranchised, was advertising and the spirit of the advertiser. The modern author specialised in the smart brevity of the short story that filled newspaper columns or magazines, and whiled away the tedium of a railway journey, and the artists who captured the spirit of these years rejected the painstakingly achieved finish of the genre painters of the mid-century for bold, Japanese-inspired poster effects that caught and held the public eye. The most trend-setting and outrageous illustrator of the period, Aubrey Beardsley, assured readers of 1894 that

> Advertisement is an absolute necessity of modern life, and if it can be made beautiful as well as obvious, so much the better for the makers of

soap and the public who are likely to wash. . . . London will soon be resplendent with advertisements.

Five years later, with the cliffs of Dover bearing an advertisement for liver pills, Henry James complained in *The Awkward Age* (1899) of a contemporary indifference to anything but 'staring, glaring, obvious, knock-down beauty, as plain as a poster on a wall, an advertisement of soap or whiskey, something that speaks to the crowd and crosses the footlights'. Writers who sought to be popular needed to 'work for the galleries', as Thackeray had advised, with a vengeance. James went on:

London doesn't love the latent or the lurking, has neither time, nor taste, nor sense for anything less discernible than the red flag in front of the steam-roller. It wants cash over the counter and letters ten feet high.

James himself had become a symbol of this gulf of taste between the discriminating reader and the common man with his newfound power in the cultural market-place: he had stood appalled before the curtain at the first night of his *Guy Domville* in 1895 and heard it howled down. The dramatic critic Bernard Shaw faced the problem of who should supply the criteria of public taste: should 'the drama's laws the drama's patrons give' in an age of democracy? 'Pray, which of its patrons?' asked Shaw: '– the cultivated majority, who, like myself and all the ablest of my colleagues, applauded Mr James on Saturday, or the handful of rowdies who brawled at him?' In his short stories of the 1890s, James was to brood to good effect over the professional writer's new enslavement to his public, and the repercussions of that insult to integrity caused by the deliberate marketing of the literary personality by agents, publishers and reviewers.

The new, expanded readership had made fundamental changes in the literary marketplace. Serious writers, contemptuous of the vulgar trivialisation of the deep and considerate bond between Dickens, Trollope, George Eliot and their readers, became suspicious of an audience that wanted details of their private lives and amusing eccentricities. Astute manipulators of a purely conventional morality, like the almost forgotten best-sellers Marie Corelli (1855–1924) and Mrs Humphrey Ward (1851–1920) unconsciously flattered their readers into a rapport that parodied the old responsibilities. Late Victorian readers existed as buyers to be captured, and for the first time publishers feared their market's boredom more than its moral outrage. Whereas Meredith's career had been temporarily frozen by the refusal of the circulating libraries to carry *The Ordeal of Richard Feverel* in 1859, the favoured novelists and playwrights of the 1890s made well-judged assaults on sexual discretion: Grant Allen (1848–99) in *The Woman Who Did* (1895), and Sir Arthur Wing Pinero in *The Second Mrs Tanqueray* (1893) and *The Notorious Mrs Ebbsmith* (1895). A chasm yawned between uncomplicated souls who enjoyed *King Solomon's Mines* (1885) by Rider Haggard (1856–1925) and Conan Doyle's *The Adventures of Sherlock Holmes* (1892), and the avant-garde who purchased *The Yellow Book* (1894–97) with its fiction by Henry James, its shocking Beardsley illustrations, and its hints at strange sexual corruption and moral exhaustion. The only figure who made genuine efforts to bridge this gap was the editor W. E. Henley with his patronage of writers of general distinction and popular appeal: Conrad, Kipling, Hardy, Shaw and Stevenson.

The form of imaginative literature was changing into a shorter and more unforgiving compass. Until the 1890s, the novel had remained one of the symbols of Victorian moral stability in the face of rapid material change; the pattern of publication established with such lucrative success by Scott remained in force for over fifty years. In 1832, the year of Scott's death, novels were priced at ten shillings and sixpence the volume, or thirty-one shillings and sixpence for three volumes complete; a sum well beyond the means of most purchasers. Successful writers such as Thackeray, Ainsworth and Dickens started to publish in a cheap serial form that reached as wide an audience as possible. A lavishly bound 'library edition' came out a year later, and then, if demand really justified it, a paper-bound one-volume reprint, revised or abridged. In 1842 a Mr Mudie opened a circulating library in Bloomsbury where books could be borrowed one volume at a time for a subscription of one guinea a year, and by 1860 he was able to open a palatial hall in Regent Street itself, with branches all over the kingdom. His ideal subscriber has been described as a provincial industrialist with a large family of women whose considerable leisure could be filled with uncontroversial, time-killing narrative that flattered a middle-class image: the three-volume format suited libraries like Mudie's and W. H. Smith's, since each novel could be borrowed simultaneously by three different subscribers. It was possible for a mildly talented writer such as the unhappy Reardon of Gissing's *New Grub Street* (1891) to stretch a slight plot into three volumes signifying hope, reversal and reconciliation, and so make a safe living that provided handsome profits for the libraries and a guaranteed product for the consumer. This generally satisfactory arrangement lasted into the 1890s, with occasional grumblings from more adventurous authors. In 1894 one hundred and eighty-four 'three-deckers' were published; then the runaway success in 1895 of the now forgotten *The Manxman* by Hall Caine (1853–1931) showed that quick returns might be preferable to slow and steady remuneration. A new public, avid for lively, even risqué fiction, had been identified, and it was prepared to buy its own books. The sway the libraries had over publishing was ended.

Censorship in England remained something inexplicable to outsiders. In 1889 the English publisher of Emile Zola was imprisoned for obscenity, and only four years later Zola himself was fêted on a visit. The poems and short fiction of the 1880s and 1890s treated homosexual feeling as it had not been dealt with in literature since the Elizabethan age, but in 1885 the criminal law was deliberately amended to outlaw such connections, and Oscar Wilde became the most notorious victim of what Lord Macaulay had called the British public in one of its periodical fits of morality. The interest in their own sex among some of the most artistically independent writers of the period (whom Hardy described compassionately as 'souls unreconciled to life') is one of the most notable traits of the period, and by no means easy to account for. It was partly a development of that admiration for a hellenistic culture that began in the Romanticism of Keats and Shelley and gathered momentum with German hellenism as understood by Walter Pater, and it was fostered by the fastidious and conscientious taste of the mid-century, and inevitably, by the ethos of the public schools. Love for one's own sex, so invariably distressing and dangerous in the late nineteenth century, was an expression of Romantic intransigence. Marriage had been the symbol of an individual's desire to conform to a social discipline; in the novels of George Eliot and Trollope it signifies a desire to transcend egotism. By the 1870s, scrupulously or vindictively analysed unhappy unions, a concentration on the solitary unamiable man or the narcissistic lover of his own sex ('The Anti-Marriage League', as more conventional writers termed this trend), gave a powerful sense of the disequilibrium between the individual and his world, and a refusal to waste imaginative sympathy on unfit objects.

This sexual distaste or revolt was accompanied by a move to clinical detachment. The modern world was too complex to be seen steadily and whole, and characters were viewed in chosen contexts, in accordance with the practice of French naturalism: Gissing looked at people moulded by economics, Hardy evaluated them as sexual beings, and Henry James's men and women were psychological subjects undergoing experiments. An interest in the lowest levels of society, what Gissing termed the 'nether world', appears at first a return to Wordsworth's fondness for the outcast, but the writers of the *fin de siècle* felt only a Romantic nausea of betrayed idealism. The working-class types, like the absinthe-drinkers of the French Impressionist painters Edouard Manet (1832–83) and Edgar Degas (1834–1917), were separated from the artist by their tongue-tied incomprehension: W. E. Henley produced a typically detached portrait of a London barmaid:

> Her head's a work of art, and, if her eyes
> Be tired and ignorant, she has a waist;
> Cheaply the mode she shadows; and she tries
> From penny novels to amend her taste;
> And, having mopped the zinc for certain years,
> And faced the gas, she fades and disappears.

London itself, the eternal subject of this metropolitan art, was no longer a conglomeration of human beings working out intricately meshed individual destinies, as in the novels of Dickens and Thackeray, but a spectacle to be enjoyed with a defiant aestheticism. The poet and critic J. A. Symonds (1840–93) looking over the city, saw not the 'mighty heart' that Wordsworth had perceived, but merely

conflagrations of jewels, a sky of burning lavender, tossed abroad like a

crumpled cloak, with broad bands of dull purple and smoky pink, slashed
with bright gold and decked with grey streamers.

The Whistler–Ruskin libel trial of 1876 was, in its most
important aspect, a collision of mid-Victorian humanism and
late-Victorian aesthetic detachment.

'The embittered hour': nature and disenchantment

Thomas Hardy (1840–1928) is the most substantial literary
figure of the late Victorian period. As a poet, he ignored the
hectic idiosyncrasies of Rossetti and Swinburne to concentrate
on the sober evaluation of experience, and his poetically
symbolic novels dramatised the dislocations between man,
nature and society.

Hardy was born into a respectable though not genteel rural
Dorset family; his father was a builder in a small way, and his
mother had been a servant. It was an inheritance similar to
that of Dickens, and an excellent one for a rising writer who
needed a firsthand knowledge of most sections of his public.
However, Hardy yearned for gentility and was perversely
ashamed of the background which nourished his art; the
intensely detailed landscapes of his 'Wessex' are those of his
native Dorset, and his poetry alludes mysteriously to family,
passions and disappointments that are ignored in the formal
biography he wrote for posthumous publication under his
second wife's name. This deliberately secretive man was at the
same time dolefully candid about rural life; its beauties, folk
ways and communal celebrations are offset by drunkenness,
boredom, promiscuity, poverty and squalor.

Hardy was articled at sixteen to a local architect, and
continued to educate himself painstakingly in his free time;
during his five years as an assistant architect in London he
discovered contemporary culture and began writing poetry.
On his return to the family cottage after a mysterious
breakdown, he wrote a subsequently suppressed satirical novel
The Poor Man and the Lady (1868) and began his first published
work, *Desperate Remedies* (1871), a blatantly commercial fiction
in the sensational style of Wilkie Collins. His sole independent
architectural commission introduced him to his first wife,
whom he married on the strength of his success at writing

serials, the form in which his rapid succession of fictions was to be published. He gave in with reasonably good grace to the censoring of franker scenes, restoring the cuts in volume publication a year later.

Under the Greenwood Tree (1872) was a deceptively gentle reconstruction of a vanished way of life; *The Trumpet Major* (1880) became a more elaborately elegiac version of how customs pass away. *Far From the Madding Crowd* (1874) was an immediate success, and scenes of Greek pastoral, Shakespearean comedy, folklore and erotic spell-binding are embedded in the melodrama Hardy was always able to transform into something rich and strange. *The Return of the Native* (1878) developed into a study of an English version of Flaubert's Madame Bovary of 1857, in the incongruous setting of an ominous landscape and Greek tragedy. Minor but hardly negligible fiction interspersed these more famous achievements: *A Pair of Blue Eyes* (1873) was a favourite of Tennyson and Coventry Patmore, and much admired by Marcel Proust as an early study of the power of images to awaken desire, and the disillusioning suspicions that corrode love.

Hardy, by now a literary lion, built himself a large and ugly house, Max Gate in Dorchester, while writing *The Mayor of Casterbridge* (1886), a fast-paced, crammed and ambitious study of a solitary egotist haunted by his drunken sale of wife and child at a country fair in the days of his youth. *The Woodlanders* (1887) marks a transition between the sunny pastoralism of the early novels and the bleak universe of the last ones; the sylvan landscape, like that of Tennyson's *Maud*, is made a crucible for natural selection. Three collections of short stories (*Wessex Tales*, *A Group of Noble Dames* and *Life's Little Ironies*) crystallise the themes of his fiction: 'The Withered Arm', 'On the Western Circuit' and 'The Fiddler of the Reels' are miniature versions of the greater novels in their treatment of folklore, sexual disillusionment and erotic magic.

Tess of the D'Urbervilles (1891) is the summit of Hardy's intense and rich art; the story of a peasant girl of surpassing beauty, placid heroism and love of life, who is casually seduced, abandoned by her inexperienced husband, and finally hanged for the murder of her lover. The many planes of the action are manipulated with assurance; Tess is both joyously individual and a timeless tragic victim, and her world is the partially mechanised one of Hardy's own day that still includes pockets of lush pastoral calm, while the intimate texture of daily life is contrasted with the far reaches of the unrecorded past on the great plain of Stonehenge.

Tess involved Hardy in trouble from the outset, and he had to mutilate the text for publication, softening his heroine's seduction into a mock-marriage, and omitting the gripping scene where Tess, abandoned by her church, christens her illegitimate child. 'If this sort of thing continues', he confided to his diary, 'no more novel-writing for me.' *Jude the Obscure* (1896), a defiantly pessimistic tale of ruined lives and blighted sexuality, brought down a storm of protest; a village boy is destroyed by his unsatisfied desires for a university education and for a girl cousin, the most uncanny of Hardy's perverse heroines. *Jude* masquerades as a novel of ideas, but its repellent strengths lie in a deeply idiosyncratic treatment of the perennial war between flesh and spirit, necessity and idealism. The right of the working man to education had already been assured by the influence and activities of writers such as Kingsley and Ruskin; the nineteenth century was, as Hardy himself proved, the age of the autodidact. The volatile extravagances of *Jude* suggest that Hardy was finished with the novel, and in 1898 he published his first collection of verse, *Wessex Poems*. He continued to write as a poet until his death, leaving a vast collection of verse that includes the curious and spasmodically absorbing *The Dynasts* (1904), a failed magnum opus on the Napoleonic years.

Hardy's influence on twentieth-century English poetry has been profound; whereas Browning conveyed Shelley's dynamic style with its confessional voice, knotty intellectualism and impatience with traditional forms to American modernism as a whole, Hardy preserved a more severe English tradition dating back to *Lyrical Ballads*: an emotional caution, a respect for the evidence of the senses, a deliberate insularity, a reverence for the past, and a concern for form. Poetry was not a vehicle for argument; instead it evoked what Coleridge had called 'the blossom and the fragrancy of all human knowledge, human passions, emotion, language'. 'The Movement' of the English mid-twentieth century grew out of Hardy's astringent scepticism, while at the same time Robert Graves (1895–) developed the compensatory aspect of Hardy's poetry: a world charged with ecstatic and baleful sexuality, with individual women the facets of eternal desire.

Hardy's belief that sexual love was a key to understanding is something he shares with Rossetti – the early poem 'Neutral Tones' could be Rossetti's own – but his poetry becomes cooler and more carefully planed away. Hardy concentrates on the intensely detailed, emotionally charged scene ('At Castle Boterel'), or the solitary, enigmatic figure ('Midnight on the Great Western'), or even the critical absence of humankind from a landscape still saturated with their emotion ('Voices from Things Growing in a Churchyard'). His best poems deal with rekindled desire; as both his wives found to their cost, he could only value love in retrospect, as in 'Thoughts of Phena at News of Her Death'.

> Not a line of her writing have I
>   Not a thread of her hair,
> No mark of her late time as dame in her dwelling, whereby
>   I may picture her there;
> And in vain do I urge my unsight
>   To conceive my lost prize
> At her close, whom I knew when her dreams were upbrimming with light,
>   And with laughter her eyes.

Hardy was an intuitive, though not an ingenuous artist. His world is that of the nineteenth century only by fits and starts; a society in the throes of change is imposed on the permanent fact of nature which is so indifferent to human suffering as to appear positively malevolent. He was a poetic novelist in an age of realism, and though he seems to share the common concerns of his colleagues (the decline of religious faith, feminism, the barriers of social caste, and the battle against censorship), his treatment of these topics is usually eccentrically conservative. Hardy, like Tennyson, was a major Victorian writer who remained steadfastly unmoved by the optimism of the age. Biology was destiny to him; after a brief sexual flowering, those of his heroines who survive decline into dull shadows of themselves, and his heroes struggle against nature and heredity as hopelessly as the protagonists of Greek tragedy against fate itself.

The critic John Bayley pointed out in his admirable 1978 study that 'the small things are more important in Hardy than the big things'. Every Hardy novel is constructed, like the *pointilliste* paintings of Georges Seurat (1859–91), of a multitude of distinct sensory impressions, and he has a Pre-Raphaelite fondness for bizarre juxtapositions: a man momentarily caught in a fall from a cliff studies the fossils in the rocks, whose partner in eternity he will shortly be; illicit lovers meet under the eye of the heavens in an observatory on a lonely plain; two men competing for a discarded mistress are unaware that her coffin has been loaded on to their train. Incongruous situations were Hardy's equivalent of Wordsworth's 'spots of time': 'My art is to intensify the expression of things . . . so that the heart and inner meaning is made vividly visible', he explained. His art is all imagery: he keeps aloof from the action of his novels in a way unthinkable to most of the novelists of his century, with their controlling commentary on the narrative flow. But the fluid symbolism of his imagery is pulsing with thought and nuance, as, for example, his Tess, 'conscious of neither time nor space' goes to meet her future husband:

> She went stealthily as a cat through the profusion of growth, gathering cuckoo-spittle on her skirts, crushing snails that were underfoot, staining her hands with thistle-milk and slug-slime, and rubbing off upon her naked arms sticky blights which, though snow-white upon the apple-tree trunks, made madder stains on her skin: thus she drew quite near . . . .

Hardy's contemporary, Richard Jefferies (1848–87) is remembered for a trio of mannered books: *Bevis* (1882), a minutely detailed study of woodcraft that has the unthreatening period charm of Kenneth Grahame (1859–1931); the festive, unstructured *Amaryllis at the Fair* (1887) which predicts the later eccentric fiction of John Cowper Powys (1872–1963); and the idiosyncratic utopia *After London* (1885) which has something in common with William Morris's *News From Nowhere* (1896) in its radical simplification of society along mediaeval and anti-intellectual lines.

Jefferies was part of a plain-spoken tradition, that included William Cobbett's intemperate politics, prickly self-confidence and countryman's eye for detail, and George Borrow's identification with the gipsy outsider living close to nature.

Jefferies shares Hardy's characteristics to a minor degree; a deep pessimism qualified by an exact response to physical life, a confidence in his intuitions that compensates for intellectual awkwardness, and a strong autobiographical drift in his fiction. 'To be human is to be sad', Jefferies wrote in *Amaryllis*, and his characters, like Hardy's, bloom briefly in a sexual awakening and are left 'warped and twisted by the pressure of years' in a universe 'designless and purposeless and without idea'.

Jefferies was not 'a born story-teller' as Hardy had called himself; he approached nature notebook in hand. His parents, who had 'come down in the world' impressed him with a class-consciousness even more morbid than Hardy's; in addition, the world of books had meant little to him as a child, and he was too proud to make up the loss as Hardy had. He claimed grandiosely that 'written tradition, systems of culture, modes of thought, have for me no existence', and made books scarce in the private world of *After London*. This aversion was an understandable, if violent reaction to the precious, coterie tastes of much of the literary world in the 1880s, where emotion seems often to have been translated from the French.

Jefferies began literary life as a journalist on a country paper, and disliked the work so thoroughly that he took to writing novels in the hope that one solid success would free him from the trade forever. He discovered, by the end of the 1870s, that he could market his notes of country life very profitably in London and Manchester: public interest had been piqued by the first farm-workers' trade unions, and there was a deep nineteenth-century urban longing for the imaginative delights of rural beauty, a cockney romanticism that Dickens had satisfied as far back as *The Old Curiosity Shop* (1841). Jefferies issued a series of popular volumes throughout the 1880s: *Round About a Great Estate, Nature Near London, The Open Air*.

The Story of My Heart (1883) was an emotional autobiography with lyric descriptions of nature that was to inspire D. H. Lawrence's early novel *The Trespasser* (1912); *Amaryllis at the Fair* was the sole success among the many novels that became the despair of his publishers. It is an exhaustive evocation of the fleeting physical impressions and the thin-skinned sufferings of an adolescence Jefferies never outgrew.

The poet and critic A. E. Housman (1859–1936) was a pallbearer at Hardy's impressive funeral in Westminster Abbey, and he shared Hardy's pared-down Romanticism, secretiveness, fondness for startlingly macabre revelations, sense of malign fate and a love for rural England that emphasised his own intellectual sophistication.

> The chestnut casts his flambeaux, and the flowers
> Stream from the hawthorn on the wind away,
> The doors clap to, the pane is blind with showers,
> Pass me the can, lad; there's an end of May.

Nature in Housman's poetry is not the indifferent entity Hardy knew, but full of a 'resourceful malevolence'. As he wrote in a letter to a friend:

> When Man gets rid of a great trouble he is easier for a little while. But not for long: Nature instantly sets to work to weaken his power of sustaining trouble . . . . It looks to me as if the state of mankind had always been and always would be a state of just tolerable discomfort.

The famous ironies of Housman's lyrics in *A Shropshire Lad* (1896) have the mechanical wiliness of the short stories of Guy de Maupassant (1850–93), and have been a parodist's delight. Hardy can be as objectionably pat, but his best 'satires of circumstance' (like 'A Sunday Morning Tragedy') explore character and social convention in no trivial way. Housman's chiselled ironies and manipulative pathos breed resistance, and his emotions seem 'literary' even when the poem is most fiercely personal: the apparently glib 'When I was one and twenty' refers back to the unforgettable humiliation of his failure in his final examinations at Oxford because of the stresses of an unacknowledged passion for a fellow student. His promising career as a classical scholar was postponed, and his pessimism confirmed.

In Housman's verse, women figure only slightly as the shadowy sexual partners who lend universality to his themes. His heroes are victims who enjoy the brief oblivion of drink, athletic effort or love-making, with none of that illusion of freedom that Hardy's more robust characters enjoy. Housman's 'lads' are given to a craven muttering against 'iniquity on high' over their tankards, or a bowed submission to fortune.

Housman is too thoroughly Romantic to refine his lyrics of private grief to the toughly elegant spareness of Landor's. He cannot resist the overemphatic phrase ('the sky-pavilioned land' or 'yon twelve-winded sky'), though he has the classicist's ruthless satisfaction in pruning the Romantic lushness of nature back to unadorned purity in 'On Wenlock Edge', just as Milton had taken austere pride in the wintry pastoral of the magnificent invocation in *Lycidas* (1638). That seventeenth-century elegy of heroic friendship echoes faintly throughout Housman despite his pert jest that 'Malt does more than Milton can, / To justify God's ways to man'. Housman plays at being a yokel, just as Milton played at being a shepherd, but he is a University man in every poem.

Housman devoted most of his creative life to the textual study of a very minor Latin poet whose 'eminent aptitude for doing sums in verse' mocked his own, carefully polished style. He remained a bitter Romantic, who had no tenderness for the feelings and intuitions that cost him so much strife.

'Coped and poisèd powers': a spectrum of late-nineteenth-century writers

The attitudes to nature implicit in the poetry of Gerard Manley Hopkins (1844–89) and the vigorous, fresh-minted language in which he wrote, are immediately at odds with the pessimism and linguistic austerity of Hardy, Jefferies and Housman. Hopkins avoided their use of the pathetic fallacy (the use of nature to amplify human emotions), since for the poet-priest nature was a symbol of the magnificence of God; vast, variable, complex and energetic, that includes man but cannot be fully understood by him.

> The world is charged with the grandeur of God.
> It will flame out, like shining from shook foil;
> It gathers to a greatness, like the ooze of oil
> Crushed. Why do men then now not reck his rod?

The distance between Hardy and his sympathisers and Hopkins can be measured by the difference between 'Spring and Fall', Hopkins's meditation on original sin, and Housman's 'On Wenlock Edge', with their similar Romantic-

Victorian autumnal woods, familiar from Tennyson's *Tithonus* (1833) and that equally rapturous elegy of defeated aspirations, Millais's *Autumn Leaves* (1856). Housman appeals to the same sentiments as Millais and Tennyson, but Hopkins gravely rejects the appeal to full but simple feeling, in his location of the source of grief outside the scene itself, and in the impasto richness of the language:

> Ah! as the heart grows older
> It will come to such sights colder
> By and by, nor spare a sigh
> Though worlds of wanwood leafmeal lie; . . . .

Hopkins was a gifted, naturally pious student, deeply moved by the spiritual turmoil of Oxford in the 1860s. He was variously buffeted by the warring forces there; his confessor, the Anglican ritualist Dr Pusey, with his personal tragedies and angry sense of betrayal; Dr Jowett, the modern Socrates championing freedom of thought and assaulting religious orthodoxy; Newman, famous once more through Kingsley's vituperative attacks, and Walter Pater, Hopkins's tutor, who replaced traditional religion with the 'conscious certainty of self' gained through 'impassioned concentration' on the senses.

Hopkins was converted in 1866 and joined the Society of Jesus two years later, destroying most of his early poems in a Pre-Raphaelite style as an act of renunciation. He wrote no more until his superiors agreed that he should treat the subject of five nuns drowned on their way to exile in 1875, and *The Wreck of the Deutschland*, a fervid and apocalyptic poem, was offered to a Jesuit periodical and never printed. From that time, Hopkins worked on his devotional poetry whenever he had leisure from his exacting parish work, teaching and spiritual exercises. Despite the assurance from his friend the Anglican poet R. W. Dixon that 'one vocation cannot destroy another', he was disturbed by the conflict between his gift for celebrating sensory delight and the humility and austerity to which his vows bound him. His deliberate aloofness from the literary life of his time enhanced his originality, and he developed rhythmic patterns which echoed the speech of ordinary conversation and the tones of blandishment and admonition in the sermon.

In a sense, Hopkins is a Victorian only by accident, and is often welcomed as a sharer in modernism. His scrupulous obedience to the benign philistinism of his Order, where culture was (as his letters explained) only 'a means to an end', and 'individual fame . . . the most dangerous and dazzling of all attractions', made Hopkins refuse to publish in his lifetime, and his friend Robert Bridges edited the short but superb volume of *Poems* in 1918, so that Hopkins's reputation flourished along with those of Eliot and Pound.

For all his experimental daring, Hopkins was a deeply conservative poet who ignored most Victorian themes and looked back to the beginnings of English Romanticism. This came about through his perfect devotion to Ruskin, that disciple of Wordsworth; Ruskin's feeling for the vast meaning of nature transmitted through the most sensitive details of grass and stone translates into the exquisite prose sketches of Hopkins's notebooks from which the poems were quarried. Ruskin's magniloquent essay on Turner's *The Slave Ship* in the first volume of *Modern Painters* lies behind Hopkins's dramatic sense of 'the horror and the havoc and the glory' of the wrath of God, and in particular *The Wreck of the Deutschland* itself.

Hopkins's poems, like Wordsworth's, relive those moments of personal insight into nature, when a dedicated concentration on what is there to be seen reveals the underlying divine presence:

> Nothing is so beautiful as spring –
>> When weeds, in wheels, shoot long and lovely and lush;
>> Thrush's eggs look like little low heavens, and thrush
> Through the echoing timber does so rise and wring
> The ear, it strikes like lightnings to hear him sing; . . . .

This poem, so similar to Browning's 'Home Thoughts From Abroad', demonstrates Hopkins's rejection of imagery employed for visual delight alone and freed from moral significance; his un-Victorian stance, in fact. 'All this juice and all this joy' mourns man's separation from this abundant natural world, as Wordsworth had done in his *Immortality Ode*. Hopkins shared Coleridge's convictions of the connection of all elements including 'dear and dogged man' within a vast and paradoxical nature, and Shelley's sense of the inexhaustible energy of the creative process; Hopkins's image of the

Christian poet as a skylark develops out of Shelley's mystical
'blithe spirit', also recalling man from his 'sordid turbid' time
to his essential liberty.

Hopkins borrowed an unsophisticated political theory from
Ruskin and Carlyle. He took a Romantic view of the labouring
poor; Harry Ploughman, Felix Randal and Tom Navvy
working with 'churlsgrace' close to God and nature. He had
Ruskin's distaste for a century 'bleared, smeared with toil',
and yearned for a pious, mediaevalised utopia. The fascinated
fear of a cleansing catastrophe that he expressed in apocalyptic
poems like *The Wreck of the Deutschland* was shared with Ruskin
and Carlyle, and balanced by a magical private vision of
England's Catholic past with its shrines, pilgrimages and folk
piety, expressed in 'The Loss of the Eurydice' with its longing
and warning and roots in the fantasies of Pugin. This visionary
aspect of Hopkins is most lyrically voiced in 'Duns Scotus's
Oxford', one of the most polished of all the many Victorian
tributes to the city; Duns Scotus (d. 1308) was the mediaeval
philosopher who had defended the individual personality and
the natural world against the orthodoxy of Thomas Aquinas
(1225–74), by claiming that the whole creation, including each
individual human soul, was a continual and sufficient proof of
God and his glory. Hopkins was able to use Scotus's argument
as a justification for his poetry; his mediaeval longings, like
those of most of the great Victorians, were part of a personal
search for intellectual stability.

Hopkins's greatest claim to excellence as a poet is the group
of 'Terrible Sonnets', expressions of spiritual drought which
stand beside the magisterial and audacious *Holy Sonnets* of John
Donne, and they have force without histrionics, using Donne's
own familiar address to the Almighty, dramatically well-
judged metaphysical conceits, and the Romantic sense of a
spiritually alienated man tormented by the fecundity of nature:
'O thou lord of life, send my roots rain'.

Alice Meynell (1847–1922), a poet, suffragist, slum-visitor,
pacifist, critic and journalist, was another writer in the
Catholic flowering in England that followed the re-
establishment of the Roman hierarchy in 1850. As a young girl
primed with an excellent private education (her sister became

Lady Elizabeth Butler, an unlikely but supremely competent painter of lively battle scenes), she confided to her diary that:

> Of all the crying evils in this depraved earth, the greatest judged by all the laws of God and humanity, is the miserable selfishness of men that keeps women from the work of the mind as well as of the body.

Women like Alice Meynell mark a change in Victorian feminism, from Charlotte Brontë's and Elizabeth Barrett Browning's limited interest in the plight of the exceptionally gifted, to the publicly active and politically radical careers of Josephine Butler, Annie Besant (1847–1933) and Beatrice Webb (1858–1943). Such a dynamic role for the sex had seemed inevitable after Mary Wollstonecraft's passionate *Vindication of the Rights of Women* (1792), but the progress of nineteenth-century feminism was skewed by her early death and the wholesale and hasty retreat from anything that suggested revolutionary principles. The career of her daughter Mary Shelley showed how absolute the shift was; the former libertine became an example of female gentility. Feminism remained a minor public issue until J. S. Mill's coolly reasonable *On the Subjection of Women* (1869). A deep moral and sexual conservatism acted as a brake on dizzying material and social change, and the transformations of religious feeling left little energy over for the revaluation of sexual roles. Women writers were fuelled by impatient resentments at the limitations imposed on their sex, and female explorers, philanthropists and reformers flourished, but public debate about the nature and mission of women was conducted in the idealised abstractions of Tennyson and Ruskin and remained largely a metaphor for those tensions within society and the individual that needed to be brought into balance. Inevitably, the Romantic polarisation of the sexes in polite society led to the infamous 'black army' of prostitutes that infested night-time London, and their recruits from the labouring class of surplus females. By the mid-century, the 'Girl of the Period' with her shorter skirts and 'fast' behaviour was caricaturing the inanity of the preferred sexual type, and the emergence of the professionally competent, Ibsen-reading 'New Woman' of the 1890s is a tribute to the quiet gains made by feminism from the 1870s onwards. By the end of the century, women had their share in universal elementary education, university colleges were opened for them, and the professions gradually admitted them; the Married Women's Property Act lifted them from chattel status, and the tacit acceptance of birth control by the middle classes in the last quarter of the century freed women from the disabilities of continuous childbearing and men from the economic necessity of marrying late, which had fostered prostitution and its attendant evils.

Alice Meynell was a Catholic convert, married to Wilfred Meynell, a former Quaker and the editor of *Merry England*, a magazine that began in 1883 and published the work of the gifted faithful, including Coventry Patmore, Cardinal Manning (1808–92), Wilfred Scawen Blunt, Hilaire Belloc (1870–1953), Lionel Johnson (1867–1902), and its special discovery, the visionary poet Francis Thompson. Alice Meynell's first volume of poems came out in 1875 to a promising reception, but while her eight children were young she devoted herself to her characteristically neat and astringent reviews and essays, and her independent brood went on to become the 'Clan Meynell', a rival to the contemporary 'Bloomsbury' of the Stephen circle.

As a poet, Alice Meynell has a distinctive, cool and sceptical voice, even when she deals with the passionate issues of her faith and sexual being. Melancholy and conscientious in her personal relationships, and forbiddingly austere in her beauty, she moved in her poetry between the engrossing egotism of Shelley and the fastidious decorum of Anne Brontë. Like W. S. Landor, for whom she was 'Portia', she magnified small emotions in a tiny compass with a sure sense of proportion; like Elizabeth Barrett Browning, she dwelt on the power of motherhood, but as a possible threat to her singleness of being rather than as a fecund source of energy. The finest moments of her spare and self-critical art come in the refined and intelligent expertise of her subtly rarefied inner landscapes, like those of a quattrocento fresco, or the earliest paintings of Rossetti:

> . . . the stony fields, where clear
> Through the thin trees the skies appear;
> In delicate spare soil and fen,
> And slender landscape, and austere.

Her private art belongs to no discernible tradition, though her preoccupations were shared by Mary Cassatt (1845–1926), the American Impressionist painter working in France, who concentrated on expressing the fleeting emotions of maternity with a stringently limited palette. There was nothing sentimental about her art, which combined with the visionary directness of American primitivism and the tactile suggestiveness of the woman painter Vigée Le Brun (1755–1842) who had brought Rousseau's revolutionary simplicity to her portraits of the women and children in the last years of the French court during the *ancien régime*.

The poetry of Francis Thompson (1859–1907) was at the farthest possible remove from the discreet art of Alice Meynell, yet they were members of the same household. Thompson was a failed medical student who modelled his life in London's underworld on that of the English Opium Eater; in a desperate period of near-starvation (food was dearer than laudanum) he sent a packet of his writings to Wilfred Meynell, who was impressed by the frantic and visionary art of one who claimed to swing the earth a trinket at his wrist, in an ecstasy of Rossettian overstatement. Thompson became the ward and wayward genius of the family, a prototype of the emotionally manipulative pseudo-Shelley of Shaw's play *Candida* (1895); the most flamboyantly gifted of *Merry England*'s contributors, but able to write only in periods of withdrawal from his addiction, or in the temporary elations of the consumption that killed him. He made himself conform to the model of the Romantic poet as his age understood it; childlike and amoral like Shelley, and self-doomed to tragedy like Chatterton, De Quincey, Poe, and the Irish James Clarence Mangan (1803–49). The real world was raw material for his opium-inspired reveries, in which he transformed the people around him into the inhabitants of a Rossettian universe.

Thompson's literary experience was wide but essentially uncritical and imitative; his fantasies, based on De Quincey's, lacked the original's poise, musicality and originality. Thompson had no use for the unadorned truth, revelled in learned quaintnesses ('to write plainly on a fine subject is to set a jewel in wood'), and filtered experience through what he had read. His themes of guilt and innocence, his religious faith and sexual idealism should have made him a more absorbing writer, but his grandiose approach actually trivialises his subjects, most notoriously in the influential posthumously published essay on Shelley, which is actually a rapturous portrait of himself, complete with the toy theatre that accompanied him through all his vicissitudes.

> The universe is his box of toys. He dabbles his fingers in the day-fall. He is gold-dusty with tumbling amidst the stars. He makes bright mischief with the moon. The meteors nuzzle their noses in his hand . . . .

The extravagances of his religious poetry, including *The Hound of Heaven* (1893), made an image-crammed counterfeit of mysticism available to unsophisticated readers, much as the stupendous canvases of John Martin (1789–1854) had cheapened the imaginative daring of Turner and Blake. Thompson was not a poet's poet; the greater a reader's experience, the more Thompson's superficial and unreliable borrowings were likely to annoy. His ambitious models for himself, particularly the extraordinary Richard Crashaw (1612?–49), merely show how little he is prepared to analyse his mysticism. The elaborate imagery is never pointed in effect.

> I fled Him, down the nights and down the days;
>   I fled Him, down the arches of the years;
> I fled Him, down the labyrinthine ways
>   Of my own mind; and in the midst of tears
> I hid from Him, and under running laughter.
>   Up vistaed hopes I sped;
>   And shot, precipitated,
> Adown Titanic glooms of chasmed fears,
> From those strong Feet that followed, followed after.

It is an imitative style that has not been much imitated itself in serious poetry, except in one remarkable case: Oscar Wilde responded to Thompson's *Sister Songs* with 'That's what I've wanted to do all my life', and his last poem, *The Ballad of Reading Gaol* (1897), succeeds in borrowing the mixed and imprecise metaphorical style of *The Hound of Heaven* and turning it into a gripping amalgam of Decadent lyricism and brutal realism that produces one of the best poems of the 1890s. This is more than Thompson could have done, and it is incisively critical of both author and culture, which Thompson could never have been, but the poem could not have been written without Thompson's example.

Wilfrid Scawen Blunt (1840–1922) was another member of the Meynell circle, and the patient nurse of Thompson in his final illness; his own very different poems with their tempered hedonism and agnostic ironies are unfairly neglected, and his extravagant life with its commitments to Irish, Islamic and Indian independence is hardly remembered. He was the son of one of the most celebrated Catholic converts of the 1850s, and was brought up after his mother's death by tolerant and worldly relations instead of the bishop she had appointed as guardian. A surreptitious reading of Darwin convinced Blunt that, as 'The Happy Warrior' was to put it:

> . . . Life's law is this:
> Pleasure is duty, duty pleasure,
> In equal measure.

His verse argues the rightness of remaining an outsider, and the sober elegy on William Morris, one of those 'intent, untiring souls who proved time till their death', admonishes the reader to

> Dare to be last, least, in good modesty,
> Nor fret thy soul for speedier heritage.
> Even as he lived, live thou, laborious, sage,
> Yielding thy flower, leaf, fruitage, seasonably.

In time, Ezra Pound was to provide an even more exalted tribute to Blunt himself in the Pisan Cantos, where the senior poet becomes a symbol of honesty of craft and conscience:

> But to have done instead of not doing
>   this is not vanity
> To have, with decency, knocked
> That a Blunt should open
>   To have gathered from the air a live tradition
> or from a fine old eye the unconquered flame
> This is not vanity.

The dinner of roast peacock to which Blunt entertained the younger Yeats and Pound was an emblem of a tradition being passed on. Blunt preserved the line between the tense, ironic and urbane Byron and Crabbe and the intellectually fastidious Yeats and Pound, who believed with Blunt that 'human nature is an earthy fruit / Mired at the stem and fleshy at the root'. Blunt selected his influences carefully from among the detached observers of the Victorian scene; Clough's marvelling treatment of the sexual instinct, and Meredith's flair for dramatising the tension between intuition and experience in a young man's sentimental education. Blunt's sexual candour has nothing of Swinburne's extremism, nor the period's usual sense of a conflict between flesh and spirit; his love is 'of body and body', and the 'serious joy' of sexual pleasure teaches the one valuable moral lesson which is 'to learn the proportion of things' by obedience to the law: 'Learn to appraise thy desires, to weigh the wares of thy heart'. 'Happiness needs to be learned' in its 'habits and customs', but, once discovered, becomes a modern version of Romantic 'joy':

> He who has once been happy is for aye
> Out of destruction's reach. His future then
> Holds nothing secret, and Eternity
> Which is a mystery to other men
> Has, like a woman, given him its joy.

Blunt's considerable wit is usually muted in favour of the complex character studies of his narrative poems, and the discreet force of their moral meaning; his portrait of the unsatisfactory husband of his *Griselda* (1893) is as meticulously devastating as the best of Crabbe's writing, and as supple in its use of the couplet form. Blunt's unusual sensitivity to proportion made him a master of Byronic bathos ('An emigration plan to Newfoundland / Which ended in disaster, and a ball') and paradox, which he exploited featly in his sequence *In Vinculis* (1889), a meditation on the prison experiences endured in the cause of Irish independence, where the material that Wilde handled with baroque verve in *De Profundis* (1905) and *The Ballad of Reading Gaol* is treated with a cool discretion. Elements of Blunt make him akin to the poets of the 1890s; his sexual frankness, an element of Byronic pessimism underneath his hedonism, his paradoxes, and technical competency. But his passionate defence of the morally intuitive self places him firmly within the Romantic tradition.

James Thomson (1834–82), who styled himself variously 'B.V.' (for Bysshe Vanolis) or 'The Great Pitiable', wrote emphatic, densely imaged and sardonically morbid poetry that insists on his separation from humanity and his distrust of a malevolent natural world. As ehe put it in 'A Real Vision of Sin', with that cockney humour that anticipated Eliot in *The Waste Land*:

> We used to spree and we don't spree now;
> A screw is loose in the world, allow,
> *We* didn't make it, anyhow.

This 'obscure, dismal, bewildered and melancholy man . . . the laureate of pessimism', as he described himself, was the product of a narrowly Calvinist schooling (which explained his later atheism) and the child of a father himself subject to 'strange mental perturbations'. He was never to lack friends, though he eventually alienated his protectors and died a pauper as his character deteriorated through drink. Thomson was a pessimist through an excess of Romantic idealism; the girl-child whom he had loved died in her teens, and he identified himself as 'Vanolis' through the German Romantic poet Novalis, who had suffered a similar loss. Like many of the minor poets of the period, Thomson modelled his verse on earlier literature but choose unusually excellent or out of the way masters: Balzac and Stendhal, Coleridge, Blake, the American Walt Whitman (1819–92) and the Italian Romantic pessimist, Leopardi (1798–1837).

Thomson's most significant encounter was with Charles Bradlaugh (1833–91), the notorious social reformer of the late nineteenth century, who had run away from home and enlisted in the army where Thomson was serving as a schoolmaster. When Thomson was dishonourably discharged, Bradlaugh gave him a home and work on his weekly *National Reformer* ('Atheist in theology, Republican in politics, and Malthusian in social theory') which had a circulation of 8000 in 1874. Thomson was a witty and independent critic, championing the cause of Blake against Tennyson and the Victorian literary establishment, but he was inevitably evicted from Bradlaugh's household as an incorrigible problem, and wandered to America and Spain on a series of ill-fated jobs. His long poem *The City of Dreadful Night* was published in 1874, and eventually Thomson was forced to sever his connection with the secularists for bringing atheism into disrepute by his denial of human progress. The *Collected Poems* of 1880 sold unexpectedly well, but this brief Indian summer of critical acceptance and a second love was cut short by a return to his old addiction, and his death.

Thomson sees human beings as a noxious, negligible or pathetic species according to his mood; his sense of scale is of Darwinian proportions, involving vast landscapes and periods of time. He anticipated the metaphysical Italian painter Giorgio de Chirico (1888–1978) in his famous image of a clock without hands, and in his ominously depopulated urban landscapes, the emotional reverse of those in Keats's *Ode on a Grecian Urn*.

> The street-lamps burn amidst the baleful glooms,
> Amidst the soundless solitudes immense
> Of rangèd mansions dark and still as tombs.
>   The silence which benumbs or strains the sense
> Fulfils with awe the soul's despair unweeping;
> Myriads of habitants are ever sleeping,
>   Or dead, or fled from nameless pestilence!

Thomson is not a poet of subtle effects; his rhymes clang and jar, and his descriptions are mechanically exhaustive. But his poetry has in its outlines a challenging originality, and *The City of Dreadful Night* is a creditable addition to that long list of nineteenth-century apocalyptic literature which developed in a time of misgivings about rapid political change and a too intense subjectivity. Thomson's poem has its roots in Blake's visions, Byron's battle-pieces and his 'Darkness', Hood's 'The Last Man', Carlyle's social prophecy and the tirades of Ruskin, Browning's 'Childe Roland', Tennyson's 'Locksley Hall Sixty Years After', Hopkins's *The Wreck of the Deutschland*, and the genre culminates in T. S. Eliot's *The Waste Land* (1922), with its retrospective vision of the genuine apocalypse of the Great War. The effects of Eliot are anticipated in the less ambitious and more approachable shorter poems of Thomson: 'A Real Vision of Sin' and 'In the Room', the first using imagery of startling bravado and incongruity (the sky 'spongy and lax' like 'a soaking blanket'), visions of doomed crowds on their meaningless rounds, and a cynically demotic speech. 'In the Room', Thomson's finest single achievement, has the pieces of furniture in a rented chamber discuss the former occupants in the manner of Hardy's poems; the body of a suicide is revealed only incidentally. It is an imaginative *tour de force* similar to that of the discovery of Esther's father in Dickens's *Bleak House*, or the painted symbol of maddening loss in *The Yellow Chair* (1888) by Vincent Van Gogh (1853–90). Thomson at his best is close to the surrealists; a gratifyingly ambitious poet willing to strive for grand effects and a total view of human existence in an age increasingly committed to minute details of stylistic refinement.

Robert Bridges (1844–1930), poet laureate from 1913, was an artist of more conventional temperament, with habits of severity and understatement that matched his leonine good looks, the 'dedicated charm' of his country estate, and his English traits of cold baths, emotional reticence and distrust of Rome. His friend Gerard Manley Hopkins's conversion caused a serious breach between them, not repaired until 1877, and the Hopkins side of their subsequent correspondence survives as an invaluable guide to the greater poet's inner life and ability to hold his own under the patronage of one who was the self-conscious and superficial heir of Tennyson. Bridges saw Hopkins's poems through the press in 1918, and is more famous by this act than through his own neglected art.

Bridges reacted against the torrent of feeling in Swinburne and Rossetti, writing gravely circumspect elegies and natural descriptions of an inattentively observed, 'literary' turn, full of 'fruitful valleys', 'starry woods', 'sweet-springing meads and bursting boughs of May'. The anthology-piece 'London Snow' has none of the nervy exhilaration of Hardy's birdlike dartings after imagery in 'Snow in the Suburbs'; Bridges is gratified by the snow's ability to deaden raw sensation as it falls, 'hiding difference, making unevenness even'. He has Arnold's austerity without his saving inconsistency, and it was not a state of mind which Hopkins, with his habitual praise of 'dappled things' and 'the horror and the havoc and the glory' could share; he maintained stoutly that what Bridges praised as 'severe' was in fact merely 'bald'. Like Hopkins, Bridges carried on elaborate metrical experiments, but where Hopkins sought to give poetry the range and urgency of the human voice, Bridges's mannerisms have the air of a stammer adopted for effect.

The Testament of Beauty (1929), an agnostic's defence, was purchased more than read in its time, and Bridges's best poems are his shorter ones. Like Hopkins, Bridges was not a committed Victorian; whereas Hopkins sought a Romantic fulness of feeling, Bridges's tastes for generalisation and decorum lay within the tradition of retirement in eighteenth-century poetry. His anachronistic and public art is seen at its best in three elegies which refine personal feeling in the spirit of Landor, but argue the vanity of human wishes in the neatest Augustan fashion. 'Elegy on a Lady Whom Grief for the Death of the Betrothed Killed' is a grave marriage-song, with Bridges's characteristic insubstantiality turned to good dramatic account:

> . . . on the banks of forgetful streams
> The pale indifferent ghosts wander, and snatch
> The sweeter moments of their broken dreams.

'The Summer-House on the Mound' is an elegy for Victorianism itself, a glad recollection of childhood that modulates into a Tennysonian warning against a baleful change in national mood. The house of infancy has become a convent, and the windows that gave out on the English Channel and its navy are now a blank, the inhabitants promised to profitless introspection. The poet's prejudices limit the force of the poem, but the balance between personal and impersonal elements has the appealing exactitude of Samuel Johnson's *The Vanity of Human Wishes* (1749). 'Elegy Among the Tombs' is a quest for escape from 'the world my solemn fancy leaves behind', and an apologia for Bridges's discriminating preference for the secluded, rural and intellectual good life, in an age that was becoming the creation of the advertising man and the noisy patriot.

Andrew Lang (1844–1912) had the Aesthetic ability to handle language with delicacy and charm without any desire to stir emotion or rouse a social conscience. He took a deprecating view of the literary arts, viewing them as useful tranquillising agents in an age when science engrossed the intellect; an attitude he described as 'Alexandrian', after the poetry of the Hellenistic decadence (c. 300–260 BC), and by the 1890s the cultivated purity of taste he exemplified was supplanted by the emotional morbidity of the Decadence itself.

Lang was what William Morris might have been without his driving energy and the ethical demands of his socialism; a man of wide interests and rapid intelligence, a translator of several European literatures, spinner of long, vapidly classical narrative poems in the manner of Leigh Hunt, an amateur of anthropology, history and book design, and deeply appreciative of the comfort and beauty of his privileged life. His epicureanism irritated the stronger talents of his time, and Henry James spoke for many in belittling 'his cultivation, absolutely, of the puerile imagination and the fourth-rate opinion'.

Lang was a Scot working within the English tradition as an essayist, poet and folklorist. His neat *Ballads in Blue China* (1873), following his *Ballads and Lyrics of Old France and Other Poems* (1872) indicated his approval of French mediaevalism and the fashionable orientalism of the time when collections of porcelain popularised by Rossetti, Whistler and Wilde needed to be 'lived up to' by wealthy amateurs. Lang was fluent and graceful as a minor essayist, often completing his assignments – he wrote for every periodical of distinction after his early retirement from academic life – at the staff meetings when they were handed out. But he was handicapped for serious writing by an inability to survive criticism or to contemplate any kind of suffering. He preferred to approach life through its decorations, as a true Aesthete.

> I have lived with the earliest Apostles of Culture, in the days when Chippendale was first a name to conjure with, and Japanese art came in like a raging lion, and Ronsard was the favourite poet, and Mr William Morris was a poet too, and blue and green were the only wear, and Paradise was Camelot.

Lang would hardly be remembered today were it not for his admirable and enduring *Fairy Books* (1889–1910), actually written under his editorial supervision by a host of translators, and illustrated in a careful, Pre-Raphaelite manner. These tales, nominally for children, were understood by Lang as a code through which momentous secrets about human nature were conveyed; a Romantic belief first given voice by the German poet Schiller, when he wrote that 'Deeper meaning resides in the fairy tales told me in my childhood than in all the truth that is taught by life'. As an academic, Lang was deeply involved in the elucidation of such hidden knowledge, and in the 1890s he was president of the Society for Psychical Research, which was to number the psychiatrists Freud and Jung among its members.

The better qualities of Lang were magnified in the achievement (not recommending itself to all tastes) of his fellow-countryman J. M. Barrie (1860–1937), where a tender reversion to the fantasies of childhood and an overwhelming desire to create oases of psychological comfort were balanced by sudden provoking and disturbing outbursts about tensions within the most outwardly happy individuals and families. 'Mr Lang', mused Barrie, approvingly, 'puzzled the Sassenach a little. Perhaps this is the first duty of a Scot.'

George du Maurier (1834–96) also worked the vein of nostalgia as a sentimental romantic novelist and as an illustrator of surpassing talent, who made the diversions of high life as glamorous in magazine illustration as they were in the paintings of the gifted James Tissot (1836–1902), whose own extraordinary career resembled a du Maurier novel, with its mysteriously sequestered mistress, elegant villa, and retreat to a religious vocation at the height of his powers. Both artists were specialists in what Ruskin contemptuously called 'vulgar society', with its late-Victorian combination of elegance, trumpery opulence and profligacy which was stringently analysed in the novels of Henry James. Du Maurier's illustrations gracefully lampooned the excesses of Aesthetic taste and invented a new female type, the antithesis of the rosebud beauty of the 1860s; 'tall, straight-backed, square-shouldered, deep-chested', at home on a bicycle or in a ballroom, in a Burne-Jones painting or with the New Women of Girton College.

The descendant of a family of French emigrés with no claim to their aristocratic title, he perfected his style of *le vrai chic anglais* while at school in France, and was admired in the highest English circles for his polished demeanour and conversation. He was a close friend of Henry James, a similarly Olympian interloper, and his life (in a period when fiction and reality were often confused) came to resemble the *donnée* of a Jamesian novel: the runaway success of *Trilby* (1894), the romance of an artist's model hypnotised into an operatic diva by the malignant Svengali, so threatened the perilous stability of this secretly neurotic man that the loss of his privacy shortened his life. His close-knit and devoted family displayed a continuity of talent common in nineteenth-century France but rare in England; his son Gerald pioneered a new, naturalistically nervous throwaway style of acting that supplanted the melodrama of the late Victorian stage (which had reached one of its high points in Beerbohm Tree's portrayal of Svengali). A grand-daughter, Daphne, continued the tradition of best-selling, actable novels that mingled historical romance, wish-fulfilment and glamorous criminality in surroundings of the utmost luxury.

When partial blindness prevented du Maurier from becoming a painter, he became Thackeray's natural successor at the *Punch* table, developing an instantly recognisable and heavily 'literary' cartoon humour where the careful drawings conveyed an impossible ideal of elegance and hauteur, and the elaborate captions were spiced with black humour, class snobbery and social embarrassment. Occasionally the self-conscious pastiches of Thackeray have the original's high spirits and self-mockery, but more often du Maurier is touchingly in love with his own illusions.

Du Maurier's fiction has its roots in the Newgate novel: his Peter Ibbetson, 'a convict and a criminal lunatic . . . who has had unrivalled opportunities for mixing with the cream of English society', is a later version of Bulwer Lytton's Eugene Aram, while Svengali is a cheaply potent version of Dickens's Fagin in *Oliver Twist*. The old fascination with criminal intelligence had a renewal in the 1890s, with the importing of the French Romantic tradition of the artist as a damned soul. In addition, du Maurier loved the popular *Scènes de la vie de bohème* (1845) by the lawyer's clerk Henri Murger (1822–61); tender pastorals of the lives of poverty-stricken artists and poets and their working-class mistresses and models, which survive today in the 'realistic' forms they inspired; Puccini's *verismo* opera *La Bohème* (1896) and the early novels of George Gissing. Murger helped to invent the myth of the artist as a natural aristocrat, whose unrewarded talent justified his treachery towards a philistine bourgeoisie. The popularity of these formulae in the 1890s underlines the developing gulf between a general public and the refined practitioners of art.

Du Maurier yearned to be a writer like the hero of his preposterous *The Martian* (1897), a fable of reincarnation and astral travel, in which a handsome young Englishman pens a consolatory story 'as universal as the Lord's Prayer'. But literature remained an enigma to this instinctive author, who portrayed himself in *Trilby* as 'a mere light amuser', and 'a wretched little over-rated follower of a poor trivial craft'. His highly imperfect fictions can still be enjoyed for their enchanting period illustrations and their natty epigrams, and valued for their outspokenness about the often baleful relationship between a writer and his frivolous and demanding public.

The hero as Punch: two iconoclasts

Samuel Butler (1835–1902) is remembered as a one-book man; *The Way of All Flesh*, begun in 1873, was published a year after his death. The jaunty but psychologically acute history of an amiably befogged young man's progress from the hypocritical religiosity of his parents to a cheerful unbelieving worldliness was a Victorian *Candide*. Its subject of the results of an appalling misconceived education was essentially that of Byron's *Don Juan*, Mill's *Autobiography*, Meredith's *The Ordeal of Richard Feverel* and Edmund Gosse's vengeful contemporary memoir, *Father and Son* (1907), but Butler's approach was comic, even when the matter was most painful. His gleeful iconoclasm, and the disclosure that the choicest imbecilities were drawn from life in the Butler parsonage, obscured the formal shapeliness of the novel and Butler's brilliant mixture of empathy and resentment; for generations *The Way of All Flesh* was loved for what it admitted as much as for what it was, and set the tone for many mocking revaluations of the Victorian age.

Nevertheless, *The Way of All Flesh* remains a quintessentially Victorian work; the recalling of a painful childhood is a common set-piece in the novels of Dickens, the Brontës, Thackeray and George Eliot. Butler provides his own version of signal moments in post-Romantic literature; from Wordsworth's grave demonstration of how the art of lying may be taught to a bewildered but inoffensive child, to George Eliot's demonstration of the power of history and heredity over the individual personality, to Carlyle's autobiography of moral improvement, and Dickens's fondness for comic monsters and cockney comedians. Bernard Shaw, who had offered similar fictions to the public in advance of the fashion set by Butler, praised his successful rival handsomely:

> Butler is the only man known to history who has immortalised and actually endeared himself by parricide and matricide long drawn out. He slew the good name (and it was such a very good name!) of his father and mother so reasonably, so wittily, so humorously, and even in a ghastly way so charitably, that he convinced us he was engaged in an execution and not in a murder.

Butler's own character was not as charming as that of his Ernest Pontifex. After his escape from the parental home, he became a dilettante whose narrow and exclusive passions for the composer Handel (1685–1759) and a clutch of early Italian painters barely concealed his inherited philistinism. The child of a Machiavellian mother had learned to be untrusting in his dealings with people, and he was alternately gullible and treacherous, possibly inclined to his own sex, but too selfish to look for much beyond his bachelor comforts. He was a blend of the disconcertingly perceptive and the deliberately obtuse, exquisite in his analysis of how the members of his own family had become what they were, but regarding the lower orders and all foreigners as not quite human creatures provided for his amusement; Dickens had invented Butler's type in Mr Meagles of *Little Dorrit*. Butler's unharnessed intelligence was dangerous, and Charles Darwin, a notable victim of one who 'hated' prominent men as a diversion, regarded Butler as 'thoroughly unscrupulous'.

Erewhon (1872) rides Butler's crotchets to death in an intermittently amusing way, as does its sequel, *Erewhon Revisited* (1901). The whimsical inversions of custom, particularly the treatment of the sick as criminals and the criminals as sick, and the generally Gilbertian satire on late

Victorian manners, are more attractive in outline than in development, and Butler's minor works, including his travel books, are often foolish in the extreme.

The Way of All Flesh remains an elegant farce that anticipates Lytton Strachey's landmark in iconoclasm; *Eminent Victorians* (1918) takes up the key virtues of the age and demonstrates their latent viciousness in language that, like Butler's, abuses the typical cadences of the period. Morally speaking, *The Way of All Flesh* identifies itself with that genre most abhorrent to Victorian moralists from Macaulay onwards, the Restoration comedy of the playhouses reopened after the puritan interregnum, which discriminates wittily and boldly between an hypocrisy that deserves unmasking and a polite discretion in pursuit of natural pleasures: *The Way of All Flesh* has half of its title and most of its outlook in common with *The Way of the World* (1700) by William Congreve (1670–1729).

George Bernard Shaw (1856–1950), first novelist, then critic, and finally dramatist, made his reputation as a jester like Butler, to whom nothing was sacred. 'It was as Punch', he recalled, 'that I emerged from obscurity.' Shaw cultivated the pose of the audacious unbeliever, but his own puritanism was offended by the 'blank materialist Hedonist atheism' of Butler, and his comedy was intended as seriously as that of his masters, Mozart and Molière (1622–73). 'By laughter only', he wrote, 'can you destroy evil without malice, and affirm good fellowship without mawkishness.' Great art, and particularly that of the theatre, was 'a factory of thought, a prompter of conscience, an elucidator of social conduct, an armoury against despair and dulness', and never a refuge from intellectual activity or an escape into 'an imaginary past, an imaginary heroism, an imaginary poetry'.

Shaw had a thoroughly Romantic conception of the artist, drawn from his models in the poet Shelley and the Norwegian dramatist Henrik Ibsen, as a risk-taker in the service of 'unsatisfied younger generations' compelled to mount to 'heights that now seem unspeakably giddy and dreadful to him, and from which the first climbers must fall and dash themselves to pieces'. He had Coleridge's conviction that 'a work of art is a growth, and not a construction', and so ignored the cast-iron conventions of the 'well-made play'. Like

Wordsworth, he was a Romantic puritan, feeling that the business of the writer was to educate and exhort by 'energy and elevation of spirit', and to draw attention to those unique moments of insight in which the individual is aware of eternal truths and universal brotherhood. For Shaw, these versions of Wordsworth's 'spots of time' occurred through the arts rather than in the natural world, to which he was largely indifferent; in Mozart's *Don Giovanni* and Wagner's *Parsifal* where music and stage illusion put an enchanted but alert audience in possession of 'those pregnant simplicities which stare the world in the face for centuries and yet are never pointed out except by great men'. Shaw the iconoclast was prepared to venerate a long line of heroes as candidly as his original master, Carlyle, who had felt similarly drawn to and repelled by contradictory aspects of Romanticism. Shaw was to defend Ibsen and Wagner against English prejudice; he revered William Morris as his political and intellectual father, and exalted John Bunyan above Shakespeare, for the 'life, strength, resolution, morning air and eternal youth' of his strenuous parable of moral growth, *The Pilgrim's Progress* (1678).

Shaw was born into a family of genteel but poor Dublin Protestants; his father was incapacitated by drink, and the talented, strong-minded and unemotional mother took her children and followed her manager and singing-teacher to London in 1873. Shaw, who had been a clerk in Dublin, set about writing novels while living on his mother's slender means; of the five he completed only the amiably clever *Cashel Byron's Profession* (1882) 'crept into print through the back door of a Socialist magazine', and in nine years he had earned only as many pounds. But Socialism was shaping his career as it had done that of William Morris, now his mentor. The Fabian Society, developed by Shaw and Beatrice and Sidney Webb (1858–1947), proposed the achievement by 'the inevitability of gradualness' of the supposedly necessary and peaceful sequels to universal suffrage: the abolition of private property, equality of income, and the emancipation of women. The late-developing, gawky youth, 'raw from eighteenth-century Ireland', and feeling 'like a peasant in the drawing-room', cured his shyness by pitching himself into street-corner political rallies and becoming an outspoken popular journalist.

'Corno di Bassetto' was the critic for 'a hapenny newspaper

. . . not catering for a fastidious audience', and under his ridiculous pseudonym Shaw took the mystery out of music, painting and the theatre for readers like Mr Pooter and his neighbours in George (1847–1912) and Weedon (1854–1919) Grossmith's endearing *Diary of a Nobody* (1892); London clerks who joined bicycle clubs and frequented music halls. He paid dry tribute to the 'positive popular attractions' of newspaper criticism with 'its cruelty, its gladiatorship, and the gratification given to envy', and this successor to Hazlitt had the same gusto and cultivated prejudices, as well as a Romantic taste for pugilism, but a cooler judgement: even when Shaw sounds his most captious in his abuse of Brahms (1833–97) and Shakespeare, he bases his aversion on a detailed knowledge of cultural history. His reviews give an exact sense of the fleeting occasions of theatre and concert room, and a bad performance leads to a vigorous analysis of the reasons for the defects and the remedies to be applied; he writes buoyantly of dreadful evenings, but never in the merely belittling spirit of his amusing minor successor, Max Beerbohm. His greatest critical essays – on Shelley, Bunyan and Mozart – are achievements equal to his plays: the series on his visit to Bayreuth, for example, are slippery mixtures of irreverence and genuine emotion.

At least three of Shaw's novels remain very readable, given that he ignored them in later life; a little more success in the traditional field of fiction could have ruined him as a dramatist. *Love Among the Artists* (1881) is more thoroughly experimental than anything of Butler's, and Shaw acknowledged a debt to the quizzical anti-Romanticism of his almost forgotten countryman, the novelist Charles Lever (1806–72). As a novelist, Shaw has deep affinities with Trollope, whose early history resembled his own; both writers develop character through a fine ear for naturalistic dialogue, and expose hypocrisy, social counterfeit, and the folly of modelling life on escapist literature. Both rejected fiction where 'the lover is the hero and the husband only the wife's mistake', as Shaw phrased it, and each is fascinated by the incompatibility of daily living and cherished secret ideals, while paying tribute to the supreme importance of work.

Cashel Byron's Profession was the first of Shaw's economic romances, analysing the effect of money and class upon the sexual instinct; *An Unsocial Socialist* (1884) developed that genre to a pitch of outrageous and good-humoured absurdity, following which, Shaw wandered into his career as a dramatist. This began as a failed collaboration with his fellow critic, the translator of Ibsen, William Archer. When it became clear that Shaw's theories of play construction were far in advance of Archer's purely conventional mechanics, Shaw was left to finish *Widowers' Houses* (1892) alone; it became the first of three Unpleasant Plays, and the start of Shaw's major career. 'You cannot write three plays and then stop', he explained.

Shaw prided himself on his modernity, even if it guaranteed eventual obsolescence. Yet his constant reference to contemporary manners and problems is built upon a meticulous understanding of layers of European culture; Shaw's desire to emancipate himself from provincial narrowness and allude to a boundless heritage resembles the art of James Joyce, another self-exile from Ireland. Shaw had no patience with the Aesthetes: works had to be judged by 'the depth and moral dignity of their conception' rather than their incidental graces. Nor did Irish nationalism in literature attract him; the underrated and bitterly ironic *John Bull's Other Island* (1904) is a swingeing attack on 'the dreaming' that so attracted Yeats and his contemporaries. For Shaw, the great events of contemporary culture were taking place elsewhere in Europe, in Germany and Scandinavia in particular, and he devoted himself to making Englishmen aware of them.

'Exact estimates of life': naturalism and the novel

When George Moore made notes on his room-mate's infatuation and enrolled himself in a provincial theatre company to get background for his first major novel, and when George Gissing visited his Nether World by the more traumatic route of prison and poverty, the pioneers of French 'naturalism' in the English novel were not copying the inhumane detachment of Edmond Goncourt (1822–96) and his brother Jules (1830–70) in *Germinie Lacerteux* (1864) and *Soeur Philomène* (1890), those self-conscious examples of the '*humble roman*'. Moore and Gissing treated men and women in their social context not in a reductive spirit, but as an attempt to trace the origin of motive more precisely and compassionately; as Walter Pater had explained in his *Appreciations* (1889):

> The relative spirit has invaded moral philosophy from the ground of the inductive sciences. There it has started a new analysis of the relations of body and mind, good and evil, freedom and necessity. Hard and abstract moralities are yielding to a more exact estimate of the subtlety and complexity of our life.

George Moore (1852–1933) was a protean literary figure; an uncanny exploiter of a contradictory variety of European styles, who became the apostle of naturalism in the English novel and finally the forerunner of such subjective writers as Virginia Woolf and D. H. Lawrence.

The awkward and ill-educated son of a wealthy Irish landlord, Moore became a painter and roué in Paris as soon as he came into his inheritance, and after seven years began writing in London under the spell of the French realists. By 1900 he had taken an interest in the Irish literary renaissance and moved back to Dublin, but within ten years he had quarrelled with the Church and the literary establishment and returned to England. His career spanned fifty years, and his remarkable absence of a personal style or permanent strong convictions enabled him to remain the pure medium through which European influences reached the insular English writer in prose.

Moore's reading of Zola and Flaubert 'inebriated' him with a new understanding of human motive in fiction: 'Change the surroundings in which a man lives, and in two or three generations, you will have changed his physical constitution, his habits of life, and a goodly number of his ideas', he quoted excitedly in his introduction to *A Mummer's Wife* (1885). Zola's realism promised more than George Eliot's early Positivism had dared: 'a new art based on science', Moore wrote; 'an art that should explain all things and embrace modern life in its entirety'. *A Mummer's Wife* combined Zola's social determinism and Flaubert's anti-Romanticism in the story of an imaginatively starved provincial wife who is drawn into the casual make-believe of the theatre and left without moral support. But by the end of the novel, Moore's desire to be 'Zola's ricochet in England' had flagged, and he rejected the 'odious pessimism' of Flaubert's blend of cynicism and pathos.

Balzac's 'winged realism' in which individuals elect quite deliberately to become members of the social process and so subject to its determinism had a greater long-term effect on Moore's fiction, with its fundamental respect for individual integrity and resilience.

In his later novels, Moore mingled his early naturalism – a close observation of how the environment influences personality – with a musical prose and a subjective outlook. This paradoxical blending of qualities was the hallmark of the French Impressionist painters, who saw objects scientifically under the influence of certain conditions of light and atmosphere, but had no inhibitions about adding a personal emotionalism and lyricism, as in the famous record of his garden at Giverny by Claude Monet (1840–1926). Moore argued that his realism was the most moral form of art, since it involved an unremitting process of decision-making; which facts were necessary, and which could be omitted without damage to the total truth of his narrative. *Esther Waters* (1894) was designed as a rebuke to Hardy's *Tess of the D'Urbervilles*, where the heroine was deliberately aggrandised by Hardy's poetry and his favourable presentation of her plight; Moore's story of a beaten-down servant girl trying to fend for herself and her illegitimate son allows for neither triumph nor tragedy, and the emotional caution of the novel is curious rather than attractive.

> All was forgotten in the happiness of that moment – the long fight for his life, and the possibility that any moment might declare him to be mere food for powder and shot. She was only conscious that she had accomplished her woman's work – she had brought him up to man's estate; and that was her sufficient reward.

Moore is one of those writers like Henry James and Meredith (other favourites of the avant-garde of the 1890s) who wrote by choice about the female consciousness, and had great faith in its power of withstanding social tyranny. *A Drama in Muslin* (1886), one of the novels by which Moore is still known in an age of comparative neglect, is a bleak study of Irish society as it portrays débutantes in the marriage market; it is close to Ibsen in its fine depiction of young women becoming sceptical of the adjustments of conscience they are asked to make. Moore's heroines, like those of Shaw and

James, affront their destinies and take their futures into their own hands in a way that runs counter to his early naturalism.

Moore's most consistent literary debt is to Turgenev, another writer who oscillated between two cultures; that of his native Russia where he too had been the son of a landowner, and that of his adopted France. Moore was deeply attached to the themes of Turgenev; the vulnerability and strength of the individual, whose sensibility is explored through a Romantic awareness of natural beauty and a deep sense of national identity. In his fiction, Moore makes constant reference (both conscious and unconscious) to *Fathers and Sons* and *A Nest of Gentlefolk* (written between 1850 and 1861): *The Untilled Field* (1903) is purely in the spirit of Turgenev. The rest of Moore's literary background is explored in the raffish autobiographical period studies, *The Confessions of a Young Man* (1888) and its eventual sequel, *Hail and Farewell* (1911–14). *Hail and Farewell* is an unbuttoned semi-fictional self-portrait, full of handsomely indulged prejudices, Shelleyan Romanticism ('my perverse mind, prone to sympathise with every revolt against common law') and a genuine love of reading. It is written in the form of an eloquent and irreverent soliloquy, occasionally directed by an unseen interviewer, in the manner of Browning's dramatic monologues.

George Gissing (1857–1903) whose sad, unwisely managed life was as melancholy as anything in his fiction, was 'a damaged, joy-loving human being', according to the more successful exploiter of the same subject-matter of low life and intellectual aspiration, H. G. Wells. Gissing wrote best when his life was most hopeless, and human misery and cruelty 'haunted him in the night', as he wrote in his *Commonplace Book*. 'I do not love the people', wrote the son of a Wakefield druggest. 'But my passion of sympathy for the suffering poor!'

With the death of his father, the thirteen-year-old Gissing became the focus of his family's hopes, and a successful scholarship pupil at a Manchester college. Just before he would have gone to university, he was summarily expelled for theft; he had stolen from his fellow-students to prevent a working-girl with whom he had a liaison from taking to the streets. He was sentenced to a month in gaol, and after a period of destitution in America and England following his release, he married the girl, sank into the lower class and began writing *Workers in the Dawn* (1880) which mingled his idealistic socialism and a contempt for the abyss just below his precarious decency. The marriage failed, and he lived apart from his disturbed and alcoholic wife while tutoring and writing a succession of working-class novels while he crept back to middle-class respectability. In 1890 he produced a grim exposé of the unfashionable end of the literary world in *New Grub Street*, and the next year made a second unsuitable marriage to a woman from a superior class; despite his unhappiness in his domestic life, *The Odd Women*, a compassionate study of the surplus female population, came out in 1892. By 1894 Gissing's career was prospering in a quiet way; his third, informal marriage to a sympathetic Frenchwoman removed him from the roots of his imaginative life. *The Private Papers of Henry Ryecroft* (1903) is the fantasy of the kind of man Gissing would have liked to have been; studious, sentimental, and rich enough for a country cottage where he could have been cared for kindly while he read great literature. There is something infinitely touching about Gissing's permanent awe of a caste and its culture from which he had been so cruelly excluded; his life has more than a touch of Hardy's *Jude the Obscure* about it.

Gissing consoled himself with the thought that his narratives of a working class trying to better itself but sinking back into squalor and discouragement would eventually achieve the status of Dickens's novels, which he had praised with more energy than perception in a critical study of 1898. In fact, Gissing's literary reputation went into an undeserved decline after his death, and when George Orwell resumed Gissing's style and subject-matter in the 1930s, he remarked indignantly that his predecessor was available only in 'soup-stained editions from public libraries'.

Gissing remains the most severe analyst of class differences in England at a time when such distinctions were not rigid, but usually based on mere appearances; respectability was proved by the wearing of a hat and the absence of a 'made-up' tie, having the price of a cab-fare, or owning an umbrella. Whereas Dickens and Kingsley had evoked the miseries of the underclass from their own secure position in the middle class, Gissing in his novels knows and fears the gutter; his attitude to the class into which his own mistaken altruistic idealism had temporarily dropped him was intriguingly ambivalent. On the one hand, as in the savage 'Io Saturnalia' chapter of *The Nether World* (1889) he saw the working class as brutal, dangerous and unreachable; on the other, he fastened on some of its more promising members who deserved to be helped towards culture and civility. For a social novelist, Gissing is surprisingly indifferent to questions of economics; he was at his best, like Elizabeth Gaskell, when depicting the daily life of the very poor in careful detail, and he was not above romanticising that of his favoured characters, in the manner of the French novelist Murger to whom he was addicted. Gissing, the most intuitive of writers, adhered to no intellectual system, and devoted himself to individuals rather than to classes. His permanent subject is the dangerous but powerful human urge to improve and offer help to one's fellows, and in his gentle and disorganised way he continues to ponder the central themes of George Eliot's *Middlemarch*, and in particular, the character of her egocentric altruist Lydgate.

'Sad company': Pater and the poets of the 1890s

Walter Pater (1839–94), retiring, self-conscious but notorious, was the mediator between the Oxford Movement of the 1830s and a new, secular aestheticism. He was the inheritor of Matthew Arnold's cult of urbanity, liberal values and a respect for European intellect, and ultimately of Coleridge's cherishing of the free imagination as the agent for discerning the ideal moral life.

The early deaths of Pater's parents led to his pervading sense of loss and the transience of all effort and emotion. Henry James called him 'the mask without the face', for his famous reticence; the witty critic Max Beerbohm described his celebrated, whispered lectures as 'a sort of self-communion', and W. H. Mallock (1849–1923) caricatured him as 'Mr Rose' in *The New Republic* (1877), a Peacockian satire on late Victorian literary life. As a young man Pater had been profoundly influenced by Keble, and had wanted to become a poet-priest; at Oxford he studied French and German philosophy and resigned his tutorship in 1881 to write *Marius the Epicurean* (1885), whose luxuriant prose conceals an austere evaluation of those sensations which, if dwelt on, lead to a perception of the truth. Subsequent generations of readers have confused Pater's Aestheticism with that languid and amoral attitude summed up in Swinburne's deliberately provocative sentence: 'A beautiful line drawn is more than a life saved; a pleasant perfume smelt is more than a soul redeemed'. But Pater's own theory of art came more from the strenuous self-criticism of Arnold than the sensuousness of Rossetti or the doctrine of 'art for art's sake' developed in France by Théophile Gautier (1811–72), the forerunner of the Decadents.

Pater argued in *Marius* and elsewhere that the appreciation of all art must be personal and direct, and without any preconceptions or external standards of excellence. The object of all aesthetic cultivation was the understanding of the self, and life could be immeasureably enriched by 'a power of distinguishing and fixing delicate and fugitive detail'. This owed much to the Hegelian theory of *Geist* popular in Oxford at the time; a principle of constant and purposeful evolution under the guise of random change.

Pater was to develop Arnold's theory of Hebraic and Hellenic states of mind, without any of Arnold's residual sympathy for the uncultivated moral sense. Pater's Hellenism (adapted from nineteenth-century Germanic thought) was the desirable and serene possession of a detached and flexible intelligence. Arnold had praised the individual striving for moral and imaginative excellence as a means of improving the community as a whole; Pater, more pessimistically, felt that the individual could not be expected to act upon society. Both Pater and Arnold justified their aesthetic position by pointing to the great achievements of periods when the nature of man had been most fully developed: fifth-century Athens, Antonine Rome, and the Renaissance itself (a period that was starting, by the 1870s, to displace the Middle Ages as an imaginative resource for Victorian writers). In his essay on 'The School of Giorgione' in *The Renaissance* (1877), Pater made the highest claim he was to urge for the aesthetic consciousness:

> a mere gesture, a look, a smile perhaps – some brief and wholly concrete moment – into which, however, all the interests and effects of a long history have condensed themselves, and which seem to absorb past and present in an intense consciousness of the present.

Such a judgement is a rationale of naturalism in art as well as aestheticism, and is far from whimsically subjective. For all Pater's stress on personal reaction, he was deeply concerned with the value of the work of art he was criticising; not, like his superficial disciple Oscar Wilde, with the engaging display of his own taste. Art began for Pater, as for Wordsworth long before, in 'the deep places of the mind', and he claimed for criticism that degree of creativity usually only allowed to poetry: each art was the result of 'impassioned contemplation'. In his Preface to *Lyrical Ballads,* Wordsworth had insisted on the need for the simultaneous revolutionising of poetry and criticism, and by Coleridge's example, critical writing became a key expression of Romantic thought and feeling. Nevertheless, Pater's criticism at the end of the century lacks the authority of Arnold, who had assured external standards: Pater's doctrine of pure relativity was inevitably misunderstood and watered-down by his followers.

The Decadent poets of the 1890s transmuted Pater's originally austere theory of art based on a rigorous attentiveness to individual sensation into a quest for sensation itself. Their verse, febrile in its subject-matter and rigidly disciplined in expression, traced a wavering course back to the beginnings of English Romanticism. They were the immediate heirs of Rossetti, who had explored those moments when the familiar world dissolves into a mystical apprehension of eternity; in Rossetti's version of Romanticism, Wordsworth's 'spots of time' were no longer the privileged insights provided by nature itself, but deliberately courted states of mind. The Decadents sought to make such heightened awareness a permanent condition, seeking it through perverse and destructive loves and addictions, and an appreciation of a 'gorgeous iridescence of decay' in the manner of Baudelaire and the French symbolists, Paul Verlaine (1844–96) and Arthur Rimbaud (1854–91), or the 'gusty gaslight' of the cheap theatres painted so atmospherically by the English Impressionist Walter Sickert (1860–1942). Inevitably, as the vision failed, the poet was left with a nauseated weariness that was valuable in itself, and captured with a wry, paradoxically classical self-deprecation in the Decadent irony of Ernest Dowson (1867–1900):

> I cried for madder music and for stronger wine,
> But when the feast is finished and the lamps expire,
> Then falls thy shadow, Cynara! the night is thine;
> And I am desolate and sick of an old passion,
>   Yea hungry for the lips of my desire:
> I have been faithful to thee, Cynara! in my fashion.

Knowingly or not, the poets of the 1890s rediscovered some of the attitudes of early Romanticism; in particular, a radical simplification of verse into the form of the ballad and the lyric. They felt that conventional poetry was no longer expressing current emotions – scepticism, and the fear of a divided world – and while they clung to the exalted view of the poet that had lasted through Tennyson and Arnold and become reinforced through a new awareness of the French Romantic tradition, they experimented with the subject-matter and language of the deprived classes. This was hardly done in a Wordsworthian spirit. Many influential poets had become acquainted with working-class life in pursuit of their sexual inclinations, and this in part explains their mingled admiration and fear of a world indifferent to beauty; the very unlikeness of London poverty to the imaginative universe of Rossetti, Burne-Jones and Japanese art made it a challenge to poetry and ripe for transformation into something rich and strange by a potent art.

> Within the town, the streets grow strange and haunted,
>   And, dark against the western lakes of green,
> The buildings change to temples, and unwonted
>   Shadows and sounds creep in where day has been.
> Within the town, the lamps of sin are flaring,
>   Poor foolish men that know not what ye are!
> Tired traffic still upon his feet is faring–
>   Two lovers meet and kiss and watch a star.

This quotation from 'Sunset in the City' (1892) by Richard Le Gallienne (1866–1947) is a representative example of this detached, aesthetic view of urban life; it could not be more different from the ironic compassion of the arresting and terrible art of John Davidson (1857–1909), the atheist son of a Scottish minister, who drifted from his fellow members of the Rhymer's Club to an interpretation of the uncompromising philosophy of Friedrich Nietzsche (1844–1900). His 'Thirty Bob a Week' (1894), which made such an impression on T. S.

Eliot, is the monologue of a London clerk that is closer to the impersonal stoicism of Wordsworth's symbolic Leech-Gatherer in *Resolution and Independence*, than to the working-class ventriloquism of Rudyard Kipling in *Barrack-Room Ballads* (1892). Davidson, who drowned himself at the age of fifty-three, is the most strongly talented associate of the Decadents who dealt in small emotions carefully amplified; Davidson chooses the immense social canvas of James Thomson, but applies himself with a delicate Decadent artistry to its minute details, and his irony is not a weary pose, but a bitter conclusion to his observations.

The Decadence was, like Romanticism of which it was a part, a European phenomenon: Max Nordau (1849–1923) in Germany saw Romanticism ending, as it had begun, in storm and stress. His *Degeneration* (*Entartung*) of 1892, rapidly translated and reprinted, attributed the present spirit of mingled lassitude and excitement to 'the excessive wear and tear suffered by nations' and in particular to the 'rank growth' of cities. The movement was full of young poets, but they were inspired not by the 'gushing youthful vigour and turbulent constructive impulses' of early Romanticism, so much as by the 'convulsions and spasms of exhaustion'. It was what W. B. Yeats called the Tragic Generation; its poets tended to die young, as suicides, as the victims of disease, or ruined by excess. There was a prevailing sense of what a character in a play by Oscar Wilde passes off as a black joke: 'Fin du siècle: fin du monde': 'End of the century: end of the world'.

The poets of the 1890s provided a strong critical commentary on their fragile and bitter art. Arthur Symons (1865–1945), a trend-setting poet of the decade, explained the period to an interested but somewhat uncomprehending American audience in 1893. This latest 'intense self-consciousness, a restless curiosity in research, an oversubtilising refinement upon refinement, a spiritual and moral perversity' had its great antecedents in the decadences of Greek and Roman culture. Classicism might still be admitted as the 'supreme art', but this 'new and beautiful and interesting disease' of a culture was more rewarding and absorbing. It was a remarkable and wilful misapplication of Goethe's famous anti-Romantic dictum that 'Classicism is health: Romanticism is disease'.

Two years before Symons's article on 'The Decadent Movement in Literature', the precious, diminutive, alcoholic Lionel Johnson had written a sophisticated satire against his style of poetry in *The Anti-Jacobin*. 'It requires a positive genius for the absurd to discover a really promising affectation . . . . But the last ten years have done it'. His Decadent art was essentially that of the Absurdist, dandified even at its most sober, and spiced with 'a tender patronage of Catholicism' that anticipates the drift of Salvador Dali (1904-); Johnson's conversion was intended 'wholly for the purposes of controversy' as far as his circle was concerned, and as a species of 'nouveau frisson' for himself. Yet for all his destructive and secretive habits, and his genuine rather than assumed attachment to vice, Johnson shared the longing of Davidson and Yeats, the most gifted figures of the decade's poetry, for an ideal and formal standard rather than the incoherent sensations of his peers. 'By the Statue of King Charles at Charing Cross' (1895) is a tacit reproof to restless modernity, and only the dexterous and oddly moving 'Ad Cinerarium' by Victor Plarr (1863-1929) of the following year suggests a similar deep dissatisfaction with the pessimistic limitation of poetry to a lament for brief life:

> They are not long, the days of wine and roses:
>   Out of a misty dream
> Our path emerges for a while, then closes
>   Within a dream.

The emotional exaggeration of the Decadents merged into a cultivated distaste for anything simply natural: Theodore Wratislaw (1871-1933), whose very name suggests strange passions but who gave up poetry in the mid-1890s to become a civil servant and so escaped the Decadent curse, announced blandly in his volume *Orchids* (1896) that 'I hate the flower of wood or common field'. Wordsworth had claimed that a poet was one who could see all the immensity of nature in a primrose by the river's brim; Romanticism, as understood by the Decadents, meant that the mind of the poet acted on the visible world and transformed it as much as possible. The most thoroughly artificial imagination of the decade belonged to Aubrey Beardsley (1872-98), the celebrated graphic artist and art editor of the first four splendid volumes of the bizarrely beautiful *Yellow Book*; his brief career was imperilled by the arrest and imprisonment of Oscar Wilde, actually his enemy, but a man with whom Beardsley was confused by his own cultivated and probably undeserved reputation for excess and immorality. If English writing of the 1890s was derivative, the graphic art of the period was received joyfully by Europe; Beardsley's immediately recognisable style certainly developed out of Manet's Impressionist love for Japanese design, but it is otherwise proudly insular, incorporating quotations from William Blake, the fake chinoiseries and absolute extravagance of the Brighton Pavilion, Victorian ecclesiastical mediaevalism, Rossetti's eroticism and Burne-Jones's Arthurian idealism, not to mention the unquestioned assumption that art existed to illustrate literature. Beardsley's own literary contributions were slight; an elegantly voyeuristic pornographic novel on the favourite nineteenth-century subject of Venus and Tannhauser, and tripplingly sardonic ballads. His establishment of a permanently attractive visual style for the period has preserved Decadent consciousness as successfully as did the plays and stories of Oscar Wilde.

Oscar Wilde (1854–1900) is the most universally recognised figure of the 1890s. He was the popular plagiarist of the sober theories of Ruskin, Morris and above all, Pater ('All influence is immoral'; 'the great sanity of the Greek attitude'; 'To realise one's nature perfectly – that is what each of us is here for') and he carefully cultivated his persona of the Decadent dandy through the alter egos of his fictional characters ('We are supposed to wear faded roses in our button-holes when we meet, and to have a sort of cult for Domitian.') Bernard Shaw, who saw in his contemporary a fellow-Dubliner trying to make the leap from the provincial 'eighteenth-century' to the centres of power in London (the power of dinner-tables and drawing-rooms rather than that of newspaper offices and the Fabian Society), left a compassionate but sharp assessment of Wilde in *Pen Portraits and Reviews*. Snobbery had led Wilde, according to Shaw, to forsake 'that fortifying body of acquaintance among plain men', and to rely on 'that Irish charm, potent with Englishmen', and 'the temptation and demoralisation of finding himself a little god on the strength of what ought to be a quite ordinary culture'. For all his sternness, Shaw was one of the few contemporary writers who did not abandon Wilde after his conviction for homosexual practices, and he paid tribute to the other dramatist's brilliant abilities, in which 'the proximity of emotion' redeems a wit that by itself would have been 'destructive and sinister'. Wilde's mask of sophistication concealed a perilous idealism and 'a most touching kindness', as Shaw knew.

Wilde thought of himself as a Romantic in an age of realism: 'Behind everything wonderful stands the individual'. He objected to writers like Moore and Gissing 'for whom the sun always rises in the East End', and believed that their art was doomed because 'life goes faster than Realism, but Romanticism is always in front of life', according to his captivating if superficial defence of the essential artifice of literature in *The Decay of Lying* (1889), his modish reworking of Plato's *Symposium*. Like the Romantics of the 1820s Wilde self-consciously created the public image of himself, but this was not safely grounded in fact, as the personae of Lamb, De Quincey and Hazlitt had been. Nor was he able, like Disraeli, to maintain an ironic distance between the reputation of an author who appeared to spend his time 'eating ortolans to the sound of soft music' and the real, unscrupulous seeker of fame. When Wilde wrote in *De Profundis* of

> The Savoy dinners – the clear turtle soup, the luscious ortolans wrapped in their crinkled Sicilian vine-leaves, the heavy amber-coloured, indeed, almost amber-scented champagne . . .

he believed, even in his deepest suffering, in the gospel of sensation and the control of life by adjectives.

Wilde was the son of a Dublin surgeon and of a mother who had adopted a flamboyant style of Irish nationalism in the 1840s, writing hectic poems under the pen-name of 'Speranza'; at Oxford he came under the influence of Pater and Ruskin and achieved academic honours as easily as he had done at Trinity College, Dublin. He developed an instantly recognisable 'aesthetic' style of dress and manners, and a wit that remains legendary. 'The voice was the medium and the ear the critic', as he phrased it in *The Critic as Artist* (1890), and he demanded, in a somewhat different spirit from that of his countryman W. B. Yeats, that there should be a 'return to the voice' in literature. The devotee of good talk charmed the dying William Morris as a raconteur, and gave up his world for a dangerous jest at his trial.

In 1881 Wilde published his *Collected Poems* (he handled the usual themes efficiently, often a trifle too robustly for the medium, and 'The Harlot's House' is one of the better examples of late nineteenth-century verse). The next year he was persuaded to make a lucrative lecture tour of America, where he played the showman with complaisance. Like other Romantics before him, he failed to make his name with two tragedies, and turned permanently to prose. Two years as a magazine editor freed him from the lecture circuit and provided for his wife and family. His volumes of short stories, *The Happy Prince* and *The House of Pomegranates*, read like the Flaubert of *Salammbô* turned loose on Hans Andersen's fairy tales; the themes of altruism betrayed and the artist destroyed are already ominous.

Wilde's one novel *The Picture of Dorian Gray* (1891) was a heady blend of R. L. Stevenson's psychological melodrama, that basic Decadent text, Théophile Gautier's *Mademoiselle de Maupin* (1836) with its sexual confusion and assertion that 'nothing beautiful can be useful', and the 'breviary' of 1890s' poets, the *A Rebours* (1884) of J. K. Huysmans (1848–1907), with its sumptuous settings and abnormal, sated hero. The outspoken perversity of Gray and his friends worried Wilde's colleagues and helped to ensure their flight from his eventual predicament; Symonds feared that this glamourised vice would only 'confirm the worst suspicions of the uninformed'. *Dorian Gray* is a basically Puritanical work, showing the inevitability of retribution, and its borrowings from the French are largely superficial.

A book of essays, *Intentions* (1891) developed Wilde's theory of individualism and artificiality, and at the same time he followed and soon led the fashion for what he disparagingly called 'those modern drawing-room plays with pink lampshades', with the sentimental comedy *Lady Windermere's Fan*. The French tragic actress Sarah Bernhardt (1844–1923) had promised to perform on the London stage in Wilde's grotesque drama *Salomé* (for which Beardsley executed wonderfully corrupt designs when it appeared in book form, and which Richard Strauss was to use as the libretto for his 1905 opera), but the Lord Chamberlain refused a licence.

Wilde continued with a series of witty comedies: *A Woman of No Importance* (1893), *An Ideal Husband* (1895) and *The Importance of Being Earnest* in the same year; the last, a classic farce that ranks with *The School of Scandal* (1777) by Richard Brinsley Sheridan (1751–1816).

At this pinnacle of his career, Wilde was encouraged to bring an action for libel against the father of his current lover, Lord Alfred Douglas. This foolhardy attempt to deny his homosexuality placed Wilde himself in the dock; he refused to listen to his friends' pleas that he cross the Channel, and he ended by serving two years in prison: 'to a man of his culture, a form of death', as he had written forebodingly in an essay on the Romantic forger Wainewright. In 1897, while in prison, Wilde wrote the extravagant 'encyclical letter' *De Profundis* to his estranged lover, and the far more touching correspondence to London papers afterwards, describing the dreary inhumanity of gaol life. In his few remaining years of self-exile in France, Wilde polished *The Portrait of Mr W. H.*, his obsessive study of Shakespeare's own alleged passionate love for a member of his own sex, first published in 1889, and *The Ballad of Reading Gaol* (1897), which uses 1890s' themes to castigate a want of human sympathy. Wilde was received into the Roman Catholic church on his deathbed in 1900.

All art was autobiography for this Romantic artist, and his career was managed so that, as Shaw and later biographers have seen, nothing should spoil 'the great situation in the last act but one'. He felt, in a more primitive and literal way than Baudelaire, that the artist was a brilliant and accursed being doomed to endure public degradation; in a telling image early in his career he had portrayed the auction of Keats's letters as a modern-day dicing for the robe of Christ. Wilde found his own alter ego in Balzac's *Human Comedy*, that series of novels (1830–50) which reach a peak with *Lost Illusions* (1837–43) and *A Harlot High and Low* (*Splendeurs et misères des courtesans*) (1839–47):

> One of the great tragedies of my life is the death of Lucien de Rubempré. It is a grief from which I have never been able to completely rid myself. It haunts me in my moments of pleasure.

Wilde presents this as an affectation, but with the underlying sense that literature *is* reality, and the visible world a 'base concession to fact'. Lucien, the natural aristocrat lured from his quest for literary greatness and his achievement of a high place in society by sexual infatuation, becomes the sinister but ennobling model for Wilde's own career.

Wilde, like the much greater artist Byron, may have been a 'charlatan of genius'. His entertaining essays give no real indication of the fine academic mind he must have possessed, and his reputation rests on the evanescent charms of his conversation, preserved in the memoirs and biographies with which the period is so well supplied. His motivation, like Byron's, is both transparent and mysterious, so that he takes on the status of a fictional creation. His plays have, as Shaw predicted, guaranteed him a niche beside the English dramatist Congreve, another artist who purports to show 'The Way of the World', but who deals sympathetically and even Romantically with the threat to individual integrity posed by social forms, and deep fears of exposure and ridicule.

Only a fragment of the long and glorious poetic career of Wilde's compatriot W. B. Yeats (1865–1939) belongs to the nineteenth century. During the 1880s and 1890s he moved tentatively but surely towards the themes and styles of his mature work, when, as T. S. Eliot wrote admiringly, in speaking as a particular man he spoke to all men. Yeats was able to build creatively on all aspects of his personal and literary background, including his artist father's late Victorian scepticism which made it impossible for the son to be an orthodox believer, and drove the natural mystic into a study of Eastern religions and the cults of Theosophy and Rosicrucianism. He fused these into a composite, personal mythology which conveyed 'human truth' by symbols which, like those of Mozart's *The Magic Flute* (1791) did not need to be intellectually analysed in order to give up a powerful meaning.

Yeats was the child of Pre-Raphaelitism; a weighty inheritance, which T. S. Eliot, born twenty-three years later, was glad to have escaped. Yet Yeats was so exceptionally gifted as to be, in his Pre-Raphaelite phase, the equal of Rossetti rather than his imitator. His admiration for Swinburne's virtuosity toughened his verse, and his conviction that his real future lay within the Irish tradition was stimulated by his reverence for William Morris's own treatment of legend as well as the example of Sir Samuel Ferguson's direct handling of Gaelic material: like Morris, he could combine dreaminess with a startling sensory exactitude, as in 'The Madness of King Goll' (1887). Rossetti's love for Jane Morris gave the initial tone to Yeats's lifelong weighing of an unhappy infatuation with dispassionate acuity; he had fallen in love with Maud Gonne, another woman of amazing beauty and obduracy, who rejected the poet for a career of passionate and revolutionary Irish nationalism.

Like his fellow-countryman Bernard Shaw, Yeats went through an unusually prolonged artistic apprenticeship, during which he created a public mask. Both men sternly eradicated their provincialism by developing high critical standards and a wide culture, and they forced themselves to speak in public without notes. Although Yeats's poetry of the 1890s often suggests a retreat to a Celtic dream-world unfixed in time, or a purely symbolic representation of Ireland's potential and her woes, his attitude is never evasive once the developing man, as well as the poetry, is taken into account. Yeats was briefly involved in radical politics, and more permanently committed to an awakening of national identity through a new and imaginative presentation of folk myth: 'To Ireland in the Coming Times' (1893) explained that

> . . . to him who ponders well,
> My rhymes more than their rhyming tell
> Of things discovered in the deep
> When only body's laid asleep.

Yeats's love for Maud Gonne was the point at which his private feeling and his awareness of the public dimension of existence coincided. *Cathleen ni Houlihan,* written for her to act in 1902, was a vivid proof of the dangerous and wonderful power of words to shape events: years later, Yeats reflected that this play, so rapturously received by its Irish audience, may have helped to 'send out certain men the English shot'. If much of the poetry of the 1890s was tentative, the man who wrote it was not; the new, astringent poetry that followed *In the Seven Woods* of 1904 and culminated in the incomparable *Responsibilities* of 1914 was the outcome of the self-criticism that had gone on in the last decade of the old century. Yeats never disowned those years; his colleagues of the Rhymers' Club who had kept him company during the experimental years remained the 'Poets with whom I learned my trade', who themselves 'kept the Muses' sterner laws'.

'England, my England': the patriotic alternative

Although the *Yellow Book*, the Rhymers' Club and Oscar Wilde have become in retrospect the very spirit of the 1890s, a contemporary, alternative group of writers existed that gave expression to the ethos of the public schools which filled the army and the administrative posts of empire. A gamut of talent from the intensely sophisticated to the barely competent supported a more aggressive militarism and imperialism; in 1890 one such voice roundly praised Alfred Austin (1835–1913), the laureate of the period:

> We do not require these foreign reinforcements: the countrymen of Shakespeare have no need to borrow either their ethics or their aesthetics from the countrymen of Baudelaire; and if we be wise we shall run more and more to whatsoever singer scents his pages, not with livid and noxious Fleurs du Mal, but with the blossoms which English children gather in their aprons . . . .

Austin gratified public taste by writing in frank enjoyment of an age when 'England's laws and England's tongue / Enfranchise half mankind!' and the titles of his poetry promised no roses and raptures of vice: 'Why England is Conservative' and 'Is Life Worth Living?' Austin has a fair claim to be one of the least distinguished of poets laureate, and his unwitting absurdities have been gathered up attentively by later generations; his elegy on George Eliot is particularly unfortunate. Nevertheless, he did speak for a large section of the reading public, and boldly attacked those 'sophists' who fumbled with the pen instead of brandishing the blade, and his narrative poems have a crude charm and a disarmingly candid nostalgia: 'The Last Night', a ballad of emigration, must have spoken to many households, and 'A Farmhouse Dirge' laments a vanished feudal security.

William Ernest Henley (1849–1903) was a far more substantial figure; a neglected genius, not only admirable in his own character, and more than creditable as a poet and essayist, but a valuable nurturer of talent in others. 'I, like many others, began under him my education', wrote Yeats. Kipling, another protegé, found him 'a jewel of an editor, with the gift of fetching the very best out of his cattle', and Henley employed Shaw briefly, recognising his talent while deploring his socialism. He attempted drama himself, collaborating with his friend R. L. Stevenson on a succession of romantic dramas which did not attract the public. In his role as the offender against Victorian prudery, Henley published a chapter from *Tess* that Hardy's original editors had refused to circulate, and, more importantly, brought Joseph Conrad before a wider public with *The Nigger of the 'Narcissus'*. Henley was a late Victorian Leigh Hunt, surrounding himself delightedly with the greatest figures of the age and temperamentally inclined to hero-worship. He was an articulate friend to conservative interests, and his preface to *Lyra Heroica: A Book of Verse for Boys*, assured his young readers of the duty of patriotism.

> To set forth, as only art can, the beauty and the joy of living, the beauty and blessedness of death, the glory of battle and adventure, the nobility of devotion – to a cause, an idea, a passion even – the dignity of existence, the sacred quality of patriotism, this is my ambition here.

This was a new version of Carlyle's transcendence of the self, or Charles Kingsley brought up to date, and it was the classic statement of what the poets of the Great War were to call 'the old lie'. In his unofficial capacity as bard to the Empire (Henley was considered for the laureateship, and would have filled the post with more distinction than Austin), he produced two of the best 'bad poems' of the century, full of feeling, technically adroit, and intensely memorable. 'England, my England' is in the tradition of Romantic public address in the spirit of Blake and Milton; 'Invictus', originally conceived as a personal meditation on a narrow escape from death, met the fate of Emily Brontë's equally undeclamatory 'No coward soul is mine . . .' as a recital piece in schools. Henley's patriotism was essentially an enhancement of the individual spirit; he had no sympathy for Prussian obedience to the state, which was winning supporters in England. 'We should', he wrote in a leader article in 1889, 'lose that enthusiasm of original effort which is the very salt of our life; and . . . all proper understanding of art and literature.' If Henley loved patriotic fervour, he loved poetry more.

Henley proposed himself, quite deliberately, as a counter-influence to Oscar Wilde and the Decadent spirit; though his reputation did not become a legend, he was known as a witty and combative talker. *The New Review*, one of his magazines, was designed as an alternative to the shocking *Yellow Book*, whose good qualities Henley was intelligent enough to perceive. Henley was perturbed by a new 'effeminacy' in literature, with its 'delicate, distinguished, aristocratic' style of 'omission, implication, suggestion', and his own publication was to be 'virile' in outlook, assuring 'healthy-minded men and honest women' that (in Henley's attractive phrase) life was 'a prolonged occasion for self-respect'. There was nothing crude about his proposal of a new and vital attitude, and the outwardly dissimilar periodicals both introduced new writers assiduously, and disdained bourgeois prejudices; Henley's Conservative magazines were banned as firmly as the *Yellow Book* itself from Coventry Patmore's devout and Tory household, since Henley's 'buxom' and 'virile' morals cancelled out his politics.

The pattern of Henley's career had been set by an unexpected new lease on life in the 1870s. He had emerged from an unpromising background into freelance journalism, and had the unbounded faith of writers of the period in the liberating power of imaginative thought. In 1867 he had lost a leg to tubercular infection, and when he was threatened with a second amputation in 1873 he put himself under the care of Joseph Lister (1827–1912), who was pioneering antiseptic surgery at the Edinburgh Infirmary. The monodrama *In Hospital* (1875) is one of the triumphs of English naturalism, taking (in its early drafts) the introspective form of the sonnet and making it describe a world outside the self. Yet the apparently clinical study of hospital routine becomes the portrait of an amorphous underworld, where personality is dissolved by illness and anaesthesia, and then remade and rededicated during slow convalescence. The Romantic reverence for the apparently divine powers of the healing physician, and for the insights of fevered illness, heightens the narrative into a development of Tennyson's *Maud* as it too explores the effects of modern stress on an unusually sensitive individual.

Henley's many single volumes of poetry have a pleasing facility, and Hardy's subject-matter of time, chance and death without Hardy's pessimism. The many poems about the appearance and characters of London show the influence of another of his heroes, J. M. Whistler, whose art he had defended from his earliest days as a journalist, for its power strenuously to transmute ignoble realities into Romantic fantasy; for Henley, there was no limit to the power of the creative artist, nor his duty to use it.

Rudyard Kipling (1865–1936) remains, in T. S. Eliot's phrase, 'the most inscrutable of authors', and also 'a writer impossible to belittle'. His poetry, with its extraordinary range of style and moods and its unmatchable technical proficiency, and the short stories which prove him to be master of the form in English, both treat men and women in relation to the human race in the largest possible sense. They are shown as sharers in history; masters and apprentices, parents and children, administering empires and suffering in war, fighting and inventing, artificers and labourers. Kipling has an unquenchable thirst to know how things work and what it is like to wield power, but an astonishing apparent indifference to what organisation is for. His stories set during the Great War of 1914–18, in which he lost his only son, are remarkable for their compassion and harrowing detail, but always so focused on a central character that Kipling's own attitudes remain a secret. It is this absolute psychological realism that permits the devotee of Kipling to take apparent prejudice and amorality in his stride; Kipling speaks as rarely as Browning with his own voice.

Kipling's art, by turns deeply ironic and flooded with feeling, was shaped like that of Thackeray by a return to England from a happy childhood in India. He was despatched from a privileged caste, a loving and talented family and that 'daybreak, light and colour' that was to make him the most visually precise and ravishing of writers, to the life of a cruelly abused and lonely young boarder in a lower middle-class villa with its rituals of sadistic piety, where God 'stood in the background and counted the strokes of the cane'. This exile, like Dickens's miserable fall in status, turned the boy into a writer; his removal from India for his education gave him a detachment which no true-born Englishman could possess ('Thanks be to Allah who gave me two / Separate sides to my head'), and his privations brought on that partial blindness that kept him out of the army for which most boys of his background were destined. He learned to be secretive, and the great documentor in his fiction of quiet suffering and cancerous griefs and resentments, and was as intuitively aware as Conrad (his intellectual superior by only a short way) of the danger that all human love poses to a hard-won stoical integrity; the mysteries of craftsmanship, soldiering, religion and Freemasonry provide the real sources of joy in his stories.

Kipling's Anglo-Indian background was indifferent to culture though appreciative of ability; when he became a young newspaperman working on *The Civil and Military Gazette* in Lahore and ironically proud of enduring the effort, tedium and absence of like minds, he produced efficient light verse (*Departmental Ditties*) and the short stories which developed into the satisfying *Plain Tales from the Hills* (1887) which rapidly transcend their know-it-all smartness and become a moving portrait of an uncertain transplanted society. He gave his readers the amusement they craved, while discreetly testing the frivolous medium to see how much intellectual weight it would bear. His parents, who encouraged his talent, were unusual members of the Anglo-Indian community; his father was an illustrator and architectural sculptor and his mother was sister-in-law to Sir Edward Burne-Jones, the eminent painter and associate of William Morris. Kipling's holidays had been spent with his uncle's household at 'The Grange', and the Pre-Raphaelite element remained strong in his work, from the strangely doomed quality of sexual love in his stories and his graphic animation of history in the manner of William Morris, to his vivid praise of the power of art to enrich human life. The short story 'Regulus', first published in 1908, shows the boy Kipling as 'Beetle', learning how literature shapes not only the individual moral sense but the future of a nation and its empire; like the later 'The Janeites', dealing with a doomed wartime battery living out its last days consoled by the bloodless social skirmishes in the pages of Jane Austen, it is an acid-test which determines whether the reader will be moved by Kipling's curious blend of personal and collective morality, or repelled by fictions which smell too much of 'tobacco and blood'.

Kipling's favourite form was the volume of short stories which permitted more ethical intricacy than the novel, in their endless refractions of a moral dilemma through apparently separate characters and situations. *Kim* (1901) is his only successful novel, amounting to a masterpiece and admired by Indian and English readers alike; Kipling's appetite for kaleidoscopic variety and his juggling of practical and metaphysical approaches to life are made elements in the picaresque and Romantic tale of a child journeying through a world at once exotic and commonplace.

Kipling's realism was a legacy of Pre-Raphaelite truth to nature rather than the late nineteenth-century vogue for de Maupassant and Zola. He aimed to be like his hero Dick Heldar in the broken-backed novel *The Light that Failed* (1890), able to hold the attention of knowledgeable practical men, and his newspaper training never left him. But at the same time he had a passionate and carefully rationed interest in 'the Dark World' or 'En-dor' of spiritualism and the supernatural; both a common concern of the period, particularly following the appalling losses of the Great War, and a private metaphor for unacknowledged emotions.

Kipling's reputation as a poet of the 1890s rests on three collections: *Barrack Room Ballads and Other Verses* (1892) *The Seven Seas* (1896) and *Five Nations* (1903). A fourth volume, a moving, terse and disquieting anthology of soldier's epitaphs which appeared at the end of the Great War, forms a necessary postscript to his analysis of all social bonds through the microcosm of the army. The popularity of these poems, at once transparent and sophisticated, was immense throughout the English-speaking world; there were houses in Edwardian England where the only books were Kipling and the Bible. *Barrack Room Ballads*, far from approving a blind patriotism, use the admitted civilian distrust of the military to suggest divisions within English society as a whole: the sour presentation of the queen in 'The Widow at Windsor' raised eyebrows at the time, and 'Loot' continues to do so today. The tone of the verse varies with a deliberate virtuosity: 'Cholera Camp' has the brio of a Gilbert lyric, and 'Mary Pity Women' goes beyond its naturalism to become a piercing lament for the sex by a man often thought of as a natural misogynist. 'Danny Deever', the finest poem in the collection, is uncannier than

Wilde's admirable *The Ballad of Reading Gaol* on the same subject. It uses the morally dispassionate approach of the original ballad form; Wilde was fiercely tender towards his condemned man, while Kipling's attitude is (as usual) more withdrawn. The poem becomes a forceful dramatisation of essential human solitude.

> 'What are the bugles blowin' for?' said Files-on-Parade.
> 'To turn you out, to turn you out', the Colour-Sergeant said.
> 'What makes you look so white, so white?' said Files-on-Parade.
> 'I'm dreadin' what I've got to watch', the Colour-Sergeant said.
>   For they're hangin' Danny Deever, you can hear the Dead March play,
>   The regiment's in 'ollow square – they're hangin' him today;
>   They've taken of his buttons off and cut his stripes away,
>   An' they're hangin' Danny Deever in the mornin'.

Sir Henry Newbolt (1862-38) was a less complicated patriot than Kipling. He provided honest, technically accomplished and direct expositions of the public school code: 'Where the strong command / Obedience is best'. Kipling's protectors of Empire are usually alone, testing their resolve among strangers and outcasts; Newbolt's are, even in their extremity, among comrades and supported by a shared concept of heroic virtue. If Kipling used the ballad to undermine his readers' secure beliefs, Newbolt writes within the simple narrative tradition and presents a straightforward decency and courage.

> They've kept the tale a hundred years,
>   They'll keep the tale a hundred more;
> Riding at dawn, riding alone,
>   Gillespie came to false Vellore.

No such singleness of purpose attaches itself to the prose of Robert Louis Stevenson (1850–94), a writer best viewed against his Scottish background but in his time hugely popular among English-speaking readers. Stevenson grew up, a sickly child, in a severely conservative, authoritarian and Calvinist household, and though destined for his father's profession of engineering, chose to become an atheist, libertine and desultory student of law. Essays and travel books, which have not worn well, failed to make a reputation for him and a liaison with a married American woman scandalised his family. When he settled in Scotland and submitted to regular habits

under the lady's régime – Stevenson was tubercular – he
began to write stories that spoke of his deepest interests; the
supernatural, involving secret guilts and fears, and the Scottish
temperament. *Treasure Island* was a popular success when it
came out in volume form in 1883, and it remains a classic for
children and for discerning adults, though its understanding of
unacknowledged motive is more complicated than anything in
the adventure stories of Charles Kingsley which it appears to
imitate. *Kidnapped* (1886) and its admirable and closely linked
sequel *Catriona* (1886) cover the same ground as Scott's
Waverley, with a prudent hero drawn into the doomed chivalric
fantasy of a wayward highlander, but Stevenson had not much
use for his great predecessor: 'Compression is the mark of a
really sovereign style', he wrote unforgivingly, and 'plain
physical sensations plainly and expressly rendered'. His own
arrow-swift narratives had no time for digressions and sub-
plots that explore the ramifications of Scott's beliefs. At a
deeper level, Stevenson was a pessimist, neither able nor
desiring to shake off his Calvinist heritage. He resented Scott's
eighteenth-century optimism, and brooded over his conviction
that men are naturally cruel, vice is fascinating, parents and
children resent one another, and that goodness is never more
than 'respectability'. His last novel *Weir of Hermiston* (1896),
left unfinished at his death at the peak of its strange excellence,
promises more than any of his other fictions in his wry
arbitration between the idealistic son and his father the
hanging judge, and a new sense of ardour and sensory delight.
Stevenson's later life had been guided by attempts to find a
cure for his tuberculosis; he wrote *The Master of Ballantrae*
(1889) while visiting hot springs in America, and shortly after
journeyed to Tahiti where he became Tusitala, the Teller of
Tales, ruling his south sea domain and his worldwide literary
fiefdom like a clan chieftain until his early death.

   The most apparent literary influence on Stevenson is not the
simple adventure story, nor the sensation novel, nor even
Gothic fiction, but a Scottish masterpiece, James Hogg's
Confessions of a Justified Sinner (1824), with its theme of the twin-
souled man betrayed into evil by the promptings of his own
nature. *Dr Jekyll and Mr Hyde* (1886) shows the wretched,
philanthropic doctor saddled with his vicious alter ego not
through the misplaced Promethean energies of Frankenstein,

but as a judgement on his secret failings. There is a strong echo of Emily Brontë in Stevenson; in the pervasive themes of disinheritance, a fierce attachment to native landscape, and the practice of using multiple narrators who change their moral colouring within the story.

Stevenson achieved a truce with his background in *A Child's Garden of Verses* (1885), a perennial favourite with its mixture of tenderness and irony, a child's own perception of scale and time, sudden acerbities, and a *fin de siècle* yearning for the lost domain of infancy with its freedom from sexual urges and moral decision. The 'virile' writers were passionately attached to their own remembered childhoods and their own young families, and to the inculcation of principle in the rising generation.

'The winter solstice': drama in the nineteenth century

The drama of the nineteenth century remained, until the last decades, a notorious wasteland. The Romantic imagination was on the whole unfriendly towards the theatre; Wordsworth had objected forthrightly to 'the degrading thirst after outrageous stimulation' among playgoers, and to 'sickly and stupic German tragedies' in particular. In her sensitively implied criticism of the unlucky amateur theatricals at Mansfield Park, Jane Austen makes the sources of Romantic aversion beautifully plain; the assumption of fictitious roles and passions threatened the new commitment to genuine feeling and an active conscience. In practice, the Romantic essayists were working reviewers who haunted theatres and idolised chosen actors, but all of them share a basic belief (traceable to Coleridge) that any performance of a play, and Shakespeare's in particular, traduces the ideal version existing in the reader's mind.

At the same time, the weakness of the theatre came about through economic and social causes. The most vital period of the English drama had come to a halt with the closing of the theatres during the puritan Commonwealth (1653–60), and the Restoration of Charles II saw only two playhouses opened under licence. The 'patent houses' of Drury Lane and Covent Garden had the sole right to present legimate drama, and other theatres were forced to circumvent the monopoly by performing plays between two halves of a concert, or interspersing the action with at least five songs per act. Naturally, such frequent additional amusement forced the patent houses to provide their own popular music and spectacle to audiences who had come to expect it elsewhere.

In the eighteenth century, patent houses were established in the larger provincial towns, and it was there that the 'stock company' developed that Bernard Shaw could still remember having seen in his youth. A troupe of local actors filled a gamut of basic types in a fixed repertory, where the leading parts would be taken by visiting London players of repute. Actors in such a company often supplemented meagre salaries with humiliating 'benefits' by which an individual would reap the rewards of his special popularity through the takings of a performance advertised in his name. The 'stock' system led to a disheartening rigidity in the repertory and had a wholly bad effect on young actors, since any spontaneity was unwelcome and no other training was available.

By the early nineteenth century the theatre was divided along lines of class and intelligence. The opulent 'Patent Houses' were run to make money, with their luxurious accommodation for wealthy patrons and barbarous indifference towards poorer spectators, and the 'Minor Theatres' were often no better than houses of assignation, as degraded in their art as in their reputation. In 1820 Hazlitt went to several of these, hoping to find a raw dramatic vitality that eluded the fashionable theatres, and voiced his disappointment in the March *London Magazine*:

> The audience did not hiss the actors (that would have implied a serious feeling of disapprobation, and something like a disappointed wish to be pleased), but they laughed, hooted at, nick-named, pelted them with oranges and witticisms, to show their unruly contempt for them and their art; while the performers, to be even with their audience, evidently slurred their parts, as if ashamed to be thought to take an interest in them, laughed in one another's faces, and in that of their friends in the pit, and most effectually marred the process of theatrical illusion, by turning the whole into a most unprincipled burlesque.

The popular audience was able to take its toll of the drama, where it did not feel the effects of its illiteracy in the pit; the infamous 'Old Price' riots at the expensively refurbished Covent Garden in 1809 had actually seen Hazlitt's 'remorseless rabble' drive a respectable audience away from the theatre, and it made managers all the more aggressive in their care for profits. In addition, the growth of Evangelical Christianity in the early nineteenth century removed a great many middle-class patrons and their families from the playhouses altogether.

In 1843 the patent system was belatedly revoked, but not before it had destroyed the craft of playmaking, damaged the acting profession, and driven away a critically responsive audience. If the middle and upper classes went to the theatre at all, they went to enjoy themselves candidly as a family at a menagerie show and spectacle, or to show themselves at fashionable Italian opera. The 'winter solstice' of English drama was made worse by a comparative absence of acting talent; Hunt and Hazlitt had been able to praise the actors John Kemble (1757–1823) and his sister Sarah Siddons (1755–1831) and Edmund Kean (1787?–1833), but the new man of the theatre tended to be a book-keeper. When G. H. Lewes became 'Vivian' of the *Leader* in the 1850s, the former actor from a theatrical family could commend only foreigners or figures from the past. The English theatre was choked with pieces plagiarised from the more lively French stage, adapted for stock companies, and the dramatic world Dickens had satirised in *Nicholas Nickleby* was still in force.

In 1865 *Society* by T. W. Robertson (1829–71) began a reform of the English stage. Robertson ignored the stock company, and followed the advice of the actor-manager David Garrick (1717–79) who had believed that 'Comedy is a serious thing'. Robertson's neatly-made, refined comedies were soon called 'cup and saucer plays' for their careful use of properties, recognisable domestic surroundings and naturalistic manners, and the dramatist became the play's director. All Robertson's innovations became traditions by the end of the century in a rapid renaissance of English drama, but they would hardly have succeeded without the simultaneous rise of a new generation of actor-managers. The first was the able and enlightened Squire Bancroft, who was determined to win back a decent and moneyed audience; he put on a single play after the dinner hour, introduced matinees, and relied on his own trained touring company instead of what provincial stock could supply. Robertson himself survives as the gently revolutionary playwright Tom Wrench in *Trelawney of the Wells* (1898) by his powerful successor Sir Arthur Wing Pinero; the 1890s tribute to the ingenuous theatre of the 1860s is frequently revived today as a complicated piece of sentimental nostalgia.

The actor-manager was now the hero of the theatre. During the profession's darkest years, an actor such as William Macready had held his audience by emotional force alone, never being able to count on the taste of his patrons, the competence or goodwill of the supporting cast, and certainly not the ability of the playwright or adapter. Henry Irving had lived through these years in a provincial company without success, and his acclamation as the murderous Polish Jew in the melodrama *The Bells* (1870) made him king of the London stage overnight, with a theatrical version of the emotions of the 'Newgate' novel. In 1878 Irving leased the Lyceum theatre and was partnered in his versions of Shakespeare by the beautiful and intelligent Ellen Terry (1848–1928). He was, judging by the emphatic accounts of the period, a mesmeric actor, as overpowering in private life as on the stage. The Lyceum became the resort of an audience which admired Aestheticism; the plays were lavishly produced with great regard for historical detail and artistic taste, but Shakespeare was ruthlessly cut and reshaped to suit the spectacle. Bernard Shaw, who was no admirer of Irving's high-handed and unintellectual style, joined the actor in pointing out the manifest unfairness of having Sir Arthur Sullivan, Lord Tennyson and Sir Edward Burne-Jones supply the music, words and design for a performance in which 'Mr' Irving took the leading role. Irving was knighted in 1895.

If actor-managers were winning back an audience for a newly respectable and gorgeous theatre, new plays were still to seek. Arthur Wing Pinero (1855–1934) was 'stage-struck' from childhood, and hard upon his father's death left his law office to become a 'general utility' actor in a stock company, ending up with five years under Irving's direction at the Lyceum. By the 1870s, a native drama of sorts had evolved through W. S. Gilbert and T. W. Robertson, and new European copyright laws made borrowing from French models more expensive. Pinero knew what he wanted to do, and had success from the beginning. He took great trouble with his many plays, writing according to a régime of inventing characters and plotting the scenario during months in country retreats, and then putting down the dialogue with each act rushed to the printer's as it came from his pen. He had begun a revolution in having the scripts printed before distribution to the cast; actors had been used to seeing only their cues and speeches, without expecting to understand the action as a whole or to prepare the part in any way. Half of his work, Pinero claimed, was done as he actually sat in the director's chair, putting his play into production.

Pinero was patriotically aware that England was lagging behind the rest of Europe in its drama, and that a new and dangerously radical theatre of ideas was being pioneered in Norway by Henrik Ibsen. Ibsen was translated into English by the critic William Archer in the early 1890s; Pinero had tried his hand at the 'problem play' with *The Profligate* in 1887, but he adapted the formulae of Ibsen's dramas to create magnificent vehicles for Mrs Patrick Campbell (1865–1940) a broodingly beautiful actress who was the Geraldine to Ellen Terry's Christabel in the theatre of the 1890s. The Second Mrs Tanqueray and The Notorious Mrs Ebbsmith were sexually experienced and free-thinking, like many of Ibsen's heroines, but they were interpreted somewhat gingerly by a cautious English moralist. *Mrs Tanqueray* (1893) is revived from time to time as a well-made period piece with gratifying parts for a large cast. It is the story of a 'woman with a past' in which she has been the kept mistress of a number of rich men, trying to make a secure future for herself through marriage to a conventional barrister. The play is a very indifferent version of Ibsen, but a touching and competent reversion to eighteenth-century sentimental comedy in its use of matched sets of characters, its theme of the need for frankness and charity in marriage, its emphasis on the superior candour and decency of women, its ritual unmasking of the hypocrite, and its sure sense of climax. Pinero may show immoral people, but his sinners genuinely want to come to repentance, and when one of his typical 'men of forty' who comment on the action from within the play itself explains that 'We can learn more from the erring than from the guilty', the remark would be absurd in Ibsen, but unexceptional in Sheridan or Goldsmith.

In time, Pinero's drama was supplanted by newer forms,

even though he went on experimenting with increasingly taut and thoughtful plays. Audiences came to prefer the intellectually more abrasive plays of Shaw, the sentimental fantasy of Barrie, or the naturalistic dramas of Galsworthy (1867–1933) and Somerset Maugham (1874–1965). The theatre itself was changing, as the generation of actor-managers gave way to speculators and investors, and the audiences of the Great War were interested in light entertainment and even moving pictures. Serious dramatists often expected to see their work performed privately, as Shaw's *Plays Unpleasant* had been.

The renaissance of the drama in England seems a qualified artistic success, hedged about with crass materialism and intellectual nostalgia. Yet the theatre of the 1890s was touched by that Romanticism which had initially shunned the drama, as the complex plays of Pinero became more and more like the fiction of the mid-century. Bernard Shaw knew that Pinero had no real relation to Ibsen, and took him to task for his pretensions; William Archer, hardly distracted by this impossible resemblance, noted perceptively in his review that the four acts of *Mrs Tanqueray* 'are like the crucial, the culminating chapters of a singularly powerful and original novel'. Pinero was in fact offering his fashionable audience something that the novel itself was ceasing to provide; the exploration of the way in which solidly portrayed characters come to terms with the consequences of their acts, achieve self-knowledge and overcome selfishness. Even Shaw was to print his plays with all the adornments of fiction; authorial interjections and long descriptions of scene, background and character study. Wordsworth's Romantic puritanism and intense and scrupulous interest in psychological cause and effect had travelled a long route to the popular stage which had seemed unredeemable to the Romantics of 1798.

'Travellers at daybreak': the end of an era

The writers of the 1890s saw themselves, in J. A. Symonds's words, as 'travellers at daybreak'. The way ahead was in no sense clear, and in fact the traditions of Romanticism were to be ruptured by the long-delayed apocalypse which Carlyle and Ruskin had predicted, and it was to take place on an unimagined scale, in a European theatre of war that would destroy most of a generation and all of its old securities.

The nineteenth century encompasses one hundred years of previously unguessed-at achievement. A democratic, peaceable, universally educated nation would have seemed a paradoxical impossibility to the approving readers of Edmund Burke in the 1790s, but every piece of social legislation, every material invention, every intellectual speculation changed perception subtly or gravely enough to make this seemingly impossible transformation possible. We need not think in terms of the grand issues of Malthus, Bentham and Darwin to understand these shifts, not always as momentous as the precipices in time Hardy spoke of, quoted at the opening to the third chapter; Hardy himself dealt, better than almost any other novelist, with the power of new inventions and discoveries to change human attitudes to self and society. Anaesthetics diminished suffering and altered people's reactions to pain in those around them to something more compassionate; photographs preserved the past, including versions of one's younger self; the wide availability of printed matter made culture available to all classes; the railway did away with old, narrow horizons as well as old securities.

During the move towards an unknown future and ever-enlarging political and social hopes, literature functioned as a guide-rail, essentially conservative in its calm emphasis on unchanging personal affections and ideal values outside the self that had nothing to do with material development. Until the very end of the century, Victorian literature remained committed to Romanticism; ideas had to be referred to feeling, rather than to system, and it was through the fictionalised history of Scott, Tennyson and Ruskin that nineteenth-century readers became aware of the roots of their culture and their part in a tradition. Literature could promise any individual alienated by his powerlessness in a more and more complex political and mechanical world a private domain, and possibly even a route by his own talent to independent greatness. Poetry and fiction provided moral and emotional support at a time when more orthodox spirituality was preoccupied with redefining itself and withstanding secular and scientific assaults.

The nineteenth century is not easily divided into 'Romantic'

and 'Victorian' periods by the simple act of Victoria's
accession. The change in sensibility which had come about by
the late eighteenth century continued to evolve until the
crumbling of the fabric in the 1890s; Victorian feelings and
ideas continue to be judged by Romantic standards, however
stern the demands of utilitarianism. On the one hand, author
and reader form a unique and mutually respectful partnership
in the search through concrete examples for the roots of
personality, the consequences of moral action, and the
obligations of the self to the community at large. On the other,
the writer or painter explores those moments of enhanced
awareness that initially console him for the endurance of daily
reality, and finally make him reject the ordinary. Shelley's
skylark, Coleridge's Aeolian harp and Wordsworth's vision of
the renovating powers of nature thread through the literature
of the century, making their last appearance in a poem
designed as a qualification of Romanticism; Thomas Hardy's
'The Darkling Thrush', written on 31 December 1900, the last
day of the nineteenth century.

I leant upon a coppice gate
  When Frost was specter-gray,
And Winter's dregs made desolate
  The weakening eye of day.
The tangled bine-stems scored the sky
  Like strings of broken lyres,
And all mankind that haunted nigh
  Had sought their household fires.

The land's sharp features seemed to be
  The century's corpse outleant,
His crypt the cloudy canopy,
  The wind his death-lament.
The ancient pulse of germ and birth
  Was shrunken hard and dry,
And every spirit upon earth
  Seemed fervourless as I.

At once a voice arose among
  The bleak twigs overhead
In a fullhearted evensong
  Of joy illimited;
An aged thrush, frail, gaunt, and small,
  In blast-beruffled plume,
Had chosen thus to fling his soul
  Upon the growing gloom.

So little cause for carollings
   Of such ecstatic sound
Was written on terrestrial things
   Afar or nigh around,
That I could think there trembled through
   His happy goodnight air
Some blessed Hope, whereof he knew
   And I was unaware.

Further reading

M. H. ABRAMS: *The Mirror and the Lamp: Romantic Theory and the Critical Tradition* (Oxford University Press, 1953)

R. D. ALTICK: *Victorian People and Ideas: A Companion for the Modern Reader of Victorian Literature* (New York, Norton, 1973)

ISOBEL ARMSTRONG (ed.): *The Major Victorian Poets: Reconsiderations* (Lincoln, University of Nebraska Press, 1969)

—— *Victorian Scrutinies: Reviews of Poetry 1830–1870* (London, Athlone Press, 1972)

PATRICIA BALL: *The Heart's Events: The Victorian Poetry of Relationships* (London, Athlone Press, 1976)

JOHN BAYLEY: *The Romantic Survival: A Study in Poetic Evolution* (London, Constable, 1957)

E. F. BENSON: *As We Were: A Victorian Peep-Show* (Harmondsworth, Penguin, 1930)

BERNARD BLACKSTONE: *The Lost Travellers: A Romantic Theme With Variations* (London, Longmans, 1962)

HAROLD BLOOM: *The Visionary Company: Readings of English Romantic Poetry* (New York, Doubleday, 1961)

T. S. R. BOASE: *English Art 1800–1870* (Oxford University Press, 1959)

C. M. BOWRA: *The Romantic Imagination* (Cambridge, Mass., Harvard University Press, 1957)

ASA BRIGGS: *Iron Bridge to Crystal Palace: Impact and Images of the Industrial Revolution* (London, Thames and Hudson, 1979)

—— *The Making of Modern England, 1783–1867: The Age of Improvement* (New York, Harper and Row, 1965)

—— (ed.): *The Nineteenth Century: The Contradictions of Progress* (London, Thames and Hudson, 1970)

—— *Victorian People: A Reassessment of Persons and Themes 1851–67* (rev. ed. Chicago, University of Chicago Press, 1970)

J. H. BUCKLEY: *The Triumph of Time: A Study of the Victorian Concepts of Time, History, Progress and Decadence* (Cambridge, Harvard University Press, 1966)

—— *The Victorian Temper: A Study in Literary Culture* (Cambridge, Mass., Harvard University Press, 1951)

—— (ed.): *The Worlds of Victorian Fiction* (Cambridge, Mass., Harvard University Press, 1975)

W. L. BURN: *The Age of Equipoise: A Study of the Mid-Victorian Generation* (New York, Norton, 1965)

JOAN N. BURSTYN: *Victorian Education and the Ideal of Womanhood* (London, Croom Helm, 1980)

ELIZABETH BURTON: *The Pageant of Early Victorian England, 1837–1861* (New York, Scribner, 1972)

MARILYN BUTLER: *Romantics, Rebels and Revolutionaries: English Literature and its Background, 1760–1830* (Oxford University Press, 1981)

JENNI CALDER: *Women and Marriage in Victorian Fiction* (London, Thames and Hudson, 1976)

JULIA CAMERON: *Victorian Photographs of Famous Men and Fair Women* (London, Hogarth Press, 1973)

LOUIS CAZAMIAN: (tr. Martin Fido) *The Social Novel in England 1830–1850: Dickens, Disraeli, Mrs Gaskell, Kingsley* (London, Routledge and Kegan Paul, 1973), from *Le roman social en Angleterre,* 1903

DAVID CECIL: *Early Victorian Novelists: Essays in Revaluation* (Harmondsworth, Penguin, 1948)

ALICE CHANDLER: *A Dream of Order: the Mediaeval Ideal in Nineteenth Century English Literature* (Lincoln, University of Nebraska Press, 1970)

RAYMOND CHAPMAN: *The Victorian Debate: English Literature and Society 1832–1901* (London, Weidenfeld and Nicolson, 1968)

BARBARA CHARLESWORTH: *Dark Passages: The Decadent Consciousness in Victorian Literature* (Madison, University of Wisconsin Press, 1965)

KELLOW CHESNEY: *The Victorian Underworld* (Harmondsworth, Penguin, 1970)

KENNETH CLARK: *The Gothic Revival: An Essay in the History of Taste* (New York, Harper and Row, 1962)

—— *The Romantic Rebellion: Romantic Versus Classic Art* (London, J. Murray, 1973)

A. J. COCKSHUTT: *Man and Woman: A Study of Love and the Novel, 1740–1940* (London, Collins, 1977)

PHILIP COLLINS: *Dickens and Crime* (London, Macmillan, 1964)

—— *Dickens and Education* (London, Macmillan, 1963)

MICHAEL COOKE: *The Romantic Will* (New Haven, Yale University Press, 1976)

VALENTINE CUNNINGHAM: *Everywhere Spoken Against: Dissent in The Victorian Novel* (Oxford, Clarendon Press, 1975)

R. T. Davies and B. G. BEATTY: *Literature of the Romantic Period* (Liverpool, Liverpool University Press, 1976)

CARL DAWSON: *Victorian Noon: English Literature in 1850* (Baltimore, Johns Hopkins University, 1979)

DAVID J. DE LAURA: *Victorian Prose: a guide to research* (New York, Modern Language Association, 1973)

ERIC DE MARÉ: *London 1851: the Year of the Great Exhibition* (London, J. M. Dent, 1973)

FRANCES DONALDSON: *The Actor-Managers* (London, Weidenfeld and Nicolson, 1970)

M. EAGLETON and D. PIERCE: *Attitudes to Class in the English Novel: from W. Scott to David Storey* (London, Thames and Hudson, 1979)

MALCOLM ELWIN: *Old Gods Falling* (Freeport, N.Y., Books for Libraries Press, 1939)

—— *Victorian Wallflowers: a panoramic survey of the popular literary periodicals* (Port Washington, N.Y., Kennikat Press, 1966)

JOHN P. FARRELL: *Revolution as Tragedy: the Dilemma of the Moderate from Scott to Arnold* (Ithaca, Cornell University Press, 1980)

F. E. FAVERTY (ed.): *The Victorian Poets: a Guide to Research* (second edition, Cambridge, Mass., Harvard University Press, 1968)

BORIS FORD (ed.) *The Pelican Guide to English Literature: From Dickens to Hardy* (vol. 6, Harmondsworth, Penguin, 1969)

NORTHROP FRYE: *A Study of English Romanticism* (New York, Random House, 1968)

ROBIN GILMOUR: *The Idea of the Gentleman in the Victorian Novel* (London, Allen and Unwin, 1981)

GEORGE GOODWIN (ed.): *The English Novel in the Nineteenth Century: Essays on the Literary Mediation of Human Values* (Urbana, University of Illinois Press, 1972)

GUINEVERE GRIEST: *Mudie's Circulating Library and the Victorian Novel* (Bloomington, Indiana University Press, 1970)

JOHN HALPERIN: *Egotism and Self-Discovery in the Victorian Novel* (New York, B. Franklin, 1974)

WENDELL V. HARRIS: *British Short Fiction in the Nineteenth Century: a Literary and Bibliographic Guide* (Detroit, Wayne State University Press, 1979)

J. R. HARVEY: *Victorian Novelists and their Illustrators* (London, Sidgwick and Jackson, 1970)

ALETHEA HAYTER: *A Sultry Month: Scenes of London Literary Life in 1846* (London, Faber and Faber, 1965)

JOHN HEATH-STUBBS: *The Darkling Plain: a Study of the Later Fortunes of Romanticism in English Poetry from George Darley to W. B. Yeats* (Folcroft, Pennsylvania, Folcroft Press, 1970)

TIMOTHY HILTON: *The Pre-Raphaelites* (London, Thames and Hudson, 1970)

JOHN HOLLOWAY: *The Victorian Sage: Studies in Argument* (London, Macmillan, 1953)

GRAHAM HOUGH: *The Last Romantics* (London, Methuen, 1947)

WALTER E. HOUGHTON: *The Victorian Frame of Mind: 1830–1870* (New Haven, Yale University Press, 1957)

HUMPHREY HOUSE: *The Dickens World* (London, Oxford University Press, 1941)

DIANA HOWARD: *London Theatres and Music-Halls, 1850–1950* (London, Library Association, 1970)

IAN JACK: *English Literature 1815–1832* (Oxford, Clarendon Press, 1963)

HOLBROOK JACKSON: *The Eighteen-Nineties: A Review of Art and Ideas at the Close of the Nineteenth Century* (Hassocks, Harvester Press, 1976, originally published 1913)

J. R. de J. JACKSON: *Poetry of the Romantic Period* (The Routledge History of English Poetry, vol. 4, London, Routledge and Kegan Paul, 1980)

LOUIS JAMES: *Fiction for the Working Man: a Study of the Literature Produced for the Working Classes in Early Victorian Urban England, 1830–1850* (Oxford, OUP, 1963)

E. D. H. JOHNSON: *The Alien Vision of Victorian Poetry: Sources of the Poetic Imaginations in Tennyson, Browning and Arnold* (Hamden, Conn., Archon Books, 1963)

P. J. KEATING: *The Working Classes in Victorian Fiction* (London, Routledge and Kegan Paul, 1971)

G. KITSON-CLARK: *The Making of Victorian England* (London, Methuen, 1962)

U. C. KNOEPFLMACHER and G. B. TENNYSON (eds.): *Nature and the Victorian Imagination* (Berkely, University of California Press, 1977)

U. C. KNOEPFLMACHER: *Religious Humanism in the Victorian Novel: George Eliot, Walter Pater and Samuel Butler* (Princeton, New Jersey, Princeton University Press, 1965)

SHIV K. KUMAR (ed.): *British Romantic Poets: Recent Revaluations* (New York, New York University Press, 1966)

CECIL Y. LANG (ed.): *The Pre-Raphaelites and their Circle* (Boston, Houghton Mifflin, 1968)

JAMES LAVER: *Manners and Morals in the Age of Optimism, 1848–1914* (New York, Harper and Row, 1966)

MARY E. LAZARUS: *Victorian Social Conditions and Attitudes 1837–71* (London, Macmillan, 1969)

F. R. LEAVIS: *The Great Tradition: George Eliot, Henry James, Joseph Conrad* (London, Chatto and Windus, 1948)

—— *Revaluation: Tradition and Development in English Poetry* (London, Chatto and Windus, 1959)

LAURENCE LERNER: *The Truth-tellers: Jane Austen, George Eliot, D. H. Lawrence* (New York, Schocken Books, 1967)

—— (ed.): *The Victorians* (The Context of English Literature Series, London, Methuen, 1978)

RICHARD LEVINE (ed.): *The Victorian Experience: the Novelists* (Backgrounds in Victorian Literature, San Francisco, Chandler, 1962)

RAYMOND LISTER: *Victorian Narrative Paintings* (London, Museum Press, 1966)

JOHN LUCAS (ed.): *Literature and Politics in the Nineteenth Century* (London, Methuen, 1971)

JEREMY MAAS: *Victorian Painters* (New York, G. Putnam's Sons, 1969)

GEORGE MACBETH: *The Penguin Book of Victorian Verse* (Harmondsworth, Penguin, 1969)

J. McMURTRY: *Victorian Life and Victorian Fiction: a Companion for the American Reader* (Hamden, Conn., Archon Books, 1979)

GRAHAM NORTON: *Victorian London* (Discovering London, 8, London, Macdonald, 1969)

J. C. OLMSTED: *A Victorian Art of Fiction: Essays on the Novel in British Periodicals, 1830–1850* (New York, Garland Publications, 1979)

T. M. PARROTT and R. B. MARTIN: *A Companion to Victorian Literature* (Clifton, New Jersey, 1974)

ROBERT PETERS: *Victorians on Literature and Art* (London, Owen, 1961)

MARIO PRAZ: *The Hero in Eclipse* (London, Oxford University Press, 1970)

—— *The Romantic Agony* (2nd edition, London, Oxford University Press, 1954)

STEPHEN PRICKETT: *Victorian Fantasy* (London, Harvester Press, 1979)

J. B. PRIESTLEY: *The Prince of Pleasure: His Regency, 1811–1820* (London, Literary Guild, 1969)

—— *Victoria's Heyday* (London, Heinemann, 1972)

V. S. PRITCHETT: *The Living Novel* (London, Chatto and Windus, 1964)

PETER QUENNELL: *Romantic England: Writing and Painting 1717–1851* (London, Weidenfeld and Nicolson, 1970)

—— *Victorian Panorama: A Survey of Life and Fashion from Contemporary Photographs* (New York, Charles Scribner's Sons, 1937)

W. J. READER: *Victorian England* (London, Batsford, 1974)

GRAHAM REYNOLDS: *Victorian Painting* (London, Studio Vista, 1966)

BERNARD RICHARDS (ed.): *English Verse, 1830–1890* (vol. 6, Longman Annotated Anthologies of English Verse, London, Longman, 1980)

GEORGE ROWELL (ed.): *Victorian Dramatic Criticism* (London, Methuen, 1971)

—— *The Victorian Theatre, 1792–1914* (Cambridge, Cambridge University Press, 1978)

EDWARD ROYLE: *Victorian Infidels: the Origins of the British Secularist Movement, 1791–1866* (Manchester, University of Manchester Press, 1974)

ANDREW SANDERS: *The Victorian Historical Novel, 1840–1880* (London, Macmillan, 1978)

J. B. SCHNEEWIND: *Backgrounds of English Victorian Literature* (New York, Random House, 1970)

L. C. B. SEAMAN: *Victorian England: Aspects of English and Imperial History 1837–1901* (London, Methuen, 1973)

AMY SHARP: *Victorian Poets* (Port Washington, New York, Kennikat Press, 1970)

RICHARD SOUTHERN: *The Victorian Theatre: a Pictorial Survey* (Newton Abbot, David and Charles, 1970)

RICHARD STANG: *The Theory of the Novel in England, 1858–1870* (New York, Columbia University Press, 1959)

LIONEL STEVENSON (ed.): *Victorian Fiction: A Guide to Research* (Cambridge, Mass., Harvard University Press, 1966)

D. D. STONE: *Novelists in a Changing World: Meredith, James, and the Transformation of English Fiction in the 1880s* (Cambridge, Mass., Harvard University Press, 1972)

—— *The Romantic Impulse in Victorian Fiction* (Cambridge, Harvard University Press, 1980)

P. W. K. STONE: *The Art of Poetry, 1750–1820: Theories of Poetic Composition and Style in the Late Neo-Classic and Early Romantic Periods* (New York, Barnes and Noble, 1967)

JACK SULLIVAN: *Elegant Nightmares: the English Ghost Story from Le Fanu to Blackwood* (Athens, Ohio University Press, 1978)

HERBERT L. SUSSMAN: *Victorians and the Machine: the Literary Response to Technology* (Cambridge, Mass., Harvard University Press, 1968)

J. A. SUTHERLAND: *Victorian Novelists and their Publishers* (London, Athlone, 1976)

G. B. TENNYSON: *Victorian Devotional Poetry: the Tractarian Mode* (Cambridge, Mass., Harvard University Press, 1981)

DAVID THOMSON: *England in the Nineteenth Century* (Harmondsworth, Penguin, 1953)

PATRICIA THOMSON: *The Victorian Heroine: a Changing Ideal, 1837–1873* (Wesport, Conn., Greenwood Press, 1978)

GEOFFREY TILLOTSON: *A View of Victorian Literature* (Oxford, Clarendon Press, 1978)

—— *Criticism and the Nineteenth Century* (Hamden, Conn., Archon Books, 1967)

G. TILLOTSON and K. TILLOTSON: *Mid-Victorian Studies* (London, Athlone Press, 1965)

KATHLEEN TILLOTSON: *Novels of the Eighteen-Forties* (Oxford, Clarendon Press, 1954)

MARTHA VICINUS: *The Industrial Muse: a Study of Nineteenth Century British Working Class Literature* (New York, Barnes and Noble, 1974)

JEREMY WARBURG (ed,): *The Industrial Muse: the Industrial Revolution in English Poetry* (London, Athlone, 1958)

J. R. WATSON: *Picturesque Landscape and English Romantic Poetry* (London, Hutchinson Education, 1970)

BASIL WILLEY: *Nineteenth Century Studies: Coleridge to Matthew Arnold* (London, Chatto and Windus, 1949)

—— *More Nineteenth Century Studies: a Group of Honest Doubters* (London, Chatto and Windus, 1956)

IOAN WILLIAMS: *The Realist Novel in England: A Study in Development* (London, Macmillan, 1974)

RAYMOND WILLIAMS: *Culture and Society, 1780–1950* (Harmondsworth, Penguin, 1961)

—— *The English Novel from Dickens to Lawrence* (London, Chatto and Windus, 1970)

G. M. YOUNG: *Victorian England: Portrait of an Age* (Oxford University Press, 1936)

—— *Victorian Essays* (Oxford University Press, 1962)

Twayne's English Authors Series, edited by Sylvia E. Bowman, and published by Twayne Publications Inc., New York, includes studies of most of the major nineteenth-century authors.

Novelists and Prose Writers in the 'Great Writers of the English Language Series,' published in New York by St. Martin's Press, and the companion volumes on *Poetry* and *Drama*, are invaluable and comprehensive guides to research and further reading.

Chronological table

Abbreviations: (D.) = drama,   (O.) = opera,   (P.) = prose,   (V.) = verse

DATE	AUTHOR	EVENT
1798	Wordsworth (1770) and Coleridge (1772): *Lyrical Ballads* (V.) Coleridge: *Fears in Solitude; Frost at Midnight* (V.)	Nelson in command in Mediterranean Income tax introduced Malthus: *Principles of Population*
1799	Wordsworth (1770) and Coleridge (1772): *Lyrical Ballads*, vol. ii (V.)	Suppression of radical groups and trade unions Bonaparte becomes First Consul Balzac (*b.*)
1800	Wordsworth (1770): Preface to *Lyrical Ballads* (P.) Edgeworth (1767): *Castle Rackrent* (P.)	Act of Union with Ireland Macaulay (*b.*) Cowper (*d.*)
1801	Southey (1774): *Thalaba* (V.)	Catholic Emancipation Bill refused royal assent Pestalozzi's progressive theory of education Barnes (*b.*)
1802	Scott (1771): *Minstrelsy of the Scottish Border* (V.)	Peace of Amiens *Edinburgh Review* founded First Factory Act
1803	Southey (1774): *The Pleasures of Hope* (V.) Landor (1775): *Gébir* (V.)	War with France resumed Beethoven's *Eroica* performed Borrow (*b.*) Bulwer Lytton (*b.*)
1804	Blake (1757): *Jerusalem* (P.), *Milton* (P.) Edgeworth (1767): *Popular Tales* (P.)	Napoleon crowned Emperor First Corn Laws Emmanuel Kant (*d.*)

DATE	AUTHOR	EVENT
1804		George Sand (*b.*)
		Disraeli (*b.*)
1805	Southey (1774): *Metrical Tales* (V.)	Battles of Trafalgar, Ulm, Austerlitz
		Beethoven's *Fidelio* performed
	Scott (1771): *Lay of the Last Minstrel* (V.)	Schiller (*d.*)
		Ainsworth (*b.*)
1806	Byron (1788): *Fugitive Pieces* (V.)	E. Barrett (*b.*)
	Scott (1771): *Ballads and Lyrical Pieces* (V.)	J. S. Mill (*b.*)
1807	Moore (1778): *Irish Melodies* (V.)	First steps towards abolition of slave trade
	Wordsworth (1770): *Poems in Two Volumes* (V.)	First public gas lighting in London
	Crabbe (1754): *Poems* (V.)	Malthus: *Letter . . . on Poor Laws*
	Hazlitt (1778): *Reply to Malthus* (P.)	Pitt (*d.*)
1808	Lamb (1775): *Specimens of English Dramatic Poets* (D.)	Hunt's *Examiner* (to 1821)
		Goethe: *Faust* (I)
	Scott (1771): *Marmion* (V.)	C. Tennyson Turner (*b.*)
1809	Blake (1757): *Descriptive Catalogue*	Battle of Corunna
	Byron (1788): *English Bards and Scottish Reviewers* (V.)	*Quarterly Review* founded
		Lamarck: *Philosophical Zoology*
	Coleridge (1772): *The Friend* (V.)	Old Price riots at Covent Garden
	Edgeworth (1767): *Tales of Fashionable Life* (P.)	Paine (*d.*)
		Darwin (*b.*)
		Kinglake (*b.*).
		Tennyson (*b.*)
1810	Crabbe (1754): *The Borough* (V.)	Lisbon besieged
	Scott (1771): *The Lady of the Lake* (V.)	Goya: *Disasters of War*
		Clergy Residence Act
	Southey (1774): *Curse of Kehama* (V.)	Coleridge lectures on Shakespeare
		Chopin (*b.*)
		Gaskell (*b.*)
1811	Austen (1775): *Sense and Sensibility* (P.)	Prince of Wales made Regent
		Luddite riots
	Lamb (1775): 'On the Tragedies of Shakespeare' (P.)	
	Shelley (1792): *The Necessity of Atheism* (P.)	
1812	Byron (1788): *Childe Harold* (V.)	Napoleon's Russian campaign

DATE	AUTHOR	EVENT
1812	Crabbe (1754): *Tales in Verse* (V.) Edgeworth (1767): *The Absentee* (P.) Landor (1775): *Count Julian* (V.)	War with America J. and W. Grimm: *Fairy Tales* Browning (*b.*) Dickens (*b.*) Lear (*b.*) Mayhew (*b.*) Wagner (*b.*)
1813	Austen (1775): *Pride and Prejudice* (P.) Byron (1788): *The Bride of Abydos, The Giaour* (V.) Scott (1771): *Rokeby* (V.) Shelley (1792): *Queen Mab* (V.)	Southey made Poet Laureate Napoleon defeated at Leipzig Hallé orchestra founded
1814	Austen (1775): *Mansfield Park* (P.) Byron (1788): *The Corsair* (V.) Scott (1771): *Waverley* (P.) Wordsworth (1770): *The Excursion* (V.)	Napoleon abdicates Congress of Vienna End of American War Stephenson's locomotive English translation of Dante completed Ingres: *La grand odalisque* Le Fanu (*b.*) Reade (*b.*)
1815	Byron (1788): *Hebrew Melodies, Collected Poems* (V.) Scott (1771): *Guy Mannering* (P.) Wordsworth (1770): *White Doe of Rylstone, Poems* (V.)	Napoleon escapes from Elba Battle of Waterloo Napoleon exiled; restoration of French monarchy Landlords carry Corn Bill Trollope (*b.*)
1816	Austen (1775): *Emma* (P.) Byron (1788): *Prisoner of Chillon, Childe Harold* iii (V.) Coleridge (1772): *Christabel, Kubla Khan* (V.) *Lay Sermons* (P.) Hunt (1784) *Rimini* (V.) 'Young Poets' (P.) Peacock (1785): *Headlong Hall* (P.) Scott (1771): *The Antiquary, Old Mortality* (P.) Shelley (1792): *Alastor* (V.)	Depression and discontent Byron leaves England Sheridan (*d.*) C. Brontë (*b.*)
1817	Byron (1788): *Manfred* (V.)	Suspension of habeas corpus

DATE	AUTHOR	EVENT
1817	Coleridge (1772): *Lay Sermons* ii, *Biographia Literaria* (P.) Hazlitt (1778): *On the Characters of Shakespeare* (P.) Keats (1795): *Poems* (V.) Moore (1779): *Lalla Rookh* (V.) Peacock (1785): *Melincourt* (P.)	Cobbett leaves for America *Blackwood's Edinburgh Magazine* founded Report on the Poor Law 'Immortal dinner' of Romantic poets Austen (*d.*)
1818	Austen (1775): *Northanger Abbey, Persuasion* (P.) Byron (1788): *Childe Harold* iv, *Beppo* (V.) Cobbett (?1763): *A Year's Residence in the U.S.* (P.) Hazlitt (1778): *Lectures on the English Poets* (P.) Keats (1795): *Endymion* (V.) Lamb (1775): *Works* Peacock (1785): *Nightmare Abbey* (P.) Scott (1771): *Rob Roy, The Heart of Midlothian* (P.) M. Shelley (1797): *Frankenstein* (P.)	Bowdler's *Family Shakespeare* E. Brontë (*b.*)
1819	Byron (1788): *Don Juan* i–ii (V.) Crabbe (1754): *Tales of the Hall* (V.) Hazlitt (1778): *Lectures on the English Comic Writers, Political Essays* (P.) Hunt (1784): *Poetical Works* (V.) Scott (1771): *The Bride of Lammermoor* (P.) Wordsworth (1770): *Peter Bell, The Waggoner* (V.)	Freedoms of press and assembly restricted 'Peterloo' massacre Géricault: *Raft of the Medusa* G. Eliot (*b.*) Clough (*b.*) Kingsley (*b.*) Ruskin (*b.*) Victoria (*b.*)
1820	Clare (1793): *Poems Descriptive of Rural Life and Scenery* (V.) Keats (1795): *Lamia, Isabella, The Eve of St Agnes, Hyperion* (V.) Lamb (1775): *Essays of Elia* (to 1822) (P.) Maturin (1780): *Melmoth the Wanderer* (P.) Peacock (1785): *Four Ages of Poetry* (P.)	George III (*d.*) Accession of George IV Trial of Queen Caroline Revolutions in Spain, Portugal, Naples *London Magazine* founded Cato Street Conspiracy; radical plots A. Brontë (*b.*)

DATE	AUTHOR	EVENT
1820	Scott (1771): *Ivanhoe* (P.) Shelley (1792): *The Cenci* (D.), *Prometheus Unbound, Oedipus Tyrannus* (V.) Southey (1774): *Life of Wesley* (P.)	
1821	Beddoes (1803): *The Improvisatore* (D.) Byron (1788): *Marino Faliero, Sardanapalus, Two Foscari, Cain* (D.), *Don Juan* iii–iv (V.) Clare (1793): *The Village Minstrel* (V.) Cobbett (1763): *Cottage Economy* (P.) De Quincey (1785): *Confessions of an English Opium Eater* (P.) Hazlitt (1778): *Table Talk* (P.) Shelley (1792): *Epipsychidion, Adonais* (V.) Southey (1774): *A Vision of Judgement* (V.) Egan (1772): *Life in London* (P.)	Greek War of Liberation begins Constable: *The Hay Wain* Weber: *Der Freischütz* Napoleon (*d.*) Keats (*d.*) Dostoevsky (*b.*)
1822	Beddoes (1803): *The Bride's Tragedy* (D.) Byron (1788): *The Vision of Judgement* (V.) Peacock (1785): *Maid Marian* (P.) Shelley (1792): *Hellas* (V.) Wordsworth (1770): *Ecclesiastical Sketches* (V.)	Suicide of Castlereagh Place's pamphlet on birth control Schubert: *Unfinished* symphony Shelley (*d.*) Arnold (*b.*)
1823	Byron (1788): *Don Juan* vi–xiv (V.) Hazlitt (1778): *Liber Amoris* (P.) Scott (1771): *Quentin Durward* (P.) Southey (1774): *History of the Peninsular War* (P.)	War between France and Spain Beethoven: Ninth Symphony Radcliffe (*d.*) Patmore (*b.*)
1824	Byron (1788): *Don Juan* xv–xvi (V.) Hogg (1770): *Confessions of a Justified Sinner* (P.) Landor (1775): *Imaginary Conversations* (P.)	National Gallery opened *Westminster Review* founded Delacroix: *Massacre at Chios* Byron (*d.*)

DATE	AUTHOR	EVENT
1824	Mitford (1787): *Our Village* (to 1832) (P.) Scott (1771): *Redgauntlet* (P.) Shelley (1792): *Posthumous Poems* (V.)	
1825	Carlyle (1795): *Life of Schiller* (P.) Coleridge (1772): *Aids to Reflection* (P.) Hazlitt (1778): *The Spirit of the Age* (P.)	Industrial and financial crisis J. S. Mill: *Essays on Government* Barbauld (*d.*) Fuseli (*d.*)
1826	Disraeli (1804): *Vivian Grey* (P.) Hazlitt (1778): *The Plain Speaker* (P.) Hood (1799): *Whims and Oddities* (V.) Borrow (1803): *Romantic Ballads* (V.)	Reform of the criminal law
1827	Bulwer Lytton (1803): *Falkland* (P.) Clare (1793): *The Shepherd's Calendar* (V.) De Quincey (1785): 'Murder . . . as one of the Fine Arts' (P.) Keble (1792): *The Christian Year* (V.) Tennyson (1804): *Poems by Two Brothers* (V.) Wordsworth (1770): *Poetical Works* (5 vols) (V.)	Battle of Navarino University College London founded Schubert: *Die Winterreise* Heine: *Buch der Lieder*
1828	Coleridge (1772): *Poetical Works* (3 vols) (V.) Hazlitt (1778): *Life of Napoleon* (to 1830) (P.) Hunt (1784): *Lord Byron and Some of His Contemporaries* (P.) Bulwer-Lytton (1803): *Pelham* (P.)	Repeal of Test Acts Thomas Arnold appointed to Rugby School Ibsen (*b.*) Meredith (*b.*) Rossetti (*b.*)
1829	Carlyle (1795): 'Signs of the Times' (P.) Peacock (1785): *Misfortunes of Elphin* (P.) Southey (1774): *Colloquies* (P.) Bulwer Lytton (1803): *Devereux* (P.)	Catholic emancipation Metropolitan police force formed Stephenson's *Rocket*

DATE	AUTHOR	EVENT
1830	Cobbett (1763): *Rural Rides, Advice to Young Men* (P.) Coleridge (1772): *On the Constitution of Church and State* (P.) Byron (1788): *Letters and Journals* (P.) Bulwer Lytton (1803): *Paul Clifford* (P.) Tennyson (1804): *Poems, Chiefly Lyrical* (V.)	George IV (*d.*) Accession of William IV Reform agitation July Revolution in France Liverpool–Manchester railway opened Faraday's dynamo Comte: *Positivism* Hazlitt (*d.*) C. Rossetti (*b.*)
1831	Elliott (1781): *Corn Law Rhymes* (V.) Martineau (1802): *Illustrations of Political Economy* (P.) Disraeli (1804): *The Young Duke* (P.)	Bristol riots Reform of game laws Anatomy Act Cholera epidemics begin (to 1833) Darwin begins *Beagle* voyage Stendhal: *The Red and the Black* Balzac: *The Human Comedy* (to 1847)
1832	Disraeli (1804): *Contarini Fleming* (P.) Bulwer Lytton (1803): *Eugene Aram* (P.) Tennyson (1804): *Poems* (V.)	First Reform Bill Last gibbetting in England Bentham (*d.*) Crabbe (*d.*) Scott (*d.*) 'Carroll' (*b.*)
1833	Browning (1812): *Pauline* (V.) Carlyle (1795): *Sartor Resartus* (P.) Disraeli (1804): *Alroy* (P.)	Abolition of colonial slavery Factory Act Oxford Movement begun Dixon (*b.*)
1834	Ainsworth (1805): *Rookwood* (P.)	Workhouses established Tolpuddle Martyrs Tamworth Manifesto Burning of Houses of Parliament William Morris (*b.*) Du Maurier (*b.*) Coleridge (*d.*) Lamb (*d.*)
1835	Browning (1812): *Paracelsus* (V.) Clare (1793): *The Rural Muse* (V.)	Reform of local government First railway boom Telegraph invented Bull and bear baiting proscribed Donizetti: *Lucia di Lammermoor* Cobbett (*d.*)

DATE	AUTHOR	EVENT
1836	E. Barrett: *Poems* (V.) Disraeli (1804): *Henrietta Temple* (P.)	The Great Trek Pugin: *Contrasts* Gautier: *Mademoiselle de Maupin* Godwin (*d.*) W. S. Gilbert (*b.*)
1837	Carlyle (1795): *The French Revolution* (P.) Dickens (1812): *The Pickwick Papers* (P.) Disraeli (1804): *Venetia* (P.) Barham (1788): *Ingoldsby Legends* (to 1847)	Accession of Victoria Daguerre's first photograph Pushkin (*d.*) Swinburne (*b.*)
1838	Bulwer Lytton (1803): *The Lady of Lyons* (D.) Dickens (1812): *Oliver Twist* (P.)	The People's Charter
1839	Ainsworth (1805): *Jack Sheppard* (P.) Carlyle (1795): *Chartism* (P.) Bailey (1816): *Festus* (V.) Dickens (1812): *Nicholas Nickleby* (P.)	'Hungry Forties' begin Formation of Anti-Corn-Law League Durham Report on Empire Young England Movement (to 1845) Penny post established Pater (*b.*)
1840	Browning (1812): *Sordello* (V.) Bulwer Lytton (1803): *Money* (D.)	Victoria marries Prince Albert F. Burney (*d.*) Hardy (*b.*) Zola (*b.*)
1841	Bulwer Lytton (1803): *Night and Morning* (P.) Borrow (1803): *The Zincali* (P.) Boucicault (?1822): *London Assurance* (D.) Browning (1812): *Pippa Passes* (V.) Carlyle (1795): *Heros and Hero-Worship* (P.) Dickens (1812): *The Old Curiosity Shop, Barnaby Rudge* (P.)	*Punch* founded
1842	Borrow (1803): *The Bible in Spain* (P.) Browning (1812): *Dramatic Lyrics* (V.) Macaulay (1800): *Lays of Ancient Rome* (V.)	No women or children in mines

DATE	AUTHOR	EVENT
1842	Tennyson (1804): *Poems* (2 vols) (V.)	
1843	Carlyle (1795): *Past and Present* (P.) Jones (1820): *Studies of Sensation and Event* (V.) Macaulay (1800): *Critical and Historical Essays* (P.) J. S. Mill (1806): *System of Logic* (P.) Ruskin (1819): *Modern Painters* i (P.) Thackeray (1811): *Irish Sketchbook* (P.)	Second cholera epidemic Bank Charter Act Theatre Regulation Act Safety regulations in factories Wordsworth made poet laureate Wagner: *The Flying Dutchman* Southey (*d.*) Henry James (*b.*)
1844	Browning (1812): *Colombe's Birthday* (D.) Disraeli (1804): *Coningsby* (P.) Kinglake (1809): *Eothen* (P.) Patmore (1823): *Poems* (V.)	Cheap Trains Act Ragged schools begun Duelling forbidden in the army *Vestiges of Creation* published Hopkins (*b.*)
1845	Browning (1812): *Dramatic Romances and Lyrics* (V.) Disraeli (1804): *Sybil* (P.)	Failure of Irish potato crop General Enclosure Act Conversion of Newman Second railway boom Barham (*d.*) Hood (*d.*)
1846	Brontës: *Poems by Currer, Ellis and Acton Bell* G. Eliot (trans.): Strauss's *Life of Jesus* (P.) Lear (1812): *A Book of Nonsense* (V.) Ruskin (1819): *Modern Painters* ii (P.) Thackeray (1811): *From Cornhill to Cairo* (P.)	Repeal of Corn Laws Browning elopement Mendelssohn: *Elijah* Berlioz: *Damnation of Faust* Haydon (*d.*)
1847	C. Brontë (1816): *Jane Eyre* (P.) E. Brontë (1818): *Wuthering Heights* (P.) A. Brontë (1820): *Agnes Grey* (P.) Disraeli (1804): *Tancred* (P.) Tennyson (1809): *The Princess* (V.)	Poor Law administration centralised First use of chloroform A. Meynell (*b.*)

DATE	AUTHOR	EVENT
1847	Thackeray (1811): *Vanity Fair* (P.)	
1848	A. Brontë (1820): *The Tenant of Wildfell Hall* (P.) Clough (1819): *The Bothie of Tober-na-Vuolich* (V.) Dickens (1812): *Dombey and Son* (P.) Gaskell (1810): *Mary Barton* (P.) Kingsley (1819): *Yeast* (P.) Mill (1806): *Principles of Political Economy* (P.) Newman (1801): *Loss and Gain* (P.)	Year of European revolution Failure of Chartist procession Pre-Raphaelite Brotherhood begun Queen's College for Women established Marx and Engels: *Communist Manifesto* Rossetti: *Girlhood of Mary Virgin* E. Brontë (*d.*)
1849	C. Brontë (1816): *Shirley* (P.) Arnold (1822): *The Strayed Reveller* (V.) Clough (1819): *Ambarvalia* (V.) Macaulay (1800): *History of England* (to 1861) (P.) Ruskin (1819): *Seven Lamps of Architecture* (P.)	Millais: *Isabella* Beddoes (*d.*) Edgeworth (*d.*) Chopin (*d.*)
1850	E. Browning (1806): *Sonnets from the Portuguese* (V.) Browning (1812): *Christmas Eve and Easter Day* (V.) Carlyle (1795): *Latter-Day Pamphlets* (P.) Dickens (1812): *David Copperfield* (P.) Kingsley (1819): *Alton Locke* (P.) Tennyson (1809): *In Memoriam* (V.) Thackeray (1811): *Pendennis* (P.) Newman (1801): *Difficulties Felt by Anglicans* (P.)	Catholic hierarchy re-established *The Germ* begun Tennyson made poet laureate Mrs Bloomer's 'dress reform' Millais: *Christ in the House of His Parents* Wordsworth (*d.*) R. L. Stevenson (*b.*)
1851	Borrow (1803): *Lavengro* (P.) Carlyle (1795): *Life of John Sterling* (P.) Ruskin (1819): *The Stones of Venice* (P.)	Great Exhibition First trade union Hunt: *The Hireling Shepherd* Landseer: *The Monarch of the Glen*
1852	Arnold (1822): *Empedocles on Etna* (V.)	Second Empire in France Millais: *Ophelia*

DATE	AUTHOR	EVENT
1852	Boucicault (1822): *The Corsican Brothers* (D.) Gaskell (1810): *Cranford* (P.) Kingsley (1819): *Hypatia* (P.) Reade (1814) and Taylor: *Masks and Faces* (D.) Thackeray (1811): *Henry Esmond* (P.)	Hunt: *The Awakening Conscience* Madox Brown begins *Work* T. Moore (*d.*)
1853	C. Brontë (1816): *Villette* (P.) Dickens (1812): *Bleak House* (P.) Gaskell (1810): *Ruth* (P.) Thackeray (1811): *The Newcomes* (P.) Yonge (1823): *The Heir of Redclyffe* (P.)	Outbreak of Crimean War Third cholera epidemic End of transportation for petty crime Gaming houses prohibited Verdi: *La Traviata*
1854	Dickens (1812): *Hard Times* (P.) Patmore (1823): *The Angel in the House* (to 1863) (V.)	Battle of Inkerman Workingmen's College movement Dispersal of PRB Japan opened to the West Frith: *Ramsgate Sands* Millais: *Ruskin at Glenfinlas*
1855	Browning (1812): *Men and Women* (V.) Gaskell (1810): *North and South* (P.) Kingsley (1819): *Westward Ho!* (P.) Tennyson (1809): *Maud* (V.) Trollope (1815): *The Warden* (P.)	Limited Liability Act Paris Exhibition C. Brontë (*d.*) D. Wordsworth (*d.*) Pinero (*b.*)
1856	Reade (1814): *It's Never Too Late to Mend* (P.) Ruskin (1819): *Modern Painters*, iii and iv (P.)	End of Crimean War National police force formed Divorce without act of parliament *Oxford and Cambridge Magazine* Shaw (*b.*)
1857	C. Brontë (1816): *The Professor* (P.) E. Browning (1806): *Aurora Leigh* (V.) Borrow (1803): *The Romany Rye* (P.) Dickens (1812): *Little Dorrit* (P.)	Albert made Prince Consort Indian Mutiny begins Pasteur's theory of disease Bessemer steel process Transportation discontinued Oxford Union murals painted Baudelaire: *Les fleurs du mal*

DATE	AUTHOR	EVENT
1857	Gaskell (1810): *Life of Charlotte Brontë* (P.) Kingsley (1819): *Two Years Ago* (P.) Thackeray (1811): *The Virginians* (P.) Trollope (1815): *Barchester Towers* (P.)	Flaubert: *Madame Bovary* Gissing (*b.*) Conrad (*b.*)
1858	Barnes (1801): *Hwomely Rhymes* (V.) Clough (1819): *Amours de Voyage* (V.) Eliot (1819): *Scenes from Clerical Life* (P.) Kingsley (1819): *Andromeda* (V.) Morris (1834): *The Defence of Guinevere* (V.) Trollope (1815): *Dr Thorne* (P.)	Jews admitted to parliament Offenbach: *Orpheus in the Underworld*
1859	Eliot (1819): *Adam Bede* (P.) Darwin (1809): *The Origin of Species* (P.) Dickens (1812): *A Tale of Two Cities* (P.) Fitzgerald (1809): *The Rubaiyat* (V.) Meredith (1828): *The Ordeal of Richard Feverel* (P.) Mill (1806): *On Liberty* (P.) Ruskin (1819): *The Two Paths* (P.) Tennyson (1809): *Idylls of the King* (V.)	Dyce: *Pegwell Bay* L. Hunt (*d.*) Macaulay (*d.*) C. Doyle (*b.*) Housman (*b.*) F. Thompson (*b.*)
1860	Boucicault (1822): *The Colleen Bawn* (D.) Collins (1824): *The Woman in White* (P.) Eliot (1819): *The Mill on the Floss, Silas Marner* (P.) Ruskin (1819): *Modern Painters*, v. *Unto This Last* (P.)	Italian 'Risorgimento' French-English tariff reduced First Food and Drug Act *Essays and Reviews*: rationalist assault on religious orthodoxy Mahler (*b.*)
1861	Dickens (1812): *Great Expectations* (P.) Dixon (1833): *Christ's Company* (V.)	Death of Prince Albert U.S. Civil War Garrotting scare Morris and Company founded

DATE	AUTHOR	EVENT
1861	Reade (1814): *The Cloister and the Heart* (P.) Rossetti (1828): *Early Italian Poets* (V.) Trollope (1815): *Framley Parsonage* (P.)	E. Browning (*d.*) Clough (*d.*)
1862	Borrow (1803): *Wild Wales* (P.) Calverley (1831): *Verses and Translations* (V.) Clough (1819): *Poems* (V.) Meredith (1828): *Modern Love* (V.) C. Rossetti (1830): *Goblin Market* (V.) Tennyson Turner (1808): *Sonnets* (V.)	Bismarck becomes Prussian Chancellor Married Women's Property Act Dostoevsky: *From the House of the Dead* Newbolt (*b.*)
1863	Barnes (1801): *Poems in the Dorset Dialect* (V.) Eliot (1819): *Romola* (P.) Kingsley (1819): *The Water Babies* (P.) Mill (1806): *Utilitarianism* (P.) Reade (1814): *Hard Cash* (P.)	Papal edict against liberalism Renan: *Vie de Jésus* Manet: *Olympia* Thackeray (*d.*)
1864	Browning (1812): *Dramatis Personae* (V.) Newman (1801): *Apologia Pro Vita Sua* (P.) Tennyson Turner (1808): *Poems* (V.) Trollope (1815): *Can You Forgive Her?, The Small House at Allington* (P.)	First International Workingmen's Association War between Prussia and Denmark Whistler: *The White Girl* Clare (*d.*) Landor (*d.*)
1865	Arnold (1822): *Essays in Criticism* (P.) 'Carroll' (1832): *Alice in Wonderland* (P.) Clough (1819): *Dipsychus* (V.) Dickens (1812): *Our Mutual Friend* (P.) Ruskin (1819): *Sesame and Lilies* (P.)	Jamaican uprising Fenian movement Slum rehabilitation Lister's aseptic surgery First woman doctor qualified Mendel's genetic experiments Gaskell (*d.*) Kipling (*b.*) Symons (*b.*) Yeats (*b.*)

DATE	AUTHOR	EVENT
1866	Gaskell (1810): *Wives and Daughters* (P.) Newman (1801): *The Dream of Gerontius* (V.) C. Rossetti (1830): *The Prince's Progress* (V.) Ruskin (1819): *The Crown of Wild Olive* (P.)	War between Prussia and Austria Field's transatlantic cable Dostoevsky: *Crime and Punishment* Keble (*d.*)
1867	Arnold (1822): *New Poems* (V.) Eliot (1819): *Felix Holt* (P.) Robertson (1829): *Caste* (D.) Trollope (1815): *The Last Chronicle of Barset* (P.)	Second Reform Act Invention of dynamite Marx: *Das Kapital* Bagehot: *The English Constitution* Dowson (*b.*) L. Johnson (*b.*)
1868	Browning (1812): *The Ring and the Book* (V.) Collins (1824): *The Moonstone* (P.) Disraeli (1804): *Lothair* (P.) Morris (1834): *The Earthly Paradise* (V.) Reade (1814): *Foul Play* (P.)	Fenian attacks Reform of army begun Trades Union Congress established Last public execution
1869	Arnold (1822): *Culture and Anarchy* (P.) Gilbert (1836): *The Bab Ballads* (V.) Mill (1806): *The Subjection of Women* (P.) Tennyson (1809): *The Holy Grail and Other Poems* (V.) Trollope (1815): *Phineas Finn* (P.)	Suez Canal opened Contagious Diseases Act against prostitution Tolstoi: *War and Peace*
1870	Dickens (1812): *Edwin Drood* (P.) Newman (1801): *The Grammar of Assent* (P.) Rossetti (1828): *Poems* (V.)	Increased grants to education Doctrine of papal infallibility Franco-Prussian War Irving's performance in *The Bells* Dickens (*d.*)
1871	'Carroll' (1832): *Through the Looking Glass* (P.) Darwin (1809): *The Descent of Man* (P.) Eliot (1819): *Middlemarch* (P.) Hardy (1840): *Desperate Remedies* (P.)	Paris Commune Irish Church disestablished Buchanan's attack on Rossetti Verdi: *Aida* Proust (*b.*) Synge (*b.*)

DATE	AUTHOR	EVENT
1871	Lear (1812): *Nonsense Songs and Stories* (V.) Ruskin (1819): *Fors Clavigera* (to 1884) (P.) Swinburne (1837): *Songs Before Sunrise* (V.)	
1872	Browning (1812): *Fifine at the Fair* (V.) Butler (1835): *Erewhon* (P.) Lang (1844): *Ballads and Lyrics of Old France* (V.)	Secret Ballot Act Licensing Act Taine: *Notes on England* Gustave Doré: *London* Rossetti: *Beata Beatrix* Beardsley (*b.*)
1873	Arnold (1822): *Literature and Dogma* (P.) Bridges (1844): *Poems* (V.) Mill (1806): *Autobiography* (P.) Pater (1839): *The Renaissance* (P.) Trollope (1815): *The Eustace Diamonds, Phineas Redux* (P.)	Beginning of world depression Mill (*d.*) Le Fanu (*d.*)
1874	Hardy (1840): *Far From the Madding Crowd* (P.) Thomson (1834): *The City of Dreadful Night* (V.)	
1875	Gilbert (1836): *Trial By Jury* (D.) Henley (1849): *In Hospital* (V.) Meynell (1847): *Poems* (V.) Ruskin (1819): *Mornings in Florence* (P.) Trollope (1815): *The Prime Minister, The Way We Live Now* (P.)	Kingsley (*d.*)
1876	Eliot (1819): *Daniel Deronda* (P.) Morris (1834): *Sigurd the Volsung* (V.)	Victoria becomes Express of India Wagner's *Ring* performed at Bayreuth Ruskin–Whistler libel suit Invention of telephone
1877	Browning (1812): *The Agamemnon of Aeschylus* (V.) Meredith (1828): *The Idea of Comedy* (P.) Patmore (1823): *The Unknown Eros* (V.)	Edison's phonograph Tolstoy: *Anna Karenina*

DATE	AUTHOR	EVENT
1877	Ruskin (1819): *St Mark's Rest* (P.)	
1878	Gilbert (1836): *H.M.S. Pinafore* (D.) Hardy (1840): *The Return of the Native* (P.)	Irving leases Lyceum Theatre Cruikshank (*d.*)
1879	Barnes (1801): *Collected Poems* (V.) Meredith (1828): *The Egoist* (P.) Reade (1814): *Drink* (D.)	Gladstone's Midlothian campaign Compulsory school attendance
1880	Blunt (1840): *Protean Sonnets* (V.) Disraeli (1804): *Endymion* (P.) Ruskin (1819): *The Bible of Amiens* (P.) Trollope (1815): *The Duke's Children* (P.)	Dostoevsky: *The Brothers Karamazov* Böcklin: *The Isle of the Dead* G. Eliot (*d.*) L. Strachey (*b.*)
1881	Wilde (1854): *Poems* (V.) Gilbert (1836): *Patience* (D.) James (1843): *Portrait of a Lady* (P.) Ruskin (1819): 'Fiction Foul and Fair' (P.)	First Boer War Savoy Theatre built Borrow (*d.*) Carlyle (*d.*) Disraeli (*d.*) Picasso (*b.*)
1882	Jefferies (1848): *Bevis* (P.) Lang (1844): *Helen of Troy* (V.) Morris (1834): *Hopes and Fears for Art* (P.) Swinburne (1837): *Tristram of Lyonesse* (V.)	Phoenix Park murders Wilde's American lecture tour Ainsworth (*d.*) Darwin (*d.*) Rossetti (*d.*) Trollope (*d.*) Thomson (*d.*) V. Woolf (*b.*)
1883	Gissing (1857): *The Unclassed* (P.) Jefferies (1848): *The Story of My Heart* (P.) Meredith (1828): *Poems and Lyrics of the Joy of the Earth* (V.) Stevenson (1850): *Treasure Island* (P.)	*Merry England* founded
1884	Dixon (1833): *Odes and Eclogues* (V.) Ruskin (1819): 'The Storm-Cloud of the Nineteenth Century' (P.)	Fabian Society founded Third Reform Act Maxim gun patented Huysman: *A Rebours* Reade (*d.*)

DATE	AUTHOR	EVENT
1885	Gilbert (1836): *The Mikado* (D.) Gissing (1857): *Demos* (P.) Jefferies (1848): *After London* (P.) Meredith (1828): *Diana of the Crossways* (P.) Moore (1852): *A Mummer's Wife* (P.) Pater (1839): *Marius the Epicurean* (P.) Pinero (1855): *The Magistrate* (D.) Ruskin (1819): *Praeterita* (to 1889) (P.) Stevenson (1850): *A Child's Garden of Verses* (V.)	Siege of Khartoum Criminal Law Amendment Act defines sexual offences Radio waves discovered D. H. Lawrence (*b.*) Ezra Pound (*b.*)
1886	Hardy (1840): *The Mayor of Casterbridge* (P.) Kipling (1865): *Departmental Ditties* (V.) Morris (1834): *A Dream of John Ball* (P.) Rossetti (1828): *Collected Works* (V.) Stevenson (1850): *Dr Jekyll and Mr Hyde* (P.)	Liberals split on Home Rule Internal combustion engine Barnes (*d.*)
1887	Doyle (1859): *A Study in Scarlet* (P.) Dixon (1833): *Lyrical Poems* (V.) Jefferies (1848): *Amaryllis at the Fair* (P.) Meredith (1828): *Ballads and Poems of Tragic Life* (V.) Pater (1839): *Imaginary Portraits* (P.)	Rhodesia founded Victoria's Golden Jubilee Edison's kinetoscope Mayhew (*d.*)
1888	Gissing (1857): *The Nether World* (P.) Henley (1849): *A Book of Verses* (V.) Kipling (1865): *Plain Tales From the Hills* (P.) Moore (1852): *Confessions of a Young Man* (P.) Wilde (1854): *The Happy Prince and Other Tales* (P.)	Scottish Labour Party formed Arnold (*d.*) Lear (*d.*) T. S. Eliot (*b.*)

DATE   AUTHOR   EVENT

1889   Browning (1812): *Asolando* (V.)   London Dock Strike
       Pater (1839): *Appreciations* (P.)   English publisher of Zola imprisoned
       Stevenson (1850): *The Master of*   Browning (*d.*)
       Ballantrae (P.)   Hopkins (*d.*)
       Swinburne (1837): *Poems and*
       Ballads, third series (V.)
       Symons (1865): *Days and Nights*
       (V.)
       Yeats (1865): *The Wanderings of*
       Oisin (V.)

1890   Bridges (1844): *Shorter Poems* (V.)   Parnell scandal
       Gissing (1857): *New Grub Street*   Van Gogh (*d.*)
       (P.)   Boucicault (*d.*)

1891   Hardy (1840): *Tess of the*   Elementary school fees abolished
       D'Urbervilles (P.)
       Austin (1835): *Lyrical Poems* (V.)
       Morris (1834): *News from Nowhere*
       (P.), *Poems By the Way* (V.)
       Wilde (1854): *The Picture of*
       Dorian Gray (P.)

1892   Blunt (1840): *Esther* (V.)   Austin made poet laureate
       Doyle (1859): *The Adventures of*   Tennyson (*d.*)
       Sherlock Holmes (P.)
       Du Maurier (1834): *Peter Ibbetson*
       (P.)
       Gissing (1857): *The Odd Women*
       (P.)
       Henley (1849): *The Song of the*
       Sword (V.)
       Kipling (1865): *Barrack Room*
       Ballads (V.)
       Meredith (1828): *Poems* (V.)
       Symons (1865): *Silhouettes* (V.)
       Tennyson (1809): *The Death of*
       Oenone (V.)
       Wilde (1854): *Lady Windermere's*
       Fan (D.)

1893   Blunt (1840): *Griselda* (V.)   Independent Labour Party formed
       Pater (1839): *Plato and Platonism*   Second Home Rule Bill rejected
       (P.)
       Pinero (1855): *The Second Mrs*
       Tanqueray (D.)
       C. Rossetti (1830): *Verses* (V.)

DATE	AUTHOR	EVENT
1893	Stephen (1832): *An Agnostic's Apology* (P.) Thompson (1859): *Poems* (V.) Yeats (1865): *The Celtic Twilight*	
1894	Kipling (1865): *The Jungle Book* (P.) Du Maurier (1834): *Trilby* (P.) Moore (1852): *Esther Waters* (P.) Pater (1839): *The Child in the House* (P.) Shaw (1856): *Arms and the Man* (D.)	Collapse of the 'three-decker' novel The *Yellow Book* Pater (*d.*) C. Rossetti (*d.*) Stevenson (*d.*)
1895	Allen (1848): *The Woman Who Did* (P.) Conrad (1857): *Almayer's Folly* (P.) Hardy (1840): *Jude the Obscure* (P.) Johnson (1867): *Poems* (V.) James (1843): *Guy Domville* (D.) Dowson (1867): *Dilemmas* (P.) Wilde (1854): *The Importance of Being Earnest* (D.) Yeats (1865): *Poems* (V.)	Trial of Oscar Wilde The *New Review* Jameson Raid Diesel engine patented Freud: *Studies in Hysteria*
1896	Dowson (1867): *Verses* (V.) Housman (1859): *A Shropshire Lad* (V.) Kipling (1865): *The Seven Seas* (V.) C. Rossetti (1830): *New Poems* (V.) Stevenson (1850): *Weir of Hermiston* (P.)	Sunday opening of museums and galleries Morris (*d.*) Patmore (*d.*)
1897	Conrad (1857): *The Nigger of the 'Narcissus'* (P.) Maugham (1874): *Liza of Lambeth* (P.) Symons (1865): *Amoris Victima* (V.) Thompson (1859): *New Poems* (V.)	Victoria's Diamond Jubilee Workmen's Compensation Act
1898	Hardy (1840): *Wessex Poems* (V.) Newbolt (1862): *The Island Race* (V.)	General Federation of Trade Unions Beardsley (*d*). Gladstone (*d*.)

DATE	AUTHOR	EVENT
1898	Pinero (1855): *Trelawney of the 'Wells'* (D.) Shaw (1856): *Plays Pleasant and Unpleasant* (D.) Wilde (1854): *The Ballad of Reading Gaol* (V.)	
1899	Yeats (1865): *The Wind Among the Reeds* (V.) Dowson (1867): *Decorations in Verse and Prose*	Boer War (to 1902)
1900	Conrad (1857): *Lord Jim* (P.) Wells (1866): *Love and Mr Lewisham* (P.)	Freud: *Interpretation of Dreams* Dixon (*d.*) Dowson (*d.*) Ruskin (*d.*) Wilde (*d.*)
1901	Hardy (1840): *Poems of the Past and the Present* (V.) Kipling (1865): *Kim* (P.) Shaw (1856): *Three Plays for Puritans* (D.)	Victoria (*d.*) Accession of Edward VII

Index